Reconstructing Chinatown

Globalization and Community

Dennis R. Judd, Series Editor

Reconstructing Chinatown

Ethnic Enclave, Global Change

Jan Lin

Globalization and Community / Volume 2
University of Minnesota Press
Minneapolis • London

Copyright 1998 by the Regents of the University of Minnesota

Published by the University of Minnesota Press
111 Third Avenue South, Suite 290
Minneapolis, MN 55401-2520
http://www.upress.umn.edu

Library of Congress Cataloging-in-Publication Data

Lin, Jan.
    Reconstructing Chinatown : ethnic enclave, global change / Jan Lin.
        p.   cm. — (Globalization and community ; v. 2)
    Includes bibliographical references and index.
    ISBN 0-8166-2904-8 (alk. paper). — ISBN 0-8166-2905-6 (pbk. : alk. paper)
    1. Chinatown (New York, N.Y.)—Politics and government.   2. Chinatown (New York, N.Y.)—Economic conditions.   3. New York (N.Y.)—Politics and government. 4. New York (N.Y.)—Economic conditions.   5. Chinese Americans—New York (State)—New York—Politics and government.   6. Chinese Americans—New York (State)—New York—Economic conditions.   I. Title.   II. Series.
    F128.68.C47L56   1998
    974.7′1—dc21
                                                                      98-10693
                                                                      CIP

Printed in the United States of America on acid-free paper

The University of Minnesota is an equal-opportunity educator and employer.

10 09 08 07 06 05 04 03 02 01 00 99 98   10 9 8 7 6 5 4 3 2 1

This book is dedicated to
my mother, Fu-yun Pan Lin, and
father, the late Ching-yuan Lin

Contents

Preface

Chinatown is a site that structures and also signifies the incorporation of Chinese immigrants into American society. As an urban space, New York's Chinatown is familiar for its residential tenement buildings, loft-manufacturing sweatshops, restaurants, and street markets. The district is jammed vigorously into the southern pocket of Manhattan's Lower East Side, the urban portal in which a succession of immigrant groups have settled and worked since the mid-nineteenth century. The labor power and small-business capital of its industrious people have constructed an ethnic enclave that is the center of economic and social life for the Chinese population throughout the New York City metropolitan area. To these denizens, Chinatown represents not just a productive arena but a place of cultural significance and a community of symbolic and sentimental attachment.

In the public imagination, however, Chinatown has historically been inscribed as an overcrowded, dilapidated place, plagued with social wretchedness and vice. The virulent anti-Oriental images of the late-nineteenth-century "yellow peril" era have faded, but the ongoing durability of negative mental constructions is evident in a variety of contemporary media representations including formulaic news reporting (the "Chinatown beat"), prime-time television serials (*NYPD Blue, Law and Order*), and classic Hollywood films. Though many people comfortably tour the district for its visual exoticism and culinary delights, this voyeurism is often backgrounded by the persisting suspicion and insinuation of a mysterious clannish quarter. This conception implicates Chinatown as a place beset with social problems such as sweatshops and undocumented immigrants, and urban pathologies such as ill sanitation, poverty, and organized criminal syndicates. The local government, similarly, treats Chinatown as a neighborhood that requires cleanup, correction, and redevelopment. In the semiotic realm, then, Chinatown as a negative symbolic representation signifies and legitimizes broader interpenetrating social projects of law and order, modernization, and cultural assimilation. In this discourse, Chinatown and Chinese Americans appear timeless, insular, and resistant to change.

As an urban "place," then, New York's Chinatown exists as a social construction as much as a material construction of circuits of immigrant labor and capital. As I interpretively deconstruct the livelihood and social life of this ethnic enclave, I will reconstruct a conception of a place that is experiencing profound economic and cultural change. This social change is both externally influenced and internally guided. At their apex, these external forces include recent global economic shifts in the structure of advanced capitalism in which the mobility of labor and capital (facilitated by innovations in transport and communications) has been heightened both temporally and geographically. Within the new global economy, these processes are locationally concentrated in particular nodal centers, or "global cities" such as New York City, as evidenced by the increasing presence of transnational banks and corporations as well as labor-intensive immigrant small-business activities in a structure of growing socioeconomic polarity (Sassen 1988, 1991). These trends are marked in microcosm in the central-city enclave of Chinatown, a district that has experienced the growth of sweatshops and foreign investments in the past three decades.

Some additional factors, notably political uncertainty, capital surplus, and economic transition in East Asia, motivate these transpacific flows of labor and capital, which both augment the supply of workers and finance new constructions of bricks and mortar in New York's Chinatown. The impacts of these flows in New York City and Chinatown occur through the intermediation of the state in a sequence of descending levels, from federal to municipal government. The federal government at the broadest level regulates the volume of foreign labor and capital inflow through its immigration policy and economic policy (particularly its trade and monetary policy). The local government manages the urban policies (in areas such as trade, banking, industry, land use and redevelopment, and social policy such as policing) that affect Chinatown. During the recent phase of New York City's ascendance to "global city" status, the local government has been prone to encourage capital inflow through banking deregulation and land-use redevelopment policy to generate revenue. These efforts have been balanced in districts such as Chinatown, however, to advance the interests of labor through an industrial policy motivated by priorities of job retention. The local government also makes periodic intrusions into the social life of the enclave through police surveillance, street-trader clearance campaigns, and redevelopment schemes.

These external processes on the level of state-labor-capital interaction in the Chinatown "politics of place" are matched by significant internal dynamics within the community power structure. The hegemony of a traditional mercantile elite from Guangdong Province has receded with the ascendance of new labor and community organizations, as well as the emergence of new Fujianese merchant associations. This considerable factionalism within the Chinatown polity turns to solidarity during the course of periodic collective actions, which have disrupted the recent social life of the district, including tenacious community-based labor disputes and community conflicts with the policing and urban renewal agencies of the local government. As the apparatus of social control and redevelopment, the local government is also the main focus of protest and collective action. These very public moments of claims-making executed by the workers and residents of Chinatown were often the formative incidents in the growth of new labor and community organizations. Besides this internal dynamic, community mobilization and social change contribute further toward a reconstruction of the public image of Chinatown among New Yorkers and the broader American public.

This book thus examines community change in Chinatown in global context through the conflicts and interactions of labor and capital, the community, and the state. Community change is considered on the material, social, and symbolic levels. I employed U.S. Census of Population and Housing statistics compiled by the U.S. Department of Commerce, and Immigration and Naturalization Service data compiled by the New York City Department of City Planning in examining the demographic characteristics and urban ecology of the enclave. To analyze the enclave economy, I utilized the Chinese American telephone book and microlevel data on business establishments compiled by the New York State Department of Labor. To develop profiles of banking activity in the enclave, I employed financial data published by the Federal Deposit Insurance Corporation and a special tabulation on regional mortgage activity collected by the New York State Banking Department in the 1980s (these data are very similar to the federal Home Mortgage Disclosure Act reports standardized by the Community Reinvestment Act).

In studying the social and political life of the enclave, I worked as a participant observer with Chinatown history and community action organizations including the Chinatown History Project, the Joint Planning Council of the Lower East Side, and the Chinese Staff and Workers' Association. While affiliated with these organizations, I was involved in a variety of tasks including research, recording of minutes at private meetings, transcribing of proceedings at public conferences, organizing of events, and participation in collective actions. As a result of my work with the Chinatown History Project (now the Museum of Chinese in the Americas), I was later invited to serve on the board of It's Time, a Chinatown housing and community organization.

In my social research as a participant observer, I make no claims to have attained the kind of objective social science intended by survey researchers. Furthermore, my ethnographic technique involved active participation in addition to neutral observation. My active "positionality" privileges what Michael Burawoy has identified as the hermeneutic dimension in social science, which seeks interpretation and understanding through a dialogue between the participant and the observed, rather than the scientific method, which is more concerned with the dialogue between theory and data in seeking explanation (1991: 3). Following Burawoy et al., I furthermore identify my fieldwork as following the extended case method (1991: 6), which investigates how micro- or community-level social situations are influenced by external forces, a methodology that also clarifies the contours and consequences of macrolevel processes by specifying their outcomes in the local context.

In addition to fieldwork, I conducted formal interviews with over sixty representatives of Chinatown economic, community, labor, and political organizations, Chinatown business leaders, and New York City urban planners, public servants, and public officials. My initial fieldwork contacts provided me with an initial cluster of interview subjects, who by association referred me to others.[1] The methodological diversity I pursued in my research is typical of the urban case study or community study and is of great utility in uncovering the manifold interconnections among individuals and institutions in these social systems, their links to other systems, and changes in these characteristics over time (Bahr and Caplow 1991).

Finally, I read or viewed a variety of novels, journalistic accounts, television serials, and films (produced by both outsiders and insiders to the Chinese American culture) in order to understand how Chinatown as a place and Chinese Americans as a people have been signified in American urban life. Through this case study of an urban immigrant community, I have attempted to inject some cultural studies into a political-economic perspective to illuminate how structural and semiotic constructions of urban places or race and ethnic categories are mutually reinforcing and necessarily intertwined. Thus, social change implicates not only a restructuring of the material foundations of the urban political economy but also a reconstructing of internal community dynamics and ethnic identities as well as the way they are externally signified.

I begin with an introduction that reviews orthodox and emerging academic literature on immigrant communities in urban sociology and race and ethnic studies. Ranging over a considerable terrain of scholarship, I forge some theoretical bridgework between academic conceptualizations of community and ethnicity as applied to urban space. These literatures are then related to cutting-edge scholarship on globalization, "global cities," and the "new urban sociology." Finally, I discuss emerging work on the political construction of race and ethnic categories.

Chapter 1 introduces the historical parameters surrounding the development of the lower-circuit ethnic enclave economy in New York's Chinatown. Chinese immigration to the United States was suspended for several decades by exclusionary legislation, a period that froze New York's Chinatown in the status of a "bachelor society" until 1965, when the lifting of the exclusion allowed the district to become a family-centered immigrant enclave. The complex internal dynamics of the enclave economy and the residential conditions of its workforce are examined. Criminal activities are seen as a historical outgrowth of the bachelor society and an outcome of recent social change.

Chapter 2 details the struggles of the working people of Chinatown in the "sweatshops" of the garment and restaurant industry and in street trading. Special features of the garment industry mediate the growth of sweatshop subcontracting. Garment sweatshop workers have by no means been quiescent; organized by the International Ladies' Garment Workers' Union (ILGWU), these workers made great gains through public collective action. Organizers have struggled to organize workers in the restaurant industry with somewhat less success.

The impact of overseas Chinese capital on the Chinatown banking industry and land market development is considered in chapter 3. These new pressures of "globalization" are set within the broader historical context of the accumulation of capital in East Asia, and the political and economic parameters surrounding its reinvestment in the United States are discussed. The structure of the Chinatown banking industry is examined in detail; locally oriented banks are gradually losing deposit share and mortgage activity to transnationally oriented banks. The Chinatown built environment is gradually being transformed with the construction of bank office headquarters, residential towers, and hotels. Close scrutiny of deposit growth rates in the mid-1990s, however, indicates somewhat of an economic slow-down. I make fine distinctions between local, regional, and global forces while interpreting recent economic change in the enclave.

Chapter 4 considers the emergence of satellite Chinatowns, which are the combined outcome of residential and commercial congestion at the core, the desire for more space and privacy, and a desire for upward mobility. Socioeconomic characteristics of residents in some outer-borough Chinese communities are compared. Ongoing growth in the satellite communities is spurred by both global and local forces. Flushing, Queens, has attracted considerable foreign capital, particularly of Taiwanese origins. Sunset Park, Brooklyn, by contrast has become a new sweatshop zone for garment shops escaping regularized union industry standards enforced in the core. The ILGWU has employed a tactic of "community-based organizing" in organizing these new underground sweatshops.

Chapter 5 moves on to detail the recent internal social changes in Chinatown's community power structure. A traditional expatriate mercantile elite bound by ties of clan kinship in China's Guangdong Province (but friendly to the anti-communist regime in Taiwan) has been supplanted since the end of the Chinese exclusion era by new Asian American workplace and community organizations that broker relationships with the broader society. A new mercantile elite of immigrants from China's Fujian Province, with a pro-Beijing orientation, has also emerged in the past decade. There is thus a considerable factionalism in the enclave polity, which fades in occasional bouts of public collective action, particularly on issues that involve state encroachment, for example, police brutality and state-led redevelopment projects such as prisons and courthouses. The organizational solidarity engendered by public collective action contrasts with weak participation among the Chinese in electoral politics. Future electoral participation promises to be deepened by voter education efforts and court-ordered implementation of bilingual balloting materials.

Community-state relationships are explored in chapter 6. The federal government was historically hostile to Chinatown until the civil rights milieu of the 1960s, when immigration exclusion was lifted and the federal presence in low-income communities was expanded through antipoverty programs. As federal revenue sharing has gradually been curtailed, however, local governments have become more reliant on local economic growth and real estate development for their revenues. New York public officials, along with regional planners and local finance capital, achieved growth through the building of the World Trade Center in lower Manhattan, which greatly augmented the metropolitan position in the global economy. The local government has similarly sought to stimulate the investment of overseas capital in Chinatown through special land-use zoning. These prerogatives of revenue enhancement have been balanced by job retention efforts in the garment industry through a unique experiment in state-labor-capital cooperation. Street traders have been cleared by a state bent on sanitary priorities. The state sanctions tourism as a revenue-generating initiative; store merchants, community development groups, and arts organizations have been involved in community preservation activities to support these efforts. The "security state," however, continues to make redevelopmental incursions into Chinatown land for prison and courthouse expansions.

Chapter 7 examines the political construction to representations of Chinatown and Chinese Americans, which has shifted through the years and clearly reflects the changing ideological purposes of federal policies concerning Chinese immigration and social policy, as well as U.S. diplomatic relations with China. These representations are changing, however, through the efforts of community activists and artists. Cultural change is thus bound up with political-economic change, as I discuss in chapter 8 while revisiting questions of globalization and community change. I also make predictions of prospective trends that may be experienced by New York's Chinatown and conclude with some comparative implications that may be drawn by urban managers.

Acknowledgments

My interest in New York's Chinatown was initially sparked in 1987 by Janet Abu-Lughod in a class she taught at the Graduate Faculty of the New School for Social Research called "Analysis of Change in World Context." Passing me a galley proof of Saskia Sassen's book *The Mobility of Labor and Capital*, Janet suggested that the garment sweatshops and overseas investors of Chinatown comprised an exemplary context to examine conceptual hypotheses regarding the influence of global forces on community change. If the dramatic socioeconomic polarization evident in postindustrial New York City increasingly converged with the dual structure of third-world cities, then these trends were also evident in the microcosm of the central-city enclave of Chinatown. Chinatown became the topic of my dissertation, and a condensation of the thesis was subsequently published as an article titled "Polarized Development and Urban Change in the Global City: New York's Chinatown," in *Urban Affairs Review*. Portions of that article have been integrated into this book.

I gratefully acknowledge Lonnie Sherrod, Dean of Student Affairs while I was a graduate student at the New School for Social Research, for approving use of federal work-study funds to affiliate with the Chinatown History Project (now the Museum of Chinese in the Americas) and to conduct research supporting an oral history project and museum exhibition on women garment workers. I later worked with the Joint Planning Council of the Lower East Side as an organizer and recording secretary. These work-study relationships were of vital importance in familiarizing me with the historical and political intricacies of a range of local issues, and helped me gain access to an initial pool of community informants. Peter Lin of the Chinese Staff and Workers' Association acquainted me with community labor issues and enlisted my participation in their campaigns. Dorothy Rony, Charlie Lai, and Sam Sue of the Chinatown History Project opened many doors and connected me with neighborhood issues. A Housing Conference held at the Chinatown History Project in June 1988 exposed me to the significant community development and planning issues affecting the neighborhood. Sam Sue later brought me onto the executive board of It's Time, a housing and community development organization.

The Community Service Society of New York gave me critical financial support as a doctoral intern during the 1989–90 academic year as I entered dissertation research. I finished writing my dissertation during my first year of teaching at the University of Houston, where I spent three congenial and productive years. Anita Bohm, Quetzil Castaneda, Janet Chafetz, Gary Dworkin, Helen Rose Ebaugh, Jacqueline Hagan, Karl Ittman, Joe Kotarba, Nestor Rodriguez, and Bill Simon were crucial to my personal and professional development while I was there. I then moved to Amherst College, which graciously extended a sabbatical after a year of teaching. I was thus able to return to New York's Chinatown in the fall of 1995 to conduct vital follow-up research and to begin writing this book.

I conducted formal interviews with dozens of individuals representing Chinatown labor, community, and political organizations, garment industry managers, Chinatown banks and realtors, Chinese businessmen, and public-sector employees who worked in Chinatown. I want to extend particular thanks to Richard Chan, David Chen, May Chen, Peter Cheng, Margaret Chin, Sherman Eng, Danyun Feng, Cristobal Garcia, Peter Kwong, Corky Lee, May Lee, M. B. Lee, JoAnn Lum, Andy Pollack, Henry Yung, John Wang, Edison Wong, Graham Wong, and Edmund Yu for sharing their knowledge and insight. I must thank photographers Corky Lee and Robert Glick for contracting with me and granting permission for reproduction of their photographs in this book.

I would also like to thank Janet Abu-Lughod, Charles Tilly, Frank de Giovanni, Diane Davis, Arthur Vidich, Margrit Mayer, Ari Zolberg, Christopher Mele, Andy Van Kleunen, Dorine Greshof, and other members of the academic community (including Perry Chang, Kim Geiger, Warren Goldstein, Amparo Hoffman-Pinilla, Hyun Kim, Dan Kryder, Darra Mulderry, Abby Scher, Joel Stillerman, and Kumru Toktamisch) at the New School for Social Research for their support, commentary, and critical reflections on my project as it developed over the years. I kindly acknowledge Carrie Mullen, acquisitions editor at the University of Minnesota Press, for guiding my manuscript through the review process and into production. Dennis R. Judd, series editor, must also be gratefully acknowledged for his faith that my manuscript had the strength to be included among the debut monographs in his new urban studies series. I thank the external reviewers, Raphael Sonenshein and Timothy P. Fong, for their comments on my book prospectus, and Peter Jackson for his able critique and suggestions for improvements on the final draft manuscript. Leland Saito provided useful commentary.

Thanks also for the professional conviviality of colleagues at Amherst College, including Carol Clark, Jan Dizard, Frank Couvares, Allen Guttman, Jerry Himmelstein, Karen Sanchez-Eppler, and Kevin Sweeney. A special nod to Ron Lembo, John Solt, and Ryan Willey. Dean of Faculty Lisa A. Raskin has been especially helpful with various expenses for photographs, graphics, and indexing. Kate Blackmer did a stellar job drawing the maps.

Finally, I recognize Jayne Lovett for her support and faithful companionship as I have written this book.

Introduction

Chinatown has traditionally occupied a chimerical position in the American popular imagination. As an urban locale, Chinatown has historically represented an extreme archetype of the clannish closed society, an immigrant enclave crowded with unassimilated newcomers who live a life of marked separation from the American mainstream.[1] An Orientalist patina of mystery and danger surrounds Chinatown; people are somewhat fearful and wary when walking there. Popular films such as Roman Polanski's *Chinatown* (1975) and Michael Cimino's *Year of the Dragon* (1985) have contributed to this iconic representation. Urban residents often mentally situate Chinatown alongside the "combat zone" or "red light district" and the African American "ghetto" in the transitional zones that surround the central city. As a district of crime and social problems, the vice industries of Chinatown are associated with the cultural insularity of a provincial, over-populated foreign colony rather than with the adolescent predators of a deprived, socially disorganized underclass. At the century's end, New York's Chinatown is commonly envisioned as a congested warren of tenements and squalid sweatshops in which deprived illegal immigrants labor in slavelike conditions under the watchful grip of organized criminal smuggling rackets.

The other image that the general public carries of Chinatown is that of the exotic foreign enclave, a dense rookery of restaurants and street emporiums tucked within the vestigial tenement recesses of the modern metropolis. Chinatown is a common stop for tourists to New York City intent on a culinary experience of foreign delicacies outside of their normal experience and a chance for shopping in a low-cost pedestrian bazaar of street hawkers, curio shops, and imported-goods stores. This view, though more

Figure 1. Headlines from the Chinatown beat. Photo by Jan Lin.

benevolent than the "ethnic vice" perspective, still leads to misunderstandings. The state has an ambivalent attitude toward this type of street-level commerce. While the throngs of leisure-seeking tourists are generally applauded by city managers, the industrious efforts of the sidewalk vendors and perishable-food merchants are often denigrated as a type of unrespectable commerce that creates a sanitary or public health hazard, causes street congestion, and evades government taxation.

The journalistic media have recently revived and heightened the vice and crime view of New York's Chinatown with a series of lurid exposés on prisonlike brothels, barracklike sweatshops, and violent killings by international smuggling rings (Figure 1).[2] These disclosures of brutality and misery in Chinatown are typically accompanied by attention to the remediating efforts of the investigative, policing, and regulatory apparatuses of the state. These government interventions are integral to the preservation of human rights and public safety in Chinatown. The fashion in which these social problems are sensationalized, however, perpetuates narrow stereotypes, which fuel nativist sentiment, particularly in the current environment of antipathy toward undocumented aliens as well as legal immigrants. To the uninformed observer, these depraved representations are taken for granted and come to embody the whole picture of what is actually a more complex and nuanced social reality of Chinatown and Chinese American life.

A more far-reaching critique of federal intervention in the livelihood of Chinese America would draw attention to the decades-long exclusions of the Chinese in U.S. immigration law, during which racist representations of Chinese Americans were commonplace. Local governments, meanwhile, have historically sought the demolition of Chinatowns and other urban ethnic enclaves to make way for expressways and to facilitate expansion of the central business district or government office buildings. The typification of Chinatown as both slum and vice district was used to rationalize these clearance schemes. Chinatown has thus been a site through which American concepts about immigrating Chinese as a racial and ethnic category were constructed and reproduced. These concepts have been largely formulated through the discourse of state action, which has been articulated on levels of federal immigration policy, urban development schemes, local policing, and federal intelligence policy. This discourse has historically treated Chinese Americans as clannish and unassimilable, and Chinatowns as beset by social problems.

The social problems perspective feeds popular cultural images of Chinatown as a defiled and degraded place that needs to be cleaned up by investigative cops and aggressive district attorneys. The social problems are viewed as an outcome of a stubborn Chineseness, an ethnic traditionalism that foils cultural integration into American society. Chinatown has historically been perceived as a cloistered, unchanging community where the residents keep to themselves. Chinatown continues to be seen as a backward, somewhat byzantine society, an urban backwater. The residents are thought to cling to ancestral traditions, resistant to change. From this perspective, Chinatown is a place that lives in the past and impedes modernization, and Chinese Americans are a group maladjusted to modernity.

Community Change in Global Context

A clearer picture of the Chinatown social reality begins with an accurate understanding of the ethnic community in the political economy and popular culture of the American city. The many small to medium-sized enterprises and sweatshops of the immigrant enclave do indeed exploit its workforce with low wages, long hours, and poor working conditions. Many immigrants, however, are eventually furnished with opportunities for upward mobility and integration into the American middle classes. Manhattan's Lower East Side has been a portal for a succession of immigrant groups since the mid-nineteenth century, including Irish, Germans, Central European and Russian Jews, Italians, Puerto Ricans, Dominicans, and Chinese. Since the 1960s, a variety of new ethnic enclaves have appeared in emerging immigration gateway cities, such as Miami's Little Havana and Little Haiti, and Los Angeles's Koreatown and Monterey Park (sometimes called "Little Taipei"). Sociological studies of these ethnic enclave economies have identified both positive and negative features. Workers suffer severe degradation in an unregulated, competitive capitalist shadow economy where bosses evade labor laws and overlook health and safety regulations. At the same time, these employers provide employees with real employment opportunities, overlooking deficiencies such as limited English skills and undocumented immigration status.

Literature has similarly attributed a double-edged character to the ethnic enclave. On one hand, the toils of contemporary Chinatown street traders reiterate Horatio Alger's celebrated "rag to riches" myth of turn-of-the-century street boys and pushcart peddlers. On the other hand, there are starker realist icons of the immigrant legacy such as the embittered Lower East Side Jewish protagonist of Abraham Cahan's *The Rise of David Levinsky*. Rather than being a marginal sidebar to American social history, it is apparent that ethnic enclaves such as Chinatown are central sites in urban development and in the formation of a national identity.

The reappearance of sweatshops and street hawkers (characteristic of an earlier precapitalist economy) in the midst of the late-twentieth-century postindustrial American economy has also prompted some observers to draw comparisons with the *informal sector* of developing economies. Typically found in third-world cities, the informal sector is an unregulated circuit of economic and residential life, which evolves as an outgrowth of rural migrant adaptation to the urban economy in the context of international capitalism. A polarized profile has commonly been identified in developing economies wherein the labor-intensive petty enterprises of the informal sector constitute a *lower circuit* of locally oriented economic activity that functions in marked disassociation from the *upper circuit* of transnational finance and corporate capitalism.

Chinatown remarkably displays signs of both the lower-circuit traditional sector and the advanced sector of transnational capitalism. The appearance since the 1970s of a number of banks in Chinatown has led to its typification as a "mini-finance zone." At the beginning of the 1990s, Chinatown banks held some $4 billion in total deposits, the combined outcome of a substantial savings rate among Chinese Americans and incoming overseas capital flow motivated by capital surplus and political uncertainty in Taiwan and Hong Kong. Among the overseas Chinese banks represented were branches of the Hong Kong and Shanghai Banking Corporation, one of the world's largest banks. Overseas Chinese banks are involved in global financial operations as well as management of import-export trade through the Port of New York. Their entrance into Chinatown retail banking is motivated by interest in capturing Chinatown deposits and financing real estate investment. Some overseas banks, such as the Ka Wah Bank and the Bank of East Asia, have built new high-rise offices for their North American operations. By taking a stake in local real estate development, they have further contributed to the restructuring of the Chinatown built environment and the enclave economy.

Since the 1970s municipal and regional officials have sought to encourage involvement of foreign corporations and banks and other producer services in New York City as a means of spurring and securing New York City's position as a national and international command center of the global economy. Local finance, corporate, and rentier capitalist interests have sought to redevelop and gentrify lower Manhattan through the construction of a postindustrial built environment, which includes the World Trade Center and World Financial Center, Battery Park City, and affiliated office and residential projects. By growing and internationalizing the local and regional economy through the stimulus of spatial restructuring, state and capital interests have coincided and have been mutually enhanced through attempts to spur an upward cycle of property values and revenue generation. In Chinatown, city planners have sought to encourage these same trends through tools of urban policy.

Along with Chinatown's increasing economic significance is a growing political conspicuousness. Workers have responded to their debased informal-sector working conditions and gained a sense of group solidarity through collective action. Through workplace pickets, street demonstrations, consumer boycotts, and hunger strikes, the Chinatown proletariat have rallied for their rights as American workers. In addition to workplace disputes, the Chinatown populace has also held public demonstrations to protest city law enforcement policy, local development schemes, and municipal employment procedures. Legal challenges have accompanied these collective actions. Community-based political organizations have penetrated local political party machinery and the municipal bureaucracy and were a significant force in city redistricting proceedings in 1991. A growing constituency of Chinese American labor and community and legal activists staff these new community and political organizations, which have challenged the traditional hegemony of Chinatown's patronage associations. They have also mobilized resources and extracted concessions from locally elected officials who regard Chinatown as an increasingly potent electoral force.

These social realities unmask the fallacy of Chinatown as an insular peer-group society run by traditional patronage associations and organized crime. More genuine is a picture of a community in the midst of change, under the impact of broader shifts in American society and the global economy. The notion of Chinatown as a solidaristic, unitary enclave must also be dispensed with. There is substantial internal differentiation along class, linguistic, and national lines. Chinatown was historically composed of lower-class and mercantile immigrants from China's Guangdong Province who spoke the Cantonese dialect. Since the liberalization of immigration policy in 1965, however, Chinatown has absorbed a more diverse array of immigrants of both lower- and upper-class origins from Hong Kong, Taiwan, and China's Fujian Province. Mandarin, Taiwanese, and Fuzhouese have been added to the repertoire of Chinese dialects used in the enclave. The affluent investors who are agents of capital flow into Chinatown emanate mainly from Hong Kong and Taiwan, nations that have recently ascended to a semiperipheral or intermediary position in the world system of states. Fujianese, the newest arrivals to New York's Chinatown, are mostly poorer immigrants.

Rather than implying that Chinatown is too internally differentiated to be a community, I would suggest that our notions of what constitutes and reproduces immigrant communities in postindustrial America must be reconceptualized to include a dynamic sense of local change within an evolving structural context. New organizational and residential solidarities have been created by labor and community organizations, resulting in an empowering sense of community as both ethnic-group consciousness and defended territory beyond the supporting framework of kinship and peer-group networks. These defensive solidarities are responses to, variously, the exploitations of co-ethnic employers, the pressures of foreign capital, or the redevelopmental interests of rentier capitalists and local governments.

Chineseness in particular and ethnicity in general are thus not primordial or ancestral. Community, similarly, is not static or resistant to change. I comprehend ethnicity and community as situational social phenomena that frame the identities of individuals and order group life, which are constructed and intensified as localities encounter and respond to broader social and economic change. As the American economy and society have globalized, social relations between constituent ethnic groups and communities have also changed.

Finally, some labor and community organizations have begun to ally with segments of small-business capital and departmental components of the local government to preserve employment or neighborhood stability. Labor-capital cooperation has occurred in the garment industry. Some community organizations have begun cooperating with local governmental agencies to revitalize Chinatown within the context of urban tourism. Neighborhood preservation has been linked with heritage tourism as an economic development strategy and a source of local revenue. This evolving multicultural urban development policy that promotes the livelihood of ethnic communities takes place within a broader agenda of "world city" promotion among city managers and regional planners.

The second-generation Chinese American professionals and activists who staff these new community organizations have interacted with community-based writers, artists, and historians to project new positive representations of the Chinatown community. These affirmative representations unearth historical memories or present a picture of a still evolving future through evocations of the quotidian struggle in a low-income enclave, or of confrontations with the enclave power elite and with the agents of power and authority within the broader society. New concepts of Chinatown as a site of community empowerment and of Chinese American ethnicity as a proactive identity rather than a cultural barrier to successful adjustment to American society have been created through these images of community change.

Community, Ethnicity, and Urban Sociology

The place, function, and future of immigrant communities and ethnic institutions in the American city have historically been of interest to academics, planners, public officials, and citizens alike. Traditional assumptions regarding the mode and direction of immigrant incorporation into American society, however, have shifted in tune with the changing political economy of American cities. The early view, derived from the human ecology school of urban sociology propagated in the early twentieth century at the University of Chicago, conceived of immigrant enclaves as impermanent "natural areas," flowering in the low-rent "zone-in-transition" ringing the central business district, which would disappear with the assimilation and upward mobility of later generations into the American middle classes (Park and Burgess 1925; Zorbaugh 1926: 223; Thomas and Znaniecki 1958).[3] Rose Hum Lee, one of the first Chinese American sociologists to apply human ecological concepts to the comparative study of a number of Chinatowns, noted their demographic decline and physical deterioration in the postwar period, and predicted their eventual "withering away" through the combined effects of the restrictive immigration laws, intergenerational occupational mobility of the immigrants, and cultural assimilation through time (1949).[4]

Anti-ethnic assumptions were implicit among the founders of human ecology theory. Robert E. Park suggested that the "keener, the more energetic, and the more ambitious" immigrants would quickly move out of their "ghettos and immigrant colonies" into secondary settlement areas in outer zones of the city, or into more cosmopolitan areas where they would associate with members of several different immigrant and racial groups (1926: 9). In separate writings on the "race relations cycle," he conceived of new immigrant groups as moving through stages of contact, conflict, and accommodation prior to their ensuing assimilation into American society (Matthews 1977). Ethnic affiliation was seen to retard Americanization, and immigrant communities were seen to harbor syndicate crime, vice, and a host of other social problems. Chicago school sociologist Walter C. Reckless wrote:

> The relationship of Chinatown to the commercialized vice areas of American cities is too well known to need elaboration. It is only fair to say, however, that the assumption of the usual parasitic activities by the Chinese in the Western World is probably to be explained by their natural segregation at the center of cities, as well as by their uncertain economic and social status. (1971: 246)

Paul Siu, another early Chinese American sociologist, who held a less critical but similarly pathological perspective on ethnic institutions, observed that Chinese laundry and restaurant workers labored in a "social isolation" and residential self-segregation that impeded their successful assimilation into American society (1952).

Louis Wirth, who later codified the thesis of "anti-urbanism" through his seminal essay "Urbanism as a Way of Life" (1938), began a shift from the anti-ethnic bias through his positive depiction of the Jewish "ghetto" of Chicago as a neighborhood of close primary ties and rich cultural life (1927). The Wirthian perspective conceived of the immigrant colony as a functioning vestige of traditional society in the face of the alienating encroachments of the dense, heterogeneously populated metropolis. The affirmative conception of the ethnic community continued with two landmark studies of Italian American communities, both in Boston. William Foote Whyte's *Street Corner Society* (1943) portrayed the efforts of his locally bound "corner boy" informant, "Doc," to gain a streetwise livelihood in marked contrast to the middle-class aspirations of "college boys" who were departing their North End neighborhood. Examining the West End neighborhood in the late 1950s before its wholesale demolition, Herbert Gans found that the close-knit "peer group society" granted its denizens a sense of identity, custom, attachment to place, and social order. His portrayal of this neighborhood in *The Urban Villagers* (1962a) countered the popular sentiment that ethnic neighborhoods were socially disorganized slums whose denizens were arguably provincial but firmly anti-assimilationist and had a resilient pride in locality and ethnicity.[5]

Gerald Suttles followed with *The Social Order of the Slum* (1968), which found that though Black, Italian, Mexican, and Puerto Rican youth gangs usually experienced tense relationships in periodic conflicts over territory in the "Addams area" (a pseudonym for his study area), a unified sense of "provincial morality" took over when there was a perceived threat from the outside. From a comparative perspective, Albert Hunter and Suttles (1972) later suggested that the strongest sense of "community" exists in the case of the "defended neighborhood," when residents come to recognize a common interest in responding to intrusions from beyond. This cohesion was strongly apparent in street-corner gangs, vigilante-like citizens' groups, and restrictive covenants. From this standpoint, "community" was not something backward, an atavistic remnant of traditional "folk society," but a socially constructed phenomenon that arose from the interaction of individuals across a defined territory in response to redevelopmental incursions or urban change.

New conceptual work on urban communities was also produced with the emergence of the community action movement in the 1950s and 1960s. A voice of urban populism came with Jane Jacobs, the notorious critic of urban renewal, who led home owners in Manhattan's West Village neighborhood in successfully opposing a redevelopment plan engineered by Mayor Robert Wagner in the late 1950s (Zukin 1989: 114–15). Another classic case of the defended community during this era involved citizen opposition to the Yerba Buena urban renewal project in the "South of Market" neighborhood of San Francisco (Hartman 1974). Ira Katznelson (1981) examined the convergences between racial/ethnic demographic succession and the political "assault" of neighborhood action movements on the established "trenches" of territorially based patronage politics in upper Manhattan in the early 1970s.[6] Ranging historically and geographically across a variety of European, Latin American, and American case studies, Manuel Castells (1983) has drawn our attention to the growth of community-based "urban social movements" as a cross-national phenomenon.[7] More recently, Janet Abu-Lughod and her research team (1994) delivered a complex, nuanced account of local resistance to redevelopmental gentrification in Manhattan's East Village.

Running parallel with these community action movements were the civil rights movement and the urban disturbances of the 1950s and 1960s, which by the early 1970s had fomented a new racial/ethnic consciousness and concern regarding inequality and intergroup relations in urban America. Liberal authors Nathan Glazer and Daniel Patrick Moynihan (1963) urged us to look "beyond the melting pot" model of U.S. society. The death knell of assimilation discourse was increasingly rung by an artillery of new conceptual paradigms that privileged cultural pluralism and ethnic persistence. The conceptual rethinking extended to conservative sociologists such as Michael Novak (1971), who noted a new group awareness among white ethnic Americans in describing the "rise of the unmeltable ethnics." Observing that the occupational and residential concentration of immigrant groups accompanies rather than impedes social change, William Yancey et al. (1976) suggested that ethnicity should be reconceptualized as an "emergent" phenomenon. Rather than being a status or attachment that was biological, primordial, or ancestral, ethnicity could now be viewed as something that was the situational product of evolving intergroup relations in a changing U.S. society.

Ethnic Enclaves

Associated with the new models of ethnic persistence is the ethnic enclave economies perspective, which highlights the economic dynamism displayed in contemporary urban ethnic enclaves such as Miami's Cuban enclave and the Chinese enclaves of San Francisco and New York City. These ethnic enclave economies are seen to proffer socioeconomic opportunity for the latest immigrants to American cities in a fashion different from the low-wage, dead-end employment in the secondary labor market experienced by African Americans. Utilizing a complex "returns on human capital" statistical methodology, proponents of this approach conceptualize immigrant occupational niches as urban subeconomies that grant labor-market rewards and upward socioeconomic mobility over time (Wilson and Portes 1980; Wilson and Martin 1982; Portes and Manning 1986; Sanders and Nee 1987; Zhou and Logan 1989). There has been some debate among these writers, however, regarding positive versus negative functions of the enclave economy, specifically over the question of different rewards conferred on employees versus employers.[8] Another concern is whether the enclave is defined by place of work, place of residence, or industry sector. Furthermore, examining New York's Chinatown, Min Zhou and John Logan found evidence of significant gender differences in enclave labor market outcomes. Positive returns on human capital for men as opposed to absent or negative returns for women led these investigators to ponder "to what degree the positive functions of the enclave for men are derived from the subordinate position of women" (1989: 818).

In summary, the ethnic enclave may be conceived as having a double-edged character that rewards bosses mainly at the expense of workers, who labor in jobs that are mostly dead-end in terms of future occupational mobility. The entrepreneurial accomplishments of the immigrant small-business sector, in other words, are based to a great extent on the exploitation of their co-ethnic workforce, who labor long hours for low wages in poor working conditions, with little employment security. As Jimy Sanders and Victor Nee have noted,

> The "embeddedness" of economic activity in networks of ethnic relations can trap immigrant workers in patron-client relation-ships that bind them, in exchange for assistance at an early stage, to low-wage jobs. A detailed analysis of the actual pattern of ex-change between bosses and workers within immigrant enclaves is needed before generalizations can be made about ethnic solidari-ty's effect on the socioeconomic mobility of immigrant workers. (1987: 765)

On the other hand, we may recognize that immigrant bosses also work hard, provide opportunities for immigrants with limited English-speaking ability, give them on-the-job training, and may overlook undocu-mented immigration status. Additionally, through the multiplier effect, en-clave earnings are recirculated through purchases in co-ethnic businesses and through forward, backward, and consumption linkages, and accumu-lated earnings are eventually reinvested in residential and commercial real estate. Thus, although there may be short-run disparities in the economic benefits conferred on enclave participants, the aggregate economic effect is positive. The local economy in ethnic enclaves is generally robust, and the built environment is in constant use or in a process of upgrading; this situa-tion is in contrast to the capital-scarce, deteriorated urban terrain of the "barrio" or "ghetto."

This focus on ethnic enclave economies differs from the earlier as-similationist studies in identifying positive rather than negative outcomes from ethnicity and ethnic solidarity. Rather than predicting the eventual dissolution of ethnic communities, the enclave thesis suggests their persis-tence. Alejandro Portes and Robert Manning (1986) point out also that ethnic enclaves have a historical dimension, using the examples of the Jewish enclave of Manhattan's Lower East Side and the Japanese of the West Coast.

Globalization and Polarized Cities

Clear demographic and geopolitical shifts prompted these conceptual reassessments of ethnicity and immigrant communities in the United States. The Hart-Cellar Immigration Act of 1965, in the spirit of the civil rights era, finally lifted decades-long immigration restrictions. Immigration to the United States after 1965 began to acquire a more nonwhite, Asian and Latin American/Caribbean character as the American economy similarly became differentially integrated into the changing global economy, forming trade and investment links with these developing world regions. In this broader context of globalization, the issue of immigrant acculturation into a prospective American melting pot was becoming less the question than that of their political and economic incorporation into a restructuring post-industrial American society. Emerging perspectives in urban political economy contextualized the transformation of American cities within this backdrop of globalization (Feagin and Smith 1987).

The globalization thesis distinguishes the post–World War II era as a new phase of capitalist production, management, and finance in the world economy. Beginning in the 1960s, analysts of industrial relations and the international economy began to call attention to an increasingly transnational strategy in the marketing as well as production activities of corporations based in the advanced capitalist nations. Fiscal uncertainty, two oil shocks, simultaneous inflation and recession (stagflation), and structural unemployment and domestic economic "crisis" in capitalist core nations such as the United States in the 1970s were increasingly attributed to global restructuring (Harvey 1989; O'Connor 1984). From this standpoint, the growth of immigrant sweatshops and new immigrant communities filled the vacuum in the United States left by economic "deindustrialization" because of the "capital flight" of American "runaway shops" to third-world locations (Bluestone and Harrison 1982; Glickman 1987).

As articulated by Frobel et al. (1980), a "new international division of labor" (NIDL) has emerged in the world economy since the 1960s, which involves the strategy of firms in advanced capitalist "core" nations shifting production facilities to lesser developed "periphery" nations to take advantage of cross-national differentials in wage rates and labor bargaining power. In many cases, governments of the less developed nations encouraged the direct investment of transnational corporations in specifically designated free-trade zones or export processing zones close to airports or harbors.

Among the inducements offered were basic infrastructure, a ready low-wage labor supply, tax reductions, and lifting of quota restrictions and tariffs on the import of intermediate inputs and the export of finished products. The NIDL was also facilitated by technological advances in global transport (especially shipping containerization) and communications (satellites, computers, and, more recently, fiber optics and facsimile machines).

In the 1970s, however, came growing shop-floor militancy, labor organizing, and rising wage levels in the less developed countries. The declining power of organized labor in the advanced industrial core and a new movement of immigrants from peripheral to core states also helped mediate an increasing switching of production from offshore locations back to onshore. Electronic assembly factories staffed particularly by Asian, Latino, and Caribbean immigrant women appeared in Silicon Valley, Southern California, New York City, and other immigration gateway locations. Garment sweatshops and other unregulated labor-intensive economic activities appeared in the same sites. The phenomenon was variously depicted as one of "reperipheralization at the core" (Sassen-Koob 1982), "bringing the Third World home" (Smith 1988: 214), and growth of "downgraded manufacturing" in postindustrial cities (Sassen 1988). Comparisons were made with trends in European cities (Portes et al. 1989). The original expositors of the NIDL thesis were compelled to acknowledge that transnational capitalism was now practicing a kind of "shifting cultivation" of production facilities in both the core and periphery (Kreye, Heinrichs, and Frobel 1986).

Associated with the concept of a global system of production sites is the notion that the headquarters of international banks and corporations have become linked through a hierarchical system of *world cities.* The term *world cities* was initially promulgated by Peter Hall (1966) in reference to the seven most influential metropolitan areas in the advanced capitalist world. Robert Cohen (1981), John Friedmann and Goetz Wolff (1982), and Warwick Armstrong and T. G. McGee (1985) subsequently associated the concept with global economic change and the notion of an urban hierarchy spanning both developed and less developed nations. Saskia Sassen (1988) finally linked "global cities" with patterns of labor and capital mobility. As codified by Sassen (1988), the global city concept rests on the notion that the emergent "producer services" sectors of advanced global capitalism are becoming structurally concentrated in certain nodal "command centers," such as New York, Los Angeles, London, and Tokyo. Sassen also suggests that growth in producer services creates low-wage work through demand for a range of personal services, domestic household services, customized construction and repair work, and building security services in offices and high-income gentrified neighborhoods. Thus postindustrial global cities require not only a corps of highly skilled and educated managers and administrators but also a phalanx of low-skilled and low-paid clerical staff, who are often recent immigrants.

These forms of high-income employment spur residential gentrification in the urban core. High-income gentrification, furthermore, creates a demand for high-priced specialized products usually manufactured via labor-intensive methods and sold through small boutiques, rather than for the standardized, mass-marketed items that historically have been produced by capital-intensive technology and marketed through department stores. Examples are custom-designed apparel, footwear, jewelry, fur, furniture, and electronics products. A highly publicized illustration of these linkages is the garment industry, in which high-fashion designers, such as Liz Claiborne and Norma Kamali, have contracted assembly work to low-paying, unregulated immigrant sweatshops (Sassen-Koob 1987).

As advanced and less developed economies have become more closely integrated, the globalization perspective suggests growing structural similarities among constituent cities in the contemporary capitalist world system. Concepts traditionally derived from studies of third-world cities have increasingly been applied to the advanced capitalist milieu. The emergence of unregulated economic activities and a marginalized underclass in postindustrial first-world cities such as New York, Los Angeles, London, and Paris has invited comparison with the *informal sector* of third-world metropolises such as Jakarta, Lima, Manila, and Mexico City, where rural-to-urban migrants have historically generated their own employment opportunities and resided in self-built squatter housing (Abu-Lughod and Hay 1979; Sassen 1988; Portes et al. 1989). The dualist paradigm classically employed in the third-world urbanization literature identifies the existence of a vast locally oriented, petty capitalist *lower circuit* of informal-sector activities operating in marked separation from an *upper circuit* of transnational sector operations oriented toward the global economy (Santos 1979; Friedmann and Wolff 1982; Armstrong and McGee 1985).[9] This economic bifurcation leads to a process of uneven development and aggravates social inequality in urban residential life.

In New York City, the recent growth of Latino, Caribbean, and Asian residential enclaves has been accompanied by the appearance of unregulated and exploitative forms of sweatshop production of apparel and footwear and other light manufacturing activities. At the same time, there has been a pronounced growth of employment in high-wage advanced corporate and managerial services in the midst of a long-term decline in medium-wage skilled manufacturing employment. Transnational interests have dramatically increased their presence. The result has been a cleavage in the New York City class structure that is reflected through polarization in housing markets, race and ethnic relations, political coalitions, and the spatial configuration of the broader metropolitan region (Mollenkopf and Castells 1991).[10]

Where migrants to the favelas, barrios, and kampongs of the developing world have largely relied on self-built squatter housing, new immigrants to New York City have settled into existing, mostly deteriorated low-rent housing stock in the urban core (Manhattan) and the inner ring of outer boroughs. To some extent, it is a story of immigrant succession; they have used housing filtered down from upwardly mobile white ethnic populations, who have dispersed into better housing in the outer ring of suburbs on the metropolitan periphery. Accelerating gentrification and redevelopment in the core and some inner-ring neighborhoods, however, cast doubt over the continued viability of the residential filtration model. Similarly, economic transition to postindustrialism clouds opportunities for occupational upward mobility for the newest immigrants to New York City.

I employ the dual city concept in examining the process of urban development under economic change in a nodal metropolis of the new world economy through the microcosm of the central-city enclave of Chinatown. Rather than unity or extreme heterogeneity, there is a pronounced polarity in the Chinatown enclave economy. Socioeconomic differentiation is further articulated through the built environment in the form of spatial differentiation. A telling illustration of these contrasts in New York's Chinatown is the sight of sidewalk peddlers plying their wares and produce from tables or canvas sheets on Canal Street in front of the guarded glass offices of transnational banks such as the Bank of East Asia and the Hong Kong and Shanghai Banking Corporation (which is the twenty-fifth largest bank in the world) (Figure 2). New York's Chinatown presents an interesting case where both processes of the informal sector and the advanced transnational sector can be observed in direct juxtaposition within the microcontext of the community.

The existing literature on New York City's Chinatown (Kuo 1977; Wong 1982, 1988; Zhou 1992) generally views the district as a unified enclave.[11] Only Peter Kwong (1987) has drawn attention, as I have, to themes of inequality and community conflict through his discussion of distinctions between affluent uptown and poorer downtown Chinese in New York City.

In contrast with Asian enclaves, Latino districts in the United States are for the most part capital-scarce lower-circuit enclaves unmarked by sig-

Figure 2. The Chinatown two-circuit economy. Photo by Jan Lin.

nificant internal socioeconomic polarization. There have been indications, however, of a sometimes surreptitious flow of Latin American investment capital into American bank deposits and real estate investments since the early 1980s. Debt crisis and slow growth in Latin American economies are the motivation for this capital flight. New York City and Miami seem to be the main host cities for this circuit of investment. By comparison, Asian enclaves have greater upper-circuit involvement. The Asian Pacific Rim, unlike the Latin American and Caribbean region, constitutes a major growth area in the late-twentieth-century global economy and thus has emerged as a main source of mobile, investable capital. Political uncertainty at home, the accumulation of substantial trade surpluses, the lure of preferential investment opportunities abroad (an effect of exchange-rate differentials), and bilateral trading ties mean that much of this upper-circuit surplus capital is being recycled into investments on American shores.

State Policy and Local Mobilization

The global cities perspective may emphasize the structural factors and systemic variables in urban development to some degree neglecting the agency of intermediate institutional forces. Cities are compared and ranked in terms of their relative economic position in the global economy, conforming to a logic of "advanced capitalism," with scant attention to local factors and urban politics. The instructive but forbidding view of polarized cities projected by some of these theorists might suggest that new immigrant workers are politically impotent pawns of the new capitalist social order. The role of local government planners and public officials may also be seen as somewhat secondary to the broader machinations of capital. Some writers friendly to the globalization perspective, however, have injected more attention to local conditions, state policy, and social action into the analysis.

The conceptual fit between the global cities perspective and a political-economic perspective that emphasizes the question of state-labor-capital relations in sociospatial organization is actually quite close and is advocated by proponents of the urban political-economy paradigm, or the "new urban sociology" (Zukin 1980; Gottdiener and Feagin 1988). These scholars come from a diversity of disciplines including sociology, political science, geography, and planning and have been variously characterized as neo-Marxist, neo-Ricardian, neo-Weberian, or postmodernist (Gottdiener and Feagin 1988). Their scholarly assault is grounded in a forceful critique of the fundamental assumptions and explanatory framework of orthodox human ecological theory, which privileged neoclassical economic principles in the study of urban development. The new urban sociologists conceptualize the urban economy and processes of urban spatial development as more fundamentally interpenetrated by political and class interests, state prerogatives, the interests of labor and communities, and extra-national processes on the level of the global economy.

Joe R. Feagin and Michael Peter Smith (1987) have instructively called for attention to political variables in equal proportion to economic factors. They cogently state:

> Cities change not only as a result of the requirements of global or local capital but also as a result of state policy at the local and national level. There are, in effect, two worldwide "logics," an economic (capitalistic) logic and a state logic; these have for a century or more been inextricably interrelated. Changing urban development patterns are best understood as the long-term outcomes of actions taken by economic and political actors operating within a complex and changing matrix of global and national economic and political forces. It is historically-specific political-economic processes through which contemporary corporations must work rather than expressing general economic laws of capitalist development. (1987: 17)

Since there is an environment of competitive positioning in the world system of cities, political actors have an active interest in influencing the pace or direction of economic and urban developmental change. Feagin (1988) has documented how local government and capital interests in Houston, Texas, parlayed a "free enterprise" business climate of non-union labor, low-cost land, and low taxes to attract international capital in successfully positioning the metropolis as a nodal center of global oil and gas production. John Logan and Harvey Molotch (1987) also have described how constellations of "place entrepreneurs" and state actors can manipulate instruments of municipal policy and regional planning to attract outside investment capital and government funding to stimulate local urban growth. While boosting the economy of municipal "growth machines," these actors serve their own investment and property interests.

Local governments, meanwhile, have historically viewed immigrant communities as obstacles to growth and modernization. Throughout most of the early twentieth century, ethnic places were perceived by city managers as unsanitary districts of blight and overcrowding, social problems, and vice. An "anti-ethnic" nativism was evident in the early years of municipal reform when liberal urban Protestants articulated a "social gospel" that sought to combat the linked evils of unrestricted immigration, unsanitary slums, and urban social pathology (Warner 1972: 174). Ethnic districts were regularly the object of slum clearance or urban renewal programs to make way for expressway arterials and new housing. In razing ethnic places, city managers linked programs of urban decentralization, developmental modernization, and cultural assimilation. These communities, meanwhile, lacked the political influence to contest these land-use decisions.

The first slum clearance projects occurred in the 1930s, for example, the destruction of Jewish and Italian tenement neighborhoods of Manhattan's Lower East Side for construction of the East River expressway and public housing (Buttenweiser 1987). Federal policy became more clearly codified with the Housing Act of 1949 and associated Supreme Court decisions, which granted powers of eminent domain to local public authorities to strategically assemble neighborhoods that were classified as "blighted slums" for wide-scale clearance and redevelopment. Demolition of the Italian American West End of Boston (subject of Herbert Gans's *Urban Villagers* study) for government offices and middle-income and luxury housing was directed first by the Boston Housing Authority and then by the newly created Boston Redevelopment Authority in the late 1950s (Kennedy 1992: 164). Even without condemnation, the period between the announcement of an intercity highway or redevelopment project and groundbreaking inevitably depressed land values through subsequent abandonment and disinvestment. Compensation for displaced homeowners and tenants was scant until the U.S. Congress passed a law in 1968, although implementation has been spotty (Warner 1972: 48–49). African American neighborhoods were disproportionately affected by slum clearance and urban renewal, which during the 1960s was sometimes dubbed "Negro removal." Some three-quarters of all people displaced by renewal projects were black residents (Robertson and Judd 1989: 307). Thus, poor race and ethnic minorities bore most of the costs of urban decentralization and redevelopment at the core.

Citing the growth of grass-roots resistance to urban renewal since the 1960s, Michael Peter Smith has called for "attention to the interplay of local and global dynamics" via consideration of the "consciousness, intentionality, everyday practices, and collective action" of common people (1987: 105). He highlights the widespread impact of community mobilizations within civil society on local government policies regarding highway expansion, commercial encroachment, housing, environmental degradation, and other social policy areas. Examining a range of Sunbelt cities, he finds that black and Hispanic activists have either joined with white middle-class reformers or lobbied for local control and political representation through ward-based mobilizations (1988: 222–23). James O'Connor has argued that informal-sector workers and other "marginalized" urban populations overrepresented in part-time and subcontracting forms of employment, such as women, youth, and the elderly, are the foundation of the "new social movements" and "post-McGovern" unity drives within organized labor and the Democratic Party (1984: 114–15). Susan Fainstein also suggests that economic polarization and social marginalization were at the heart of the race/ethnic mobilizations of the 1960s and the neighborhood movement of the 1970s (1987: 323–42).

The Political Construction of Racial/Ethnic Representations

Recent literature in race and ethnic studies (Omi and Winant 1994; Feagin and Vera 1995; Smith and Feagin 1995) has drawn attention to the historically and politically constructed character of racial categories and ethnic status. Representations of racial and ethnic inferiority that validated the subordination of nonwhite peoples during the historical project of European colonialism were extended to the American milieu during its own period of state-building and imperialist expansion. White economic and cultural hegemony in the American social formation was achieved through a legal apparatus that relegated African Americans to slave status (defined as three-fifths of a citizen), Native Americans to removal (as subordinated nations), Asians to immigrant exclusion (ineligible for citizenship), and Latinos to expatriation and semicolonial guest-worker status. Although these formal subordinations were overturned by racial/ethnic social movements and civil rights legislation, negative racial/ethnic representations persist in an era of ongoing contestation for political hegemony in the U.S. social order.

Adverse stereotypes and xenophobic images of race and ethnic minorities have thus resurfaced recently in the guise of culture wars, media panics, and policy debates over social issues such as language policy and illegal immigration, the urban underclass, and gang violence. The major areas of contestation and debate in the federal arena include immigration, citizenship, and social welfare policy, while law enforcement, housing, and urban development are among the main issues on the local level. Furthermore, the mass media are complicitous in the formation and reinforcement of stigmatized representations (Smith and Feagin 1995: 12–13).[12]

Similar work has recently been undertaken by social and cultural geographers to root our knowledge and perception of race, ethnicity, and other cultural categories within historical processes and relations of power, with an emphasis on the pivotal significance of place and territory (Anderson and Gale 1992; Duncan and Ley 1993). Geographic terrains and sites figure centrally in the deployment of state policies and nationalist discourses, processes in the social construction of race and ethnic categories (Jackson and Penrose 1994). Kay Anderson's work (1987, 1991) on the impact of Canadian federal immigration restriction laws in defining Chinese as undesirable "outsiders" and of municipal slum clearance policies in framing Vancouver's Chinatown as a morally depraved and unsanitary "celestial cesspool" is particularly instructive. Conceptualizing Chinatown as an "evaluative" rather than a "neutral" term (1991: 30), she observes that built environments and physical landscapes are not "objectively given," but "negotiated realities" (1991: 28). Examining parliamentary debates, period journalism, and the writings of health inspectors and other municipal officials, Anderson suggests that Canadian representations of Chinatown as a place and the Chinese as a racial category fundamentally bear the inscription of racial ideological purpose in exercising white political domination rather than objectively describing the Chinese themselves. Anderson invokes Edward Said's compelling concept of "Orientalism" as a historical "discourse," not a pure but a political field of knowledge (Said 1979: 9) produced through the cumulative writings, since Antiquity, of European scholars, diplomats, administrators, and philosophers in validating Western authority and imperialist hegemony over the East via an imaginative distancing that both demonized and exoticized the Orient as the Occident's polar oppositional "Other."

Historians of Asian American studies have similarly examined Orientalism in the American context. Gary Okihiro suggests that American Orientalism was incarnated in the form of a "yellow peril"[13] hysteria that signified Asian immigrants as a barbarous menace to America's Far West in the late nineteenth century (1994: 118–47). This menacing personification sharply contrasts with a more benign image projected by traders, diplomats, and missionaries (particularly from the Yankee East Coast) from the 1780s to the Opium War in the 1840s of the "Celestial" civilization as a source of fine commodities (such as china, silk, and tea), governed by an advanced bureaucracy.[14] During the era of manifest destiny following the completion of the transcontinental railroad (achieved through the contribution of "Asiatic muscle"), however, writers and commentators began to warn that Chinese laborers threatened to undermine the superiority of American technology and the energies of Yankee inventiveness (Takaki 1979: 215–49). At the turn of the century, there were also admonitions regarding the potential competitive threat of Asian manufacturers in the American market, a public sentiment that has been revived in the late twentieth century despite the rise of a more benevolent "model minority" stereotype of Asian Americans.

The model minority myth of the contemporary era belies a continued double-edged ambivalence within the American public imagination toward the Asian and the Asian American in a time of declining U.S. hegemony and increased competitiveness in the global economy. The notion of Asian Americans as an entrepreneurial, achievement-oriented minority group whose strong work ethic, family values, education, and self-reliance (in alleged contradistinction to blacks and other welfare-dependent minorities) was initially propagated in a *U.S. News and World Report* story in December 1966 at the height of the decade's urban social unrest (Osajima 1988). In the following decades, this benevolent imagery has been counterposed by the resurfacing of a "yellow perilism" derived from white fears of hyper-acquisitive Japanese investors and overachieving Asians on university campuses (e.g., M.I.T. as "Made in Taiwan" and U.C.L.A. as the "University of Caucasians Lost among Asians").

The changeability of popular cultural images of the Asian in contemporary America is partly a by-product of technological innovation and communicative immediacy; the new electronic mass media reach larger numbers of homes and viewers more quickly than the traditional print and visual media. The mutability of these portrayals may also reflect a growing condition of American public uncertainty within the volatile dynamics of the new global economy, a political-economic terrain in which the United States is no longer an undisputed hegemon. Globalization thus circumscribes not only the contours of Chinese labor and capital inflow in the contemporary era but the mode of their representational inscription in the American collective imagination.

From Bachelor Society
to Immigrant Enclave

Chinatowns have historically been enclaves of petty capitalism and proletarian labor, like many other ethnic communities of the American city, such as Little Italy or Greek Town. Unlike European immigrants, however, Chinese arrivals were excluded from American citizenship by the Naturalization Law of 1790, and remained in the status of resident aliens until the McCarran-Walter Act of 1952.[1] The Chinese Exclusion Act of 1882, furthermore, prohibited new arrivals for six decades, and Chinatowns were frozen in the status of bachelor societies of "sojourners" until immigration laws were liberalized in the mid-twentieth century. After a period of participation in frontier industries such as mining and railroad construction, anti-Chinese agitation and discrimination in the labor market relegated the Chinese to labor-intensive, low-wage occupations deemed socially undesirable by established Americans, such as laundry and restaurant work. The male-dominated profile of American Chinatowns during the exclusion era provided markets for a range of vice industries, which assisted the emergence of syndicated crime within these communities.

The liberalization of U.S. immigration policy in 1965 provided the opportunity for American Chinatowns to become family-centered communities. New York's Chinatown began to grow expansively into the nation's largest Chinese American settlement, absorbing both legal and illegal immigrants. This enclave of small to medium-sized proprietors and labor operating in labor-intensive areas such as restaurants and other retail trade activities, garment manufacturing, and street vending, which use a built environment of tenement apartments and loft-manufacturing space, essentially constitutes a lower-circuit, or small-enterprise, sector of immigrant incorporation into the livelihood of the modern city.

From Bachelor Society to Immigrant Enclave

Chinese immigrants first began arriving in the United States in the 1850s, during the waning decades of the Qing dynasty. After losing the Opium War to the Western powers (1839–42), China was plagued by economic chaos, famine, flood, and political unrest, which included civil war and an extensive peasant protest in southeast China known as the Taiping Rebellion. Meanwhile, the resolution of the Opium War had led to the designation of coastal cities such as Hong Kong, Canton, and Macao as treaty ports open to Western trade and influence. Southeast China was thus opened up not only to commodity trade but to labor export in the form of contract laborers.

Asian contract labor filled the labor demand in the Americas brought about by the British cessation of the Atlantic slave trade in the 1830s. Some Asian laborers were shanghaied into forced slave labor in Mexico, Cuba, and Peru, but arrivals in Australia and North America were more commonly transported via a contract or credit ticket system. Chinese immigrants to the United States thus generally financed their trans-Pacific passage via a period of debenture to a sponsoring ocean transport company or an employer in the receiving nation. The discovery of gold in California in the 1840s stimulated the migration to America, which the Chinese called "Gum Shan" (Mountain of Gold). Many also journeyed to Hawaii to work as agricultural laborers, to British Columbia to work in fisheries and canneries, and to Australia to mine gold. The migration coincided with a period during which the production of fast sailing ships was perfected; many a Yankee-built China clipper plied the waters of the Pacific with cargoes of commodities and humanity.

Chinese immigrants during this period were primarily rural peasants from Guangdong Province on the southeast coast of China near Canton (Guangzhou) and Hong Kong (Map 1). The "fountainhead" from which these immigrants originated was the districts surrounding the Pearl River delta, with sixty percent coming from the county of Toishan (Sung 1967: 10). A rocky and austere region that yielded a scant agricultural output, Toishan (which translates as "Mountain Plateau") was historically inhabited by a peasantry that spent much of the year as itinerant peddlers, laborers, and merchants among neighboring provinces.

Concentrating in the Pacific and western states during their first decades of settlement, Chinese laborers scattered throughout surrounding states with the end of the gold rush to work on railroad construction, in land reclamation projects, seasonal agriculture, fishing, canning, and urban factory work, and as cooks, domestics, and laundry workers. Exclud-

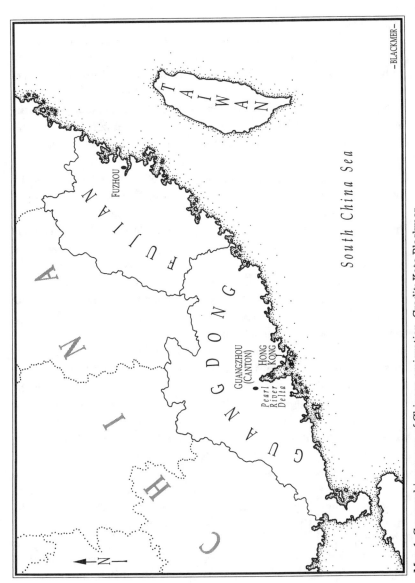

Map 1. Geographic sources of Chinese emigration. Credit: Kate Blackmer.

ed from rights of U.S. citizenship by the Naturalization Law of 1790, Chinese immigrants remained in the status of resident alien laborers and acquired a reputation among American workers as "bachelor sojourners" only interested in a temporary stay in the United States. The completion of the transcontinental railroad in 1869 spelled the end of the frontier, and labor-market competition increased as eastern migrants arrived in the West. Anti-Chinese rioting and lynchings took place in many western states in the 1870s and 1880s, and nativist regional politicians lobbied for immigrant restriction.

The resulting Chinese Exclusion Act of 1882, the first federal legislation ever passed to bar any group of immigrants based on national origin, was renewed periodically for the next sixty years.[2] New arrivals were prohibited, and the Chinese population in the United States fell from a high of nearly 110,000 in 1890 to barely over 60,000 in ensuing decades. Wives generally remained in the home village by Chinese custom and because the transoceanic journey was prohibitively expensive and considered extremely arduous. The ratio of men to women reached its high point in 1890 at nearly twenty-seven men to every woman. Chinese exclusion and the naturalization restriction effectively forestalled the development of permanent family-centered communities, and Chinatowns remained bachelor outposts well into the twentieth century. An immigration opportunity was created by the San Francisco earthquake of 1906, during which municipal records were destroyed by fire allowing many Chinese men to claim for some years that they were Chinese Americans born in the United States and thus eligible to sponsor the arrival of wives (Takaki 1987: 234). Furthermore, with the Nationalist Revolution of 1910, women increasingly broke historical tradition and journeyed to the United States. Chinese exclusion finally came to an end during World War II, and the overall number of Chinese immigrants began to increase. The gender ratio finally reached parity in 1990 (Sung 1967; Lyman 1974; U.S. Census of Population and Housing 1980–90).

The male sojourners of exclusion-era Chinatowns supported their families in China via remittances. They lived an austere life in frontier towns and encampments or crowded into tenement rooming houses in urban Chinatowns, parsimoniously saving any nonremitted earnings to make periodic visits to the homeland. These visits were accompanied by great pomp and circumstance. Whole villages came out to greet the visiting sojourner. Any children fathered on home visits by Chinese American citizens were recognized by U.S. law as American by birth and eligible to enter the United States. Children's "slots" were sometimes given or sold to members of the extended family or to other villagers. Some slots were sold through brokers. These underground entries were known as "paper sons."

The sojourner who had saved substantial money was able to buy improved housing and more land for his extended family. Other kin and friends expected gifts and loans. As a measure of his growing status in the home village, he was expected to contribute toward projects such as the building of schools and hospitals. This type of circular migration, and the associated remittance economy, is common in much international migration. Among European American flows, it was common among Italian immigrants to the United States, who voluntarily took to sojourning at the turn of the century, when the cost of trans-Atlantic steamship travel became affordable. It is also common now among Mexican American and Central American immigrant communities.

There was a geographic dispersion of the Chinese from the western to the midwestern and eastern states during the early exclusion years from 1880 to 1910. From 1910 to 1940, there was a reconcentration in urban centers as Chinese settled into restaurant and laundry work as major sources of employment. Anti-Chinese sentiment, exclusions from entering certain occupations in some states, and discrimination in the labor market led to their settling into retail trade and personal services occupations generally undesired by Americans. Many of the original frontier and rural Chinatowns either disintegrated or dwindled to a few elderly Chinese living the rest of their lives in isolation (Lee 1949). In cities, meanwhile, Chinatowns typically grew in the "urban frontier" of low-rent districts of central-city areas near waterfront locations or transportation termini (such as bus and train stations) and in locales often near skid rows and red-light districts generally undesired as residential areas by established white Americans. Over time, they have moved out of the central city and into surrounding metropolitan areas.

An alliance between the United States and China against Japan during World War II created a favorable diplomatic climate, and Congress rescinded the Chinese Exclusion Act in 1943, allowing a quota of 105 Chinese a year to enter the United States for the first time since 1882. The War Brides Act of 1946 allowed thousands of Chinese American veterans of World War II to bring wives and children to the United States as special nonquota entries. Almost 90 percent of Chinese immigrants admitted to the United States from 1947 to 1953 were women (Sung 1967: 22). Many Chinese students and professionals also entered the United States during the war, courtesy of government training programs established at many U.S. universities for Chinese students as a gesture of the wartime alliance between the two countries. Following the Chinese Communist Revolution of 1949, a series of displaced persons and refugee acts in the 1950s enabled several thousand students, trainees, professionals, and government workers stranded in the United States to become American citizens.

It was the Hart-Cellar Immigration Act of 1965, however, that really changed the demographic profile of American Chinatowns. National-origin quotas (imposed in 1924), which gave preference to northern and western European immigrants, were lifted, and a new top quota of 20,000 for any one country was set, with an overall limitation of 170,000 from the Eastern Hemisphere. Members of immediate families of U.S. Chinese, including parents, spouses, and children, were allowed to enter as nonquota immigrants. The Communist government in China was not issuing exit visas, however, so most new Chinese immigrants had to come via Hong Kong and Taiwan. Separate quotas were allowed for Taiwan and China. In 1979, improving diplomatic relations between the People's Republic of China and the United States led to a relaxation of the Chinese ban on exit visas. The 1965 law established seven quota-enforced preference categories based on family reunification principles and special manpower requirements. Professionals and skilled workers who arrived through manpower preferences were mainly from the middle classes, but the larger flow resulting from family reunification preferences brought immigrants from all socioeconomic classes.

San Francisco is home to America's oldest Chinatown, but New York City's has grown steadily since the passage of the 1965 immigration act, to become (with a population of 238,919 in 1990) the largest Chinese enclave in any individual American city. As such, it represents a critical illustrative case for examination of the recent effects of global economic change on Chinese immigration. Slightly different patterns are evident, however, when Chinese settlements in broader metropolitan areas are compared. The San Francisco Bay consolidated metropolitan statistical area (which includes San Francisco, Oakland, and San Jose), with 332,033 Chinese in 1990, overtakes the New York–New Jersey consolidated metropolitan area, which had 320,541 Chinese in 1990. The Los Angeles–Long Beach consolidated metropolitan area (which includes Los Angeles, Long Beach, Monterey Park, and a host of other municipalities) follows with a 1990 Chinese population of 307,781 (U.S. Census of Population and Housing 1990).

Data from the Immigration and Naturalization Service for the 1982–89 period enlarges our understanding of Chinese immigration flows relative to other groups. Chinese immigrants numbered 71,881, a 10.5 percent share of the 684,819 immigrants to New York City during this five-year interval;

they were the third largest group, following Dominicans and Jamaicans (New York City Department of City Planning 1992: 29). Furthermore, Chinese immigrants to New York City comprised one-fifth of total Chinese arrivals in the United States during the same period. Significantly, Chinese immigrants were also the most likely to become naturalized during the past two decades. Fifty-nine percent of Chinese immigrants admitted in 1977 had converted to American citizenship by 1990, the highest rate among all immigrants to New York City, with the exception of Romanians, who also had a 59 percent naturalization rate (New York Department of City Planning 1992: 140). This percentage compared with a naturalization rate of 32.2 percent among all immigrants to New York City.

Not enumerated in these official statistics are undocumented entries. The issue of illegal Chinese immigration to New York City was driven home by the grounding of a rusting, unregistered freighter carrying some three hundred smuggled passengers, called the *Golden Venture,* on Rockaway Beach in the New York City borough of Queens, on June 6, 1993. An analysis conducted in September 1993 by the New York Department of City Planning, however, revealed that Chinese were thirteenth on a list of the largest illegal alien groups in New York City, with Ecuadoreans, Italians, and Polish topping the list (Sontag 1993). Contrary to popular opinion, the predominant illegal aliens in New York City are not surreptitious land and coastal border crossers such as the *Golden Venture* arrivals, but visitors who arrive through the "front door" of seaports and airports and overstay their visas.

Table 1 shows the occupational profile of Chinese immigrants by gender as compared with all immigrants to New York City from 1982 to 1989. Chinese immigrants of both genders are clearly overrepresented in rural occupations (farming, forestry, and fishing) relative to all immigrants (by nearly four to one among men, and seven to one among women). Chinese women are overrepresented (by nearly two to one) in unskilled manufacturing occupations (operator, fabricator, laborer) relative to all immigrants. Chinese men, meanwhile, are underrepresented (by nearly one to three) in skilled manufacturing occupations (precision production, craft, and repair), relative to all immigrants, while Chinese women are underrepresented in service occupations (by one to five). In the professional, specialty, and technical occupational categories, Chinese immigrants of both genders have a slight edge over immigrants in general. Chinese immigrants to New York City very clearly come from much poorer rural and working-class origins than immigrants in general. These origins explain the proletarian profile of New York's Chinatown in the most recent era of globalization.

Table 1

Occupational profile of Chinese immigrants compared to all immigrants to New York City by gender, 1982–89

Occupational Profile	Male Chinese	All male	Female Chinese	All female
Total number reporting occupation	18,824	168,497	15,103	110,404
Professional/Specialty/ Technical	14.0%	12.9%	12.3%	15.9%
Executive/Administrative/ Managerial	10.9%	10.1%	6.4%	4.7%
Sales	4.8%	4.8%	5.0%	4.2%
Clerical	6.3%	7.5%	10.6%	17.8%
Precision Production/ Craft/Repair	6.3%	17.9%	6.3%	8.3%
Operator/Fabricator/Laborer	22.5%	22.9%	24.7%	12.9%
Farming/Forestry/Fishing	19.6%	5.6%	28.4%	4.2%
Service	15.6%	18.3%	6.2%	31.9%

Source: New York Department of City Planning 1992: 83.

The Historical Development of New York's Chinatown

The first Chinese to appear in New York City were reported as crew members of a junk, the *Keying,* which docked on July 10, 1847, and attracted many curious onlookers to its berth in the harbor (to view both its foreign crew and the curious architecture of the vessel). Some of the crew were reported to have jumped ship before it departed (Lee 1965). Fuller documentation is provided for Quimbo Appo (or Lee Ah Bow),[3] who disembarked from the U.S. ship *Valencia* sometime in the late 1840s or early 1850s. Originally settled in San Francisco in 1844, he apparently decided to move to New York City after having acquired some money operating a tea business. Reports of his life are somewhat conflicting. Louis Beck (1898) described him as a boozer and a womanizer who was eventually committed to a state hospital for the mentally insane, where he died at the age of ninety. A *New York Times* article of 1856, in contrast, said he was a confirmed Methodist who offered his services as a missionary to the colony of 150 Chinese (mainly marooned and jump-ship sailors) already in New York City (Miller 1969: 184). The next reported immigrant, a Cantonese named Ah Ken, established his residence on Mott Street, opening a cigar store on Park Row in 1858 (Wong 1982: 6). A sailor named Loy Hoy Sing settled on Cherry Street in 1862. A contingent of workers looking for employment after the completion of the transcontinental railroad arrived from the West Coast in 1869.

The first New York Chinese began congregating in the southern periphery of the Lower East Side on what had been called the "plow and harrow site" (where a farm and tavern were situated in the seventeenth century) around Mott, Pell, and Doyers Streets. A general store operated by the merchant Wo Kee at 8 Mott Street became an early center of social and commercial life in the immigrant enclave. Chinese settled here because native New Yorkers did not consider it a very desirable residential area. It was adjacent to the Bowery and the Five Points area, which attracted criminal elements and vagrants and was notorious for its dangerousness, including perennial violence between rival street gangs.

The 1870 census enumerated just 19 Chinese living in Manhattan or Brooklyn (Chow 1984: 38). This was almost certainly an underestimate. That same year Barth (1964: 198–205) reported the arrival of 300 Chinese laborers imported from the West Coast to work as laundry workers in Belleville, New Jersey (near Newark). There were also reports of Chinese being imported to work in potato fields in Long Island and in Manhattan cigar factories (Miller 1969: 175). Many of the migrants to the region eventually made their way to the "plow and harrow site," and an 1873 *New York Times* article reported 500 Chinese residents in Manhattan's Chinatown (Miller 1969: 184).

During the next two decades, thousands more Chinese laborers made the eastward trek, some sponsored by employers and others on their own. The official 1900 census for New York City counted 6,321 Chinese, although this figure is probably too low. Beck (1898) provided a perhaps inflated estimate in 1898 of 17,000 in the whole metropolitan area, including New Jersey and Long Island, with 4,000 in the core Chinatown area of lower Manhattan. Seven farms on Long Island employed farmers who kept the Chinese community stocked with Oriental produce. Mobile peddlers, with wicker baskets balanced on opposite sides of shoulder poles, made daily rounds throughout the metropolitan region selling produce and imported items to the dispersed Chinese (Beck 1898). Even if his numbers are suspect, Beck makes the significant point that the bulk of the Chinese laborers not residing in the Chinatown core at this time were dispersed laundrymen, whom he estimated to number 8,000.

New York City's Chinatown during the exclusion era thus had a curious spatial geography. The laundrymen, who constituted nearly half of the population, were scattered throughout the metropolitan area. Commercial activity, however, was concentrated in the core Chinatown enclave in the vicinity of the old "plow and harrow site," which was also the center of social and political activities, where the clan and district associations kept their headquarters. The scattered laundrymen worked in daily isolation (in the company of partners), journeying to Chinatown on weekends for social interaction.

Chinese immigrants concentrated in laundries not so much by choice as because of exclusion. In the decades of exclusion, Chinese were denied citizenship rights and thus were ineligible for municipal, state, and federal employment. Citizenship was also required for many other professional occupations of high and low status, ranging from physicians and attorneys to barbers, plumbers, and chauffeurs. According to Edna Bonacich's theory of "middleman minorities," specialization in niche operations is common among immigrants and ethnic groups facing prejudice and discrimination from the host society (1973).

Since New York's Chinatown was primarily a male-dominated bachelor society during the exclusion era, an avid market existed for a range of vice industries including prostitution, gambling (mainly fan-tan, a Chinese card game), and drug distribution (mainly opium). Two organized criminal syndicates controlled Chinatown; the Hip Sing tong claimed Pell Street as its territory, while the more powerful On Leong tong controlled Mott Street, Chinatown's main thoroughfare. Demand for these activities also extended to the host white society; middle-class New Yorkers were clients of Chinatown vice establishments, just as they frequented the speakeasies, brothels, and gambling halls of the Tenderloin, Harlem, or Little Italy, particularly during Prohibition (Light 1977). The onset of World War II and the end of Chinese exclusion after 1943 led to the establishment of a family-oriented society in New York's Chinatown, and vice industries declined in significance.

Residential Conditions in the Immigrant Enclave

Some 80 percent of Chinatown residents inhabit private tenement housing, with public housing and private middle-income housing serving the remainder. Constructed quickly to house an immigrant proletariat, the tenement housing of the Lower East Side has steadily deteriorated over the past century to deplorable conditions with rampant building-code violations in the contemporary era. Some tenements are still cold-water flats, and some units do not have private kitchens or bathrooms. As Table 2 shows, units without plumbing facilities comprised 2.8 percent of Chinatown households in 1990, as compared with 2.1 percent of all households in Manhattan. China-town apartments are also overcrowded, with a median of 2.99 persons per unit, nearly twice as high as the median of 1.55 persons among all house-holds in Manhattan. When overcrowding is defined in persons per room, 49 percent of Chinatown households squeezed in more than 1 person per room, as opposed to just 10 percent of Manhattan households in general.

Table 2

Housing conditions in Chinatown and Manhattan, 1990

Housing condition indicators	Chinatown[a]	Manhattan
Occupied units lacking complete plumbing	2.8%	2.1%
Median persons in unit[b]	2.99	1.55
Persons per room		
1.00 or less	51%	90%
1.01 to 1.50	14%	5%
1.50 or more	35%	5%

[a] Manhattan census tracts 6, 8, 16, 18, 25, 27, 29, and 41.
[b] Weighted average across same census tracts.
Source: U.S. Census of Population and Housing, 1990.

New York City rent control regulations keep average monthly rent pay-ments among Chinatown households generally low. High demand and low vacancy rates have led to an exorbitant "key money" payment system, where up to several thousand dollars may be demanded by landlords or other agents in the securing of a lease. Vacancy decontrol statutes have allowed some tenement rents to rise somewhat, but dramatic rent increases may only occur when a whole building is vacated and renovated or demolished to make way for new construction. These trends have kept housing organi-zations busy advising Chinatown tenants about the details of rent-control laws and giving them protective legal advice when landlords are seeking to vacate a building through property abandonment or through tenant harassment. Some Chinatown landlords have sought to improve housing conditions through rehabilitation or to build new affordable housing, but generally area property owners have preferred investment in more prof-itable, upmarket new construction, particularly in condominiums rather than rental apartments. While upgrading the housing inventory, these prop-erty owners are restricting housing opportunities for the low-income immi-

Figure 3. Family in tenement kitchen. Photo by Robert Glick. Copyright Robert Glick; used by permission of the photographer.

grant population that depends on affordable housing for their survival (Figure 3). This situation has led Chinatown community organizations to begin moving into the business of affordable housing development, generally through acquisition of city-foreclosed and fire-damaged properties, which are then renovated with public and charitable funds.

The mismatch between supply and demand for affordable housing in Chinatown has also led to some illegal conversion of commercial and manufacturing space to residential uses. Severe overcrowding can occur in these dormitory-style Chinatown apartments, where bunk beds may allow up to twenty tenants to be squeezed into one room. Tenants may even share the same bed, with one worker employed during the day, the other at night. Illegal residential conversions have even occurred in building basements with no heat, hot water, or fire exits. In one of these basement apartments, fire investigators found that an area that previously served as a giant freezer compartment was being used for living quarters. In these most deplorable living situations are found illegal immigrants afraid to seek housing in the legitimate market (Chan 1994).

During the course of my fieldwork in Chinatown, I visited two of these dormitory-style residences, both of them illegal residential conversions of loft manufacturing buildings. I visited one with a Chinese graduate student attending Michigan State University, who had obtained summer employment in New York City. Located on Canal Street, the building was owned by traders who operated a sidewalk stall selling gifts and clothing on the ground floor. There were residences on the second and third floor of the loft building, each floor of which was subdivided by drywall that did not reach the ceiling, so that sound carried throughout the sagging loft interior. Bare light bulbs hung from the ceiling. At the end of the narrow corridor on the second floor was the hallway kitchen, which was comprised of a small stove and shelves of produce and pots and pans. Five or six double bunk beds were squeezed into each bedroom. Some beds were shared by workers on opposite day-and-night employment shifts. The residents I met were Chinese and Malaysian in origin, mainly undocumented aliens who had entered illegally or overstayed their visas. Many were still seeking employment or worked in restaurants, like the graduate student. A car picked up the graduate student and other workers in the mornings on Canal Street for the drive to a restaurant in New Jersey. I was told there were about one hundred people living in the illegal dormitory building.

The other building I visited was on Broome Street, near the Bowery. This loft manufacturing building was in substantially better shape than the Canal Street building. The drywall partitions in the interior of this building were much better constructed, and there was a separate room that functioned as a communal kitchen. My acquaintance, who was a volunteer with the Chinatown Staff and Workers' Association, had his own single bedroom. This arrangement was typical of buildings with single-room occupancy units (SROs), which are rooming houses with tenants or families living in single rooms and sharing communal toilet and kitchen facilities. Landlords offering living arrangements of this sort must be officially registered for inspection with the City of New York, but the phenomenon is spreading rapidly in unregulated fashion in Chinatown. Undocumented aliens are particularly common tenants in the illegal SROs.[4] Landlords found to be operating unregistered establishments are forced to clear the premises, but it is common for them to open new facilities later. Tenants meanwhile have little legal recourse because they do not usually have an official lease.

Residential congestion and the unavailability and inadequacy of housing in Manhattan's core Chinatown (combined with an ongoing immigrant inflow) have led to a pervasive movement of the Chinese to satellite Chinatowns in the outer boroughs, a phenomenon that is systematically explored in chapter 4. Upwardly mobile families seeking the superior housing and quality of life available in the outer boroughs proliferate in these areas, although there are indications that some new immigrants are also leapfrogging the core because of housing unavailability. From all indications, the profile of Chinese living in Manhattan's Chinatown includes (1) some newer immigrants in overcrowded communal housing; (2) some non–upwardly mobile established households who have been left behind in the core, or who choose to stay in the core because of the conveniences of central-city location, and tolerate the poor housing conditions; and (3) elderly Chinese who tolerate the poor housing conditions at the core but appreciate the locational conveniences as well as the cultural familiarity of the immigrant enclave. Many of the elderly were privileged to obtain subsidized housing in the scattering of housing projects that are contained in the core (including Confucius Plaza, which at forty-four stories is Chinatown's highest building).

There are also a number of newer housing units of moderate-income or luxury upmarket character arising in Manhattan's Chinatown, partly through the impact of overseas capital investment. As discussed in chapter 3, upwardly mobile Chinese Americans have been slow to purchase these condominiums because of the frantic pace of life in the core Chinatown. As indicated by some bankers and realtors, overseas investors sometimes sublet their condominiums to local immigrants. Local buyers also purchase new housing on behalf of their elderly parents, who may prefer the hectic quotidian life of the immigrant enclave to the space and privacy available in the less familiar outer boroughs and suburbs (Figures 4 and 5).

Profile of the Immigrant Enclave Economy

On the economic front, the Chinese American Restaurant Association of Greater New York enumerated a total of 2,646 laundries, 505 restaurants, and 144 "other" businesses in the five-borough New York City area in 1960. A profile of businesses within Chinatown itself was provided by Kung (1962). I recategorized Kung's data into industry groupings using the 1987 Standard Industrial Classification Manual to permit ease of comparison with later trends. Manufacturing represented only 10 percent of all firms in the enclave at this time. Garment shops were just beginning to emerge, with 18 counted in 1960. Wholesale and retail trade accounted for the most businesses (248, or 71 percent of the total) with restaurants and groceries being the main categories. Financial and service enterprises comprised only 19 percent of all firms at this date.

Table 3 shows an industrial profile of Chinatown businesses, which I constructed using the 1989 Chinese Business Guide and Directory, a telephone directory of Chinese businesses printed by Key Publications, Inc. Some clear trends are immediately apparent. The total number of enter-

Figure 4. Elderly woman in Chinatown tenement. Photo by Robert Glick. Copyright Robert Glick; used by permission of the photographer.

prises has grown since 1960 by a factor of eight, from 348 to over 2,833. The industrial profile is much more diversified, with firms represented in all categories except agriculture, fishing, and mining. The two fastest growing sectors are manufacturing and services. Manufacturing's share of total enterprises has risen from 10 percent to 19 percent, with garment shops being the main factor in the increase. Services expanded even more dramatically, from 19 percent to 34 percent of all firms.

Figure 5. Elderly man on landing. Photo by Robert Glick. Copyright Robert Glick; used by permission of the photographer.

Table 3

**Industry profile of Chinatown businesses
compared with all firms in Manhattan, 1989**

Industry group	Chinese firms in Chinatown[a]		All firms in Manhattan[b]	
Construction	81	3%	8,627	8%
Manufacturing	533	19%	2,086	2%
Garment factories	(436)	(15%)		
Transportation/Communications/ Utilities	115	4%	2,955	3%
Wholesale trade	143	5%	14,880	14%
Retail trade	758	26%	15,775	15%
Restaurants	(192)	(7%)		
Finance/Insurance/Real Estate	253	9%	15,738	15%
Services	985	34%	45,004	43%
Total	2,833	100%	105,065	100%

[a] Data compiled from *Chinese Business Guide and Directory: 1989–1990* (Key Publications, Inc.). Chinese-owned establishments in zip code areas 10002, 10007, 10013, and 10038 were counted, then classified using the 1987 Standard Industrial Classification Manual (U.S. Office of Management and Budget).
[b] These numbers were obtained from the Division of Research and Statistics at the New York State Department of Labor, and reflect activity in the first quarter of 1988. Figures in the "other" category (agriculture, mining, fishing, forestry, and not elsewhere classified) were omitted for ease of comparison.

Table 3 also compares Chinatown's industry profile with that of Manhattan as a whole. Manufacturing and retail trade pursuits are more highly represented among Chinatown businesses, reflecting the proliferation of garment shops, restaurants, and ethnic food markets. The proportion of Chinatown enterprises involved in finance, insurance, real estate (FIRE), and "producer services" (nonpersonal services in higher-wage professional occupations) categories remains low, however, relative to Manhattan, which has a high percentage due to New York City's role as a command center in the domestic as well as the world economy.

The growth of Chinatown businesses in the FIRE and producer services categories, however, is a significant trend. This growth can be seen as part and parcel of the increasing diversification of the enclave economy in the post-exclusionary period. Matters of law, business development, citizenship, licensing, and accountancy are now increasingly handled by Chinese American law firms, accountants, travel agencies, employment agencies, and management services firms, rather than non-enclave firms.

The growth in garment shops has been particularly dramatic. Although garment factories accounted for only 15 percent of the total firms in Chinatown, their economic impact has been monumental. The Chinatown garment production zone is the main source of employment for some twenty-five thousand Chinese immigrant women. The primary occupations among men are in restaurants, groceries, and other retail shops. These economic activities serve both the Chinese enclave itself as well as non-enclave residents of New York City and tourists from out of town.

Abeles, Schwartz, Haeckel, and Silverblatt, Inc. (1983: 173–74) estimated that retail trade (including restaurants) occupied 80 percent of the commercial space in the Chinatown area, predominantly on the ground floors of tenement and loft buildings. These retail establishments include grocers, pharmacies, jewelers, curio shops, newsagents, fruit and vegetable sellers, and fish and meat sellers. Personal services establishments, such as barbers and beauty salons, fortune-tellers, acupuncturists, and video rental centers compete for space with the retailers. The competition for space grows even greater with the arrival of new groups such as the Vietnamese and the Fujianese.

Exorbitant "key money" payments, commonplace in acquisition of residential apartment leases, are also common when Chinese business people are securing commercial leases. A study by the Real Estate Board of New York amortized these key money payments over the length of a lease and found that these payments brought the typical annual rent for retail space on Canal Street to $275 per square foot, among the highest rates in New York City. Comparable rates in high-rent commercial districts were $400 annual rent per square foot on Fifth Avenue (above 51st Street) and $255 on Madison Avenue above 42nd Street (Scardino 1986).

As an outgrowth of high demand and short supply of commercial space, a number of Vietnamese-Chinese mini-malls have sprung up in recent years in ground-floor loft buildings along Canal Street and the Bowery. Recalling the indoor markets for peddlers found throughout Southeast Asia, they are called *thuong xa* among the Vietnamese. An example is the Vietnamese-Chinese Tung Nam Har Mall, completed in 1986, in a former hardware store on Canal Street, and now occupied by forty small-business owners operating stalls offering a collection of very low-cost jewelry, sportswear, and electronic products, as well as prepared food.

Wholesale trade is one area in which Chinatown businesses are underrepresented. This is because Chinese American wholesalers are mainly located in the midtown area between 14th Street and 42nd Street, popular with import-export companies because of the loft-type building stock. These businesses mainly handle wholesale import-export trade in a variety of products including apparel, jewelry, souvenirs and gift items, toys, artworks, antiques, and furniture. According to Henry Yung, former head of the 2,500-member New York Chinese Businessmen's Association, China, Hong Kong, Taiwan, Korea, and Japan are the main sources of their products. Nations such as Brazil, Senegal, and the West Indies are among the major destinations they export to. Goods sold in Chinatown to Chinatown retailers include souvenirs, gifts, and toys.

Once the main occupation of Chinese immigrants during the exclusion era, laundry work now plays a very minor role. Laundry work began diminishing as a business pursuit among the New York Chinese in the 1930s, when machine-washing technology began to enter the industry. Few Chinese entrepreneurs had the investment capital required to purchase the heavy machinery to establish washing and drying "workshops" (Chow 1984: 87–88). After World War II, mechanized steam laundries restructured the industry to such an extent that hand laundry shops operated by white owners had been completely phased out, replaced by laundry and dry-cleaning chain stores. The Chinese Hand Laundry Alliance regulated industrial change in the Chinese enclave, however, allowing only a few mechanized steam laundries to open, while hand laundries continued to do finer operations. Because of mechanization, the hours of physical work in the hand laundries were actually reduced while still allowing for an adequate financial return (Light 1972: 93–94).

This trend continued into the 1960s, when, according to Sung (1967: 188), Chinese mechanized "wet-washes" still did the bulk of the actual washing of clothing. Costing a minimum of $100,000 to start up, some thirty-four wet-washes operated in the New York City area and four in New Jersey. These huge mechanized wet-wash factories sent vans daily to collect work from some twenty-five hundred dispersed small Chinese hand laundries. The next day, laundry washed in the mechanized establishments would be returned, damp dried, to the individual hand laundries, where clothes were then starched, dried, and ironed by hand. A third, intermediary category of establishment was the shirt-processing shop, which did no washing but did pressing and ironing. Home laundering and coin-operated Laundromats continued to cut into the market, however, and only a handful of Chinese hand laundries now survive.

Linkages and Multipliers in the Enclave Economy

Chinatown's contemporary economy is considerably more diversified than during the exclusion era. This economic diversification is connected with a greater incidence of tight interindustry linkages among co-ethnic enterprises. No economic system is ever completely closed, but tight linkages between co-ethnic enterprises ensure that income and expenditures are circulated and multiplied within the enclave rather than leaking out.

Linkages may be classified into three types: backward, forward, and consumption. Backward linkages result from the demand of enterprises for productive inputs (e.g., agricultural produce, textile "bundlework"), machinery and other equipment, and ancillary supplies. Forward linkages result from the need to market and distribute the finished products or output produced by enclave enterprises. Consumption linkages emanate from the expenditure of income that is earned by workers in enterprises. Consumption linkages may be particularly significant if there is a high demand for co-ethnic goods.

Immigrant restaurants and groceries (both in the retail trade industry category), for example, are enterprises that produce few forward linkages but a number of backward and consumption linkages. Backward linkages appear in the form of immigrant firms and distributors that supply restaurants and groceries with equipment, agricultural produce, meats and seafood, and imported processed foods. The consumption linkage functions via workers' purchases of food, clothing, and other commodities from co-ethnic enclave establishments. An example of an industry with strong forward linkages is garment production (manufacturing category), which may stimulate the establishment of immigrant-owned clothing distribution and retailing firms (transportation, wholesale and retail trade sectors). Potential backward linkages include textile suppliers and sewing equipment suppliers, but so far these roles are still held by non-Chinese immigrant groups in New York City, including Jews and Italians.[5]

Earnings in the form of wages and business receipts are multiplied to a greater extent in ethnic enclaves that exhibit strong linkages between industries. New York City's Chinese-owned business enclave falls into this category. In the words of one economic development representative, the Chinatown enclave economy is like a "mini-ecosystem" in which a dollar once earned "never leaves."[6] Its value is instead perpetually multiplied within the enclave, reverberating through the enclave economy via the interindustry linkages just identified.

The result in the Chinese enclave is a relatively low unemployment rate, rehabilitation of the built environment (property owners are generally not in tax arrears), and generation of additional business tax revenues for city and state coffers. African American enclaves in the New York City metropolitan area, in contrast, are still commonly plagued by high rates of unemployment, deteriorated built environments, and capital scarcity. From the standpoint of the aforementioned analysis, the deprivation of the black "ghetto" can be attributed to a weak level of interindustry integration. Indeed, a general scarcity of black-owned businesses leads to a situation whereby African American earnings (from wages as well as transfer payments) flow out of their residential enclaves via purchases of goods from non-black enterprises (such as white-owned chain supermarkets).[7]

There must be some links, however, with the non-enclave economy, because the enclave economy must export goods outside of the system to derive new income and keep growing. The two principal sources of export income are garment production and tourism. Garment shops are the dominant source of export earnings. In 1983, it was estimated that the 450 shops of the Chinatown production zone produced some $125 million in annual income in the form of salaries of workers and employers, and company profits (Abeles, Schwartz, Haeckel, and Silverblatt 1983). The other major source of export earnings comes from tourist spending in the restaurants, ethnic grocers, and curio shops of the retail trade category. The enclave is a major stop for out-of-town tourists. In addition, Chinatown is located near many local and federal government offices in the City Hall area of lower Manhattan, whose employees frequent the restaurants during lunch and dinner.

Another agglomeration of retail enterprises that has recently emerged in Chinatown is a "mini–jewelry district" along Canal Street on Chinatown's border with Little Italy. Previously dominated by Jewish and Italian proprietors, the district has grown tremendously with the entrance of Vietnamese and Hong Kong Chinese. Specializing in low-price gold and diamond objects, the district attracts buyers from throughout the city because it is seen as a "discount" jewelry area distinct from the wholesale and upscale trade proliferating uptown. Many New York Chinese who "trust gold" make purchases (to be kept in bank safety deposit boxes) as a hedge against inflation, a dependable form of investment relatively protected from economic cycles. It is likely that jewelry purchases are also a way of laundering Hong Kong flight capital as well as local money made through criminal channels.[8]

Demographic growth in Chinatown, coupled with the concomitant

Map 2. Chinatown and Lower Manhattan. Credit: Kate Blackmer.

expansion of the enclave economy since the liberalization of the immigration law in 1965, has led to the steady overflow of the Chinese enclave beyond the "plow and harrow site" of the exclusion era into nearby districts, including the City Hall area, Little Italy, and the "East Village" (also known as "Loisaida," which is a Latino transliteration of "Lower East Side"). Map 2 depicts the approximate boundaries of Chinatown relative to other districts of lower Manhattan in the 1990s. Chinatown's expansion into neighboring districts has produced some tensions, notably in Little Italy (Jackson 1978).

Capital Formation in the Immigrant Enclave

Some of the petty enterprises in early U.S. Chinatowns were established by merchants who had sufficient capital to transfer to the United States to start up their own businesses. Most immigrants, however, were capital-scarce laborers who often acquired a long-term debt with their sponsoring clan or district associations. These same associations, however, helped members set up their own small businesses by sponsoring rotating credit associations. Rotating credit associations were the typical avenue of capital formation in Chinatowns in the bachelor stage.

The rotating credit association, a general informal device for the raising of small amounts of pooled capital, can also be referred to as a contribution club, slate, mutual lending society, or pooling club.[9] The anthropologist Clifford Geertz first observed that the phenomenon occurs (in varying permutations) in various societies from the Far East to Africa. It is called *hui* in southern China, *ko* in Japan, *ho* in Vietnam, *arisan* in Indonesia, *dashi* among the Nupe of central Nigeria, and *esusu* among the Yoruba (Geertz 1956: 3–4). Ivan Light (1972: 23) later drew attention to the transplanting of the rotating credit device from East Asia (by Chinese and Japanese) and West Africa (via the Caribbean West Indies) to the United States as a means of small-scale capital formation in immigrant communities. Not at all unique to these three ethnic groups, however, the device has been observed in a range of European, Asian, Latino, and Caribbean immigrant communities in the United States.[10]

The basic premise of the rotating credit association rests on the precept of opportunity for participating members to periodically bid on (or receive by allotment) a lump sum of pooled capital in exchange for having made a regular contribution. There is substantial variation at this point: (1) meetings may be weekly or monthly, (2) the duration of the association may be for a period of months or years, (3) members may be rural peasants or urban traders and exclusively male or female or drawn from both sexes, (4) contributions may be in kind or in cash, (5) the periodic rewarding of pooled funds may be by agreement, by lot, or by bidding, and (6) there may or may not be an interest rate charged on withdrawn funds (Geertz 1956: 25–42).

Behind this substantial variability in the specific characteristics of rotating credit associations can be discerned a continuum that varies from simple/benevolent to complex/economistic. The earliest *hui* in China were thought to originate in collections for weddings and funerals. Geertz suggests that the rotating credit association can be seen as a "device by means of which traditionalistic forms of social relationships are mobilized so as to fulfill non-traditionalistic economic functions . . . an 'interstitial' institution growing up within peasant social structure to mediate between agrarian economic patterns and commercial ones, as a bridge between peasant and trade attitudes towards money and its uses" (1956: 3–4).

Thus, the phenomenon served as a socializing mechanism in social change in the move from a particularistic to a more universalistic value framework and economy. The feasting and other benevolent rituals that accompanied meetings of the more traditional variety were seen to decline relative to an increasing concern with financial probity, legal enforcement, and commercial calculation, whereupon some rotating credit associations acquired aspects like a "firm" (Geertz 1956: 42–44). Geertz has elsewhere defined the phenomenon of rotating credit societies as a "middle rung" in the process of economic development from agrarian to economic systems in which trade plays a greater role (1963: 262).

Shirley Ardener notes (1964: 217–18) that rather than being a vestigial remnant of traditional societies, rotating credit associations persist in modern systems, being preferred to conventional banking because they are less impersonal, not taxed, a way of inducing compulsory saving, and a way of acquiring smaller amounts of credit than banks are generally willing to bother with. Immigrants to the United States may utilize both forms of credit. Aubrey Bonnett (1981) found this kind of "interfacing" occurring in his study of rotating credit in a Caribbean enclave of Brooklyn, New York. Rotating credit was useful for short-term savings to purchase clothing and gifts with small loans in the amount of about $100. It was also important for illegal immigrants who did not have the papers required by banks.

Ivan Light makes similar points in his research on rotating credit associations among East Asian immigrants to America. Whereas commercial banking practice required some sort of formal collateral to balance the risk of lending, rotating credit associations relied on the strength of informal moralistic social relations. Decorum, honor, and family reputation were at stake when a rotating credit association member died, disappeared, or defaulted on his loan. By contrast, all ten of the conventional banks established in the early twentieth century by Chinese and Japanese migrants to the West Coast ultimately failed. Credit-raising through community-based institutions is often limited, however, in terms of the scale of capital. When massive sums are required, conventional banks are necessary (Light 1972: 46–60).

Rotating credit associations, known as *hui*, were the major means of raising investment capital among the bachelor members of exclusion-era

Chinatowns, especially in start-up of the laundries and restaurants that were their principal occupations after mining and railroad work ended. One writer has described them as the "economic nerve system" of Chinatown (Leong 1936). Traditional associations were the institutional foundation of the Chinatown hui, particularly the village association, or *fong*. The fong was the smallest unit in the patchwork of regional/dialect (*hui-guan*) and clan/surname (*tsu*) associations that existed in Chinatown. Usually constituted of from ten to one hundred members, they existed at the intersection of the district and clan association, where name and location coincided, and social relationships were closest (Light 1972: 86). In New York City, the largest village associations had eight hundred to nine hundred members (Heyer 1953: 57).

Betty Lee Sung has described the operation of a hui in which her father participated in Washington, D.C.'s Chinatown during the 1940s. The family did not actually live in Chinatown, but he went to the one-room dormitory that was the fong headquarters to run the hui every Sunday. The contribution from each member was $10 a week for one hundred weeks and was of the bidding variety, with an interest rate of 50 cents or 75 cents being the average bid. If there was no bid, someone was chosen for a minimum of 25 cents interest. Bids were made at 3:00 P.M., and deposits were made in the next two hours. Participants who were delinquent on their payments suffered the disgrace of having their immediate relatives notified (1967: 140–42). Shih-Shan Henry Tsai describes another hui in San Francisco, which involved a group of twelve contributing $50 a month for twelve months (1986: 148).

Smaller fongs maintained their headquarters on the ground floors of Chinatown apartment houses, in a few rooms or perhaps only one. Larger clan associations owned the whole building, which in New York City typically meant a tenement building. In Chinese, the word *fong* means "room" or "residence" (Heyer 1953: 57). This definitional homology between the organizational and the spatial definition of the word *fong* can doubtless be traced to the functions of traditional rural-to-urban associations in the cities of southeast China. The priority of the spatial meaning is perhaps derived from the concrete experience of the immigrant laborer— the physical environment of the fong. In first-stage American Chinatowns, merchants were generally the only Chinese immigrants able to afford private apartments. Thus, the bachelor workers commonly lived communally in dormitory-style fongs maintained by their sponsoring clan or village association. Many slept in the back rooms of their restaurants and laundries, which were generally scattered throughout a metropolitan area.

Figure 6. Resident at Ng Family Association. Photo by Robert Glick. Copyright Robert Glick; used by permission of the photographer.

Village or clan "cousins" who did not live at the association headquarters would join their compatriots there at Sunday meetings when association business was conducted, including the weekly or monthly hui. The fong to which the bachelor sojourners came to relax and socialize after a hard week's work was the center of social life. For the restaurant or laundry workers who toiled in establishments far from Chinatown, Sunday meetings were particularly significant. After purchasing Chinatown produce and imported goods that could not normally be acquired in their scattered places of residence, members would visit the fong. There they could smoke, drink, eat, exchange stories and information, and play parlor games such as mah-jongg with their closest kin and countrymen.

In a survey of 137 Chinatown small-business owners, Bernard Wong (1988: 134) found that 40 percent acquired their start-up capital from rotating credit associations. Personal savings, family, kinsmen, and friends were the other common sources of start-up capital. It is significant to observe that none of the 137 enterprises initially capitalized their operations from institutional sources such as banks or credit unions. Limited English and a lack of understanding of loan procedures were barriers to use of American banks since there were no Chinese American banks operating in Chinatown until the 1960s.

Chinese small-business owners do not usually work alone. Chen

Figure 7. Mealtime at Ng Family Association. Photo by Robert Glick. Copyright Robert Glick; used by permission of the photographer.

(1980: 182) reported that the ownership structure of Chinese restaurants in 1938 was 57 percent partnerships, 33 percent individuals, and 10 percent incorporated. Chinese laundries, on the other hand, were estimated to consist of 60 percent sole proprietors, with the remaining percentage mainly partnerships (183).

Paul Siu (1952) found, based on his survey of sixty-seven Chinese laundries in five selected communities of Chicago in 1940, that 60 percent were cousin partnerships, 28 percent sole proprietors, and 10 percent non-cousin partnerships. The hui was the primary source of start-up capital, and personal borrowing was usually reserved for very small amounts of financing (seldom exceeding $200 to $300). Hui were sometimes arranged for new immigrants by a mediator already in America and a standing member of a traditional association. In these cases the formal petition for the loan was written to include an intermediary. The hui usually started at the beginning of the lunar New Year. The number of members varied from fifteen to thirty. The last Sunday of each month was generally the day for bidding. The interest bid was usually about 5 percent but ranged as high as 20 percent (Wong 1987b: 83–94).

After 1943, American Chinatowns began the transition from bachelor societies to family-centered communities, and the influence of the traditional associations began to fade. The family reunification clauses of the

1965 immigration act allowed wives, children, and extended families to join the bachelor laborers. Directly related blood kin rather than "clan cousins" united on the basis of surname or district-of-origin relationships gained importance as sources of start-up capital.

The traditional associations, in keeping with the changes, gradually abandoned the hui system and began to institutionalize more-formal credit-raising methods. The experience of the Lee Family Association office in New York City illustrates such a trend. In 1964, the elders of the association decided that the hui were not financially sound and were ridden by too many defaults. A Lee Family Credit Union was formed in 1965 and officially secured with the Federal Deposit Insurance Corporation. In 1991, this credit union held $5.7 million in total assets and $4.7 million in deposits. The average loan disbursed was in the $15,000 to $20,000 range. There were 321 outstanding loans in 1991. Bridge loans for real estate purchase were the main type of lending, primarily to families making down payments on new homes in the outer boroughs. Loans for opening garment factories were common, usually in the $25,000 to $50,000 range. Restaurant start-ups were another popular reason for taking out loans. Among the newest businesses funded by the credit union were car service businesses specializing in luxury Lincolns and Cadillacs, catering to clients in the Manhattan central business district.

Larger family associations such as the Lee Family Association have modernized over the years, but there are still small family associations that operate fongs for bachelor workers in the traditional style. The Ng Family Association is one example (Figures 6 and 7).

Criminal Activities

A significant sector of activity not captured by the official statistics documented in tables 1 and 3 are criminal activities. The influence of the tongs, which receded after the 1930s, began to revive in the 1960s with the onset of new migration. A new element is the entrance of delinquent youth gangs, which now carry out the coercive activities undertaken in the past by the bachelor "hatchetmen." Vietnamese and Taiwanese street gangs, some supervised by newly emerging organized crime syndicates, compete with more established gangs. In addition to the Hip Sing and On Leong, Chinatown's traditional syndicates, the Tung On, the Chih Kung (Chinese Freemasons), and the Fujianese American Association have appeared (Kinkead 1992). The Hip Sing and On Leong tongs have chapters in many other cities, but New York City is their headquarters.

The U.S. Justice Department now believes that organized crime in

New York's Chinatown has taken over much of the international narcotics smuggling previously controlled by the Italian Cosa Nostra, which operated a "French Connection" from Turkey to New York City by way of Marseilles. The "Chinese Connection" now brings in heroin grown in the Golden Triangle of Laos, Thailand, and Burma through Hong Kong to New York City (Kinkead 1992). Organized criminal "triads" in Hong Kong cooperate with New York City tongs in this international drug trade. In 1989, Shu Yan Eng, affiliated with Hip Sing tong, was indicted by federal agents along with Peter Fok-lueng Woo for smuggling 820 pounds of heroin (estimated street value $120 million). One of the biggest heroin seizures in U.S. history, the drug was found packed inside small rubber golf-cart tires imported from Southeast Asia. Three Chinatown properties, allegedly bought with laundered profits from heroin sales, were also impounded (Buder 1989; Hays 1989; Kinkead 1992). The Fujianese American Association is also believed to be linked with the heroin trade (Kinkead 1992).

The New York City syndicates are additionally involved in a range of local activities, including gambling, massage parlors, protection rackets, prostitution, and immigrant smuggling. Drug smuggling and basement gambling parlors (which are raided by local police but often reopen later in new locations) are their main sources of income. Protection rackets are tied in with tong "turf" or "territory." Restaurants and other retail establishments in a particular tong's territory are coerced into making regular payments. Behind the counter in many stores and restaurants can be found a framed printed "certificate of appreciation" from the sponsoring tong, a sign to others that the premises are already protected (Kwong 1987: 112). Police estimate that up to 50 percent of Chinatown businesses are under the protection of a tong (Kwong 1987: 121).

Beginning in the late 1960s, the Chinese crime syndicates began to incorporate new Chinatown youth into street gangs with names like Ghost Shadows (affiliated with the On Leong), Flying Dragons (affiliated with the Hip Sing), Fuk Chin, and Gum Sing. Initially formed from delinquent gangs of Hong Kong–born youth involved in petty misdemeanors, the street gangs have gained greater structure and financial backing from their affiliation with organized crime and are able to purchase the weapons, cars, and radio systems that enable them to engage in more serious criminal activities. Elder brothers, named *dai lo*, (usually in their twenties) connected with tong leadership supervise street youth (*sai lo*—as young as the early teens), who do not have direct contact with the leadership. These street gangs are runners in the drug trade, protect tong gambling parlors from competitors, and regularly extort protection monies from retail establishments on home turf. Gangs compete for recruits at Chinatown high schools, gaining new members through fear and intimidation, or luring them with promise of money, girls, luxury goods, and status.

One of the new tongs, the Chinese Freemasons, emerged in the early 1980s and tried to carve out East Broadway as territory. Previously dominated by Jewish merchants, East Broadway is one thoroughfare where Chinese enterprises have multiplied in the post-1965 era. The Freemasons recruited some break-away gang members and opened a headquarters and gambling hall. Three of their gang recruits were killed in a 1982 shoot-out at an East Broadway restaurant, the Golden Star Bar (Daly 1983: 31), allegedly by Hip Sing gunmen.

In the mid-1980s, Vietnamese and Taiwanese gangs began to enter the fray, mainly carving out turf in satellite Chinatowns in the outer boroughs (particularly in Queens) but also infringing on the turf of the established gangs in Chinatown. The Chinatown gangs, meanwhile, are also expanding operations into outer-borough Chinatowns. In September 1990, the powerful On Leong tong was jolted by federal indictments on racketeering charges in Chicago. These indictments had the effect of dampening the influence of their affiliated gang, the Ghost Shadows. A particularly bold newcomer Vietnamese gang, Born to Kill (believed to be led by disaffiliated Ghost Shadows members), took these events, it is thought, as an opportunity to accelerate their move into the Ghost Shadows' turf by robbing On Leong gambling dens and massage parlors and killing Ghost Shadows members. Ghost Shadows members then apparently retaliated (police believe) by assassinating in extremely bloody fashion three members of Born to Kill in October 1990 in a parking lot just south of Chinatown near City Hall. At the funeral held in New Jersey shortly thereafter, mourners were sprayed with gunfire by assailants, who hid their machine guns behind wreaths (Lorch 1990; Gelman 1990; Kifner 1991).

On a list of new Asian gangs compiled by the New York City police department are the Blue Dragons (a Vietnamese gang operating in Queens), White Tigers, Taiwan Boys, White Dragons, and Green Dragons (all small Chinese gangs coexisting in Queens). The Korean Fuk Chin also operate in Queens (DeStefano 1990). These gangs do not necessarily have close ties with organized crime syndicates. The formation of delinquent youth gangs is a common feature in the process of adolescent transition among many race and ethnic groups, particularly in urban areas. By themselves, youth gangs may be involved in some informally organized local rackets or fencing activities, but it is highly unlikely they will develop organized criminal operations on their own.

The linking of youth street gangs with organized crime in the Chinese community should be seen partially as an outcome of the historical pre-existence of organized crime networks (the tongs) in Chinese American communities. The tongs have been able to revive their activities with the appearance of these self-organized corps of "street soldiers," which they have strengthened with money and weaponry. A tremendous growth in the number of petty enterprises (such as restaurants and groceries) also provides the tongs with a greater field from which to harvest "protection taxes." Additionally, the greater aggregate size and dynamic circulation of capital within the Chinatown local economy now provide a greater demand for the underground criminal operations in which the tongs specialize, such as prostitution, gambling, massage parlors, and drugs. A lucrative new activity that has just emerged is immigrant smuggling.

Evidence of immigrant smuggling rings has recently been discovered by police investigators. These rings charge clients in China amounts as much as $25,000 for forged documents and transportation to illegally enter the United States, often through Latin America or Canada. Detectives estimated that there were some twenty-two people-smuggling rings operating in Fujian province in 1989. Involvement of Chinatown tongs is yet to be proven, but the rings thus far uncovered in New York City have been Fujianese. One particularly sophisticated operation involved a Chinatown woman named Cheng Chui Ping and her husband, Cheung Yick Tak (who is a contributing member to the Fujianese American Association, which is suspected to have some drug-smuggling links). They illegally smuggled immigrants (mainly from Fujian) by a Canadian route that involved a raft trip over the Niagara River north of Buffalo, where cab drivers then picked them up and drove them to New York City for $800. In January 1989, four people drowned when an overloaded raft capsized 30 feet from the Canadian shore. Many of the clients of this ring came from Cheng Chui Ping's home village in Fujian, Shengmei.

Other smuggling outfits advertise in Hong Kong newspapers, offering forged passports and transportation to many Latin American countries as well as the United States. Reporters have interviewed Chinese in Bangkok hotels and "safehouses" who spend weeks waiting for documents and airline tickets (Chan et al. 1990). The migrants sometimes pay for their passage in installments. Delays or failure to pay can bring severe repercussions from the smuggling rings in the form of severe beatings and burns. In January 1991, thirteen undocumented Fujianese were arrested in New York City for kidnapping and brutally beating a Fujianese "client" of their smuggling ring who had not paid in full (Strom 1991).

The working and living conditions experienced by the smuggled immigrants once they arrive in the United States may be appalling by conventional standards. One newspaper report documented the despair of one migrant, Zhou Aiming, who left a respectable job as a barefoot doctor in Fujian province and borrowed $26,000 from relatives and local business-men to be smuggled to New York City via Bolivia. He earned $1,300 a month for a 100-hour-a-week job in a battered Chinese takeout restaurant in Newark, New Jersey, working to pay off his debt and remit earnings to his family. He slept in a storage room that doubled as a bedroom. After an attack by one customer that sent him to the hospital, Zhou felt fearful about leaving the restaurant after dark and is now a virtual captive. The contrast between previous expectations and reality can be dramatic, as Zhou recounted: "In the village, we thought America was heaven on Earth. . . . Now it seems like jail" (Chan et al. 1990).

If history seems to have repeated itself with regard to the residential congestion and economic brutality of the immigrant enclave economy in the Lower East Side, history also seems cyclical with the revival of illegitimate and "criminal" activities in Chinatown's lower-circuit economy. Criminal operations, however, are not fully articulated with the rest of the immigrant enclave. Illegitimate activities are "parasitic" to the enclave in that they are a source of income leakage rather than revenue multiplication.

It is these illegitimate activities, however, that are frequently highlighted by the journalistic media, television police-detective serials, and cinematic treatments of New York's Chinatown. Investigative journalistic reports of the Chinatown underworld, especially, can usefully and importantly expose human smuggling, criminal syndicate racketeering, and armed violence as real urban social problems that require control and correction. To the extent that these lurid images from the "urban front line" provide sensational fodder for local news broadcasters and television and Hollywood producers, however, representations of Chinese American vice and violence may become regularized mental associations in the American public imagination. These constructions obscure our collective understanding of the daily struggles of the low-income proletariat who predominantly occupy the legitimate sector of the Chinatown local economy. Chinatown youth, like inner-city African American and Latino young men, can too easily be labeled as subcultural "hoods." We should not assume at a glance that they are participants in the aberrant behaviors of the criminal underworld. Chinatown youth experience many of the barriers to (and distractions from) successful school-to-work transition commonly experienced by youth in a variety of urban poor communities. They may be consumers of American popular youth culture as much as they are proponents of the culture of the Chinese enclave (Figure 8).

Figure 8. The urban grittiness of American punk rock appeals to Chinatown youth. Hip-hop styles have more recently become popular. Photo by Robert Glick. Copyright Robert Glick; used by permission of the photographer.

2

Labor Struggles: Sweatshop Workers and Street Traders

The working people of contemporary Chinatown are highly concentrated in employment in the sweatshops of the garment and restaurant industries and small retail trade establishments. Sweatshops may be defined as workplaces where employees are paid low wages, with few benefits and little employment security, under poor occupational conditions of light, health, and safety. Sweatshops often evade government regulation and labor law and may frequently shift location in order to evade investigation. Strong ties of ethnicity, kinship, and paternalistic social relations nevertheless permeate workplace affairs in the garment and restaurant sweatshops. Immigrant Chinese workers obtain employment largely through word of mouth and social connections. Many receive on-the-job training from their employers. Because many are limited in their English-speaking abilities or may be undocumented aliens, employment in a Chinatown sweatshop may be a unique job opportunity. Profitability in these enclave enterprises, meanwhile, greatly depends on the extent to which bosses can derive maximal productivity from their co-ethnic workforce by exploiting them with low wages, poor working conditions, and minimal fringe benefits and employment security.

There have been dramatic bouts of worker resistance to these oppressive working conditions in vociferous collective actions that have taken place on Chinatown's streets and sidewalks and in public parks. In the relatively dense and insular social world of the immigrant enclave, these contentious labor disputes have been highly visible intrusions in the routine of daily life. Residents, workers, bosses, and other members of the community have been drawn into these contestations or have been spectators with strong opinions of either sympathy or opposition. In the case of the garment industry, strong support from organized labor and intershop co-operation among the rank and file have advanced the claims of labor in the Chinatown production zone. In the Chinatown restaurant industry, meanwhile, the struggle for workers' rights has been less effective. There has been less solidarity among restaurant workers, and restaurant owners have withstood unionization through a somewhat unified front. Labor activists, furthermore, have asserted that their organizing efforts have been countered by collusion between the bosses, criminal syndicate tongs, and the local police.

It is important to reiterate that the immigrant sweatshop economy has been a recurrent historical phenomenon in Manhattan's Lower East Side since the turn of the century, when southern and eastern European immigrants labored in the needle trades. Not at all a quiescent or docile labor force, these immigrant workers staged periodic strikes and demonstrations that stand as classic episodes in American labor history. The celebrated "huddled masses" that steamed through New York harbor reassembled as a militant proletariat in the tenement barracks of the East River shoreline.

The entrance of the Chinese into New York City beginning in the 1960s revived some segments of the regional garment industry after a long period of postwar decline, which had accompanied the flight of "runaway shops" to southern states or sites in the third world. Globalization has come full circle, as exported jobs have been reimported home. The entrance of immigrant Chinese workers has also revived the status of organized labor in the regional garment trades, which has met the challenge of the "global factory" on American shores.

Chinese women workers figure prominently in the five hundred shops of the Chinatown garment production zone. As important wage earners in the working-class households of Chinatown, their take-home pay and health benefits are critical to the livelihood of many families in the immigrant enclave. Shaking the traditional stereotype of the docile, subservient Asian woman, the Chinese women garment workers have extended their growing economic independence into political awareness through collective action in industrial disputes.

I consider also the livelihood of Chinatown street traders in this chapter. Being self-employed petty entrepreneurs, they have not been involved in contentious workplace disputes as have the garment and restaurant industry workers. Since their livelihood depends on working in the public space of the street, they have, however, come into conflict with the local government, an issue that is explored further in chapter 6.

The Lower East Side Garment Trade

The Chinatown garment production zone is a spatial agglomeration of some four hundred to five hundred (the number fluctuates from year to year) contractors that is now acknowledged as the most concentrated garment assembly area outside of the midtown Garment District. The Garment District, which covers several square blocks around the Pennsylvania Station area, is where the majority of the management offices, retailers, cutting rooms, and labor union offices associated with the apparel trades are located. The development and persistence of the Chinatown production zone are of vital importance not only because the zone is a source of employment and income generation for local Chinese Americans, but also because of its importance to the regional economy in perpetuating New York City's position as a key domestic and international center for apparel design, manufacturing, and retailing.

Significantly, the Lower East Side tenement district of Manhattan has been both an immigrant residential quarter and a garment production area since the nineteenth century. Irish and German immigrants beginning in the mid-nineteenth century, then Jewish and Italian arrivals at the turn of the century, followed by Latinos and Asians after World War II have inhabited the district's deteriorated tenement housing and labored in the sweatshops of the garment trade. Special characteristics of the garment industry encourage a tendency toward an industrial segmentation into jobbers and contractors. This subcontracting system is what has historically stimulated the informal sector of sweatshops and homework.

Along with service occupations such as laundry work, sanitation, and kitchen work, garment work is among the more socially undesirable forms of employment and thus is typically taken by immigrants. Like the footwear, toy, and electronics assembly industries, the garment trade is a labor-intensive manufacturing activity, sharing the same chief locational requirement of a pool of low-wage workers, usually women. Trends toward automation and fixed capital investment are counterposed by the profitability of the existing technology, sewing machines, which can be manned by low-wage labor. Labor constitutes 27 percent of production costs in garment manufacture, compared to only 10 percent in manufacturing as a whole. Mass production and product standardization are furthermore impeded by the variability of demand, particularly in the women's and children's apparel segments, which are traditionally riskier because of volatility in tastes and fashion. Seasonality of fashion adds to market uncertainty. Economies of scale involving full-scale mechanization, large production facilities, and vertical integration of firms are more common in men's and boys' apparel, undergarments, and the miscellaneous apparel and accessories category (which includes gloves, robes, and belts).

Women's and children's apparel production tends toward segmentation into *jobber* and *contractor* establishments. The vertically integrated factory, or "inside shop," which is more common in standardized clothing manufacture, involves the manufacture, design, and marketing of clothing under one roof. In the more fashion-conscious segments, the jobber-contractor system evolves to split these processes; marketing, design, and cloth cutting are carried out by the jobber, and clothing assembly by the contractor. Because some large inside shops may have better facilities to market and distribute the product (as well as the appeal of a recognized name), some jobbers may be involved only with design and cloth cutting, and act as intermediaries between the larger manufacturers and smaller contractors. Most jobbers are generally more independent, however, purchasing materials directly from textile manufacturers, operating a showroom to directly market their own designs to retailers, and maintaining a cutting room, where cloth is prepared for distribution to contractors.

The contractor, who operates the "outside shop," takes the designs and cut cloth from the jobber and does the actual job of manufacture. The costs of procuring and maintaining a commercial space, sewing machines, and other equipment and of recruiting and paying workers are thus shunted on to the contractor. Start-up costs for such ventures are not prohibitive by any standard; a perpetual pool of emerging contractors may compete fiercely for jobber "bundlework." Jobbers may split piece-clothing work into smaller section-work processes, effectively opening up the bidding process to even more contractors. Greater competition among contractors for work exercises downward pressure on the wages they give their employees. Workers effectively "sweat out" the differential between one bid and another. In the effort to offer the lowest bids, contractors will often cut corners on working conditions. Garment workplaces may be fraught with problems of poor light, fire and safety hazards, and poor job security and pay (Figure 9). Frequent turnover among garment shops leads to recurring bouts of unemployment among garment workers.

The traditional explanation given by management for why garment workers are so often women is that they have nimble fingers, patience, and an eye for detail. More to the point is that they are willing to accept lower wages, given their subordinate position in the labor force. They are not seen as "heads of households" according to the patriarchal standards of the wider society (Safa 1981: 419–20). Women are led to take work home be-

Figure 9. Sweatshop interior. Photo by Robert Glick. Copyright Robert Glick; used by permission of the photographer.

cause wages are so low. This is possible because the production economy of garment manufacture at the level of the sewing machine makes homework feasible for women (Holmes 1986: 94–95). Homework rather than shop work may also be a necessity because women bear the burden of child rearing and housekeeping obligations, responsibilities that are reinforced and reproduced by patriarchal ideology and custom as well as by wage discrimination in the labor market. Immigrant women are especially prone to engage in homework because their lack of English-speaking skills is a barrier to finding work in the structured labor market. Garment worker mothers may find it necessary to take children to work with them during after-school hours; child work is now illegal (Figure 10).

Workers began organizing at the turn of the century. Cloak makers formed the core of the International Ladies' Garment Workers' Union (ILGWU), which met for the first time in 1900. The Uprising of the Twenty Thousand, a bitter strike led largely by women shirtwaist workers (first sparked by teenage firebrand Clara Lemlich at an Astor Place rally) in 1909, and the Great Revolt of 60,000 cloak makers in 1910 brought many into the ranks of the ILGWU after ten difficult years of organizing. Richly chronicled by labor historians, these two strikes remain heroic episodes in labor and women's history (Schofield 1984: 180). The Triangle Shirtwaist Factory fire of 1911 drew public attention to the conditions of the garment trade. Trapped

Figure 10. Working mothers must sometimes combine child-care responsibilities with work. Photo by Corky Lee. Copyright Corky Lee; used by permission of the photographer.

in the burning building with the fire doors locked, almost 150 women jumped to their deaths or were burned within the building. Government investigations led to the Factory Laws of 1912, which established safety and health standards and set regulations on the length of the work week.

Luminaries of American socialism and labor history such as the novelist Jack London, labor spokeswoman Mother Jones, and Industrial Workers of the World (IWW) leader William "Big Bill" Haywood could be found in New York's Lower East Side at demonstrations in Union Square or Astor Place. Emma Goldman was a resident of the East Village at 210 East 13th Street. Young garment-worker women grew radicalized in the environment of labor unrest, breaking the patriarchal orthodoxy of their immigrant Catholic or Jewish upbringing, an experience which Chinese immigrant women would experience several decades later.

The Chinatown Garment Production Zone

All of the officially registered Chinese garment firms are contractors and have been organized by Local 23-25 of the ILGWU. They are generally involved in producing women's outerwear, particularly in the sportswear lines (which represent the "not elsewhere classified" category not included under skirts, dresses, blouses, or suits—i.e., slacks, pants, athletic clothing,

and other casual wear). Chinatown has evolved to become the major production center in women's outerwear; its portion of employment in Manhattan women's outerwear production nearly tripled, from 12.6 percent in
1969 to 31.9 percent in 1980 (Abeles, Schwartz, Haeckel, and Silverblatt
1983: 43).

The critical infrastructural variable in the emergence of Chinatown
contractors was commercial space. Low-cost factory loft space, a by-
product of long-term declines in Manhattan's manufacturing infrastructure
and the financial crisis in the early 1970s, was readily available in lower
Manhattan with the arrival of post–exclusion era Chinese immigrants. Factory space in lower Manhattan rented for as little as $1.00 to $2.00 a square
foot as late as 1980 (Waldinger 1986b: 142). By 1985, prices ranged from
$5.00 to $8.00 a square foot (193). Key money was sometimes necessary to
procure a lease for loft space. Vacancy rates for lower Manhattan loft space
dropped from 35 percent in the mid-1970s to 5 percent in the mid-1980s
(Abeles, Schwartz, Haeckel, and Silverblatt 1983: 156). The 500 shops that
constituted the Chinatown production center in 1981 were located in 130
loft buildings, with up to 14 shops in a single building (Sullivan 1986: 29). By
the early 1980s, the ILGWU Local 23-25 had organized some twenty thousand Chinese American workers in the Chinatown garment production
zone, primarily women.

Garment industry labor organizations, such as the Amalgamated
Clothing and Textile Workers Union (ACTWU) and the ILGWU, have been
attempting to stem the worst excesses of the contracting system ever since
the early twentieth century. The historical tendency for garment shops to
cluster in the Lower East Side and the Garment District has abetted their organizing efforts; they have negotiated with the larger jobbers and manufacturers in the Garment District to regularize prices, wages, and workplace
standards in the subcontracting system. In agreeing to certain rules according to which their bundlework is put out to bid, the manufacturers are then
assured of a dependable, industrious workforce. The lower bids offered by
nonunion shops may be a continuing attraction, but so is a certain standard of production offered by a regularized relationship with union shops.
Unionized subcontracting shops also benefit from the system by being assured of a fairly continuous flow of bundlework.

Since World War II, the numerical strength of the union membership
has shrunk in tune with the overall decline in the position of the New York
City garment industry. With the arrival of new immigrant labor beginning
in the 1960s, however, some industry sectors have revived, and organized
labor has moved to regularize relationships with the new immigrant con-

tractors. Local 23-25 of the ILGWU began organizing the shops of the Chinatown garment production zone in the 1960s, and by the 1980s could count the majority of Chinatown workers within its ranks.

In 1982, however, Chinese contractors broke with the ILGWU in the course of negotiations over the 1982–85 contract, causing the first industry-wide dispute in more than twenty years. The leadership of the jobber associations and non-Chinese contractor associations had already agreed to the contract when most Chinese contractors (who were not well represented on the contractor association's board) voted not to sign on June 10, 1982. The Chinese contractors then split, and a group of larger, more well established contractors decided to negotiate. Local 23-25, meanwhile, had formed a Committee to Defend the Union Contract, armed with five thousand initial signatures from their rank and file. On June 24, some fifteen thousand Local 23-25 members along with other ILGWU leadership and rank-and-file supporters staged a rally in Chinatown, which was well documented by news media. The established Chinatown firms had by now endorsed the contract, but the dissenting contractors again voted to reject on July 1. Despite this July 1 vote, the ILGWU continued to negotiate interim agreements with other Chinatown contractors rather than calling for a strike. The dissident contractors took the initiative, however, staging a lockout of workers on July 9. The union responded on July 15 with a walkout of ten thousand workers and a second demonstration, this time followed by a march through the streets of Chinatown. By this time, the tide had turned, and interim agreements were signed by many sweatshop owners during the course of the demonstration. Sweatshop-owner opposition to the contract had collapsed by day's end (Abeles, Schwartz, Haeckel, and Silverblatt 1983: 77–78) (Figure 11).

The prominence of Local 23-25's manager, Jay Mazur (who was also the ILGWU general secretary-treasurer), in leading workers' interests to an advantageous conclusion during the course of the 1982 dispute helped to catapult him to the position of president of the ILGWU in 1986. Local 23-25 benefited somewhat from his rise within the organization, but some have complained that the ILGWU leadership remains a white male domain, while most of the rank and file remain nonwhite women. Through their shop stewards and business agents and the formation of a local Chinese chapter of the Coalition of Labor Union Women (CLUW), Local 23-25 workers have lobbied for increased services. One area of concern is the Garment Industry Day Care Center of Chinatown, which as of 1989 served eighty children between two and six years old but had a waiting list for another five hundred. The ILGWU also operates a Chinatown Health Clinic for the

Figure 11. Garment workers' demonstration, 1982. Photo by Corky Lee. Copyright Corky Lee; used by permission of the photographer.

benefit of its members. A van service shuttles members from this clinic to the midtown ILGWU Health Center for more serious medical attention.

The ILGWU's top-down organizing strategy (organizing first among manufacturers, then among contractors) was successful in winning Local 23-25's 1982 contract dispute, but the union has also been working in the more difficult area of bottom-up organizing. Until recently, New York City garment manufacturers were roundly union, and the top-down organizing strategy worked because the source of work for contractors was union bundlework from established companies like Macy's and Calvin Klein, which honored union rules. Newer garment manufacturers, however, such as The Gap, The Limited, Express, JCPenney, Eddie Bauer, and other retailers with private labels (such as Norma Kamali and Kathy Lee Gifford) have increasingly shown a willingness to send bundlework to nonunion contractors, for which they pay a penalty if the union finds out. Andy Pollack, an organizer with the Chinese Staff and Workers' Association (which organizes Chinatown workers from outside the organized labor movement), argues:

> Worker rights have eroded since the 1980s with a series of ineffective collective bargaining agreements. The ILGWU is complicitous in this growing situation in which Chinese contractor bosses pit workers against each other. The union effectively "turns a blind eye" since nonunion manufacturers still pay a penalty to organized

labor unions for giving bundlework to nonunion Chinese contractors. Penalty fees may contribute as much to ILGWU coffers as
dues money from union workers.

Many Chinese sweatshop contractors, however, still find it economically
beneficial to take union bundlework because these manufacturers take
over the costs of medical benefits. The ILGWU Health Fund is diminishing
meanwhile because contributions are not keeping pace with member
usage. The ILGWU has increasingly filed grievances with the National Labor
Relations Board (NLRB) and continued on to labor arbitration as a means
of legally threatening contractors who operate outside of union rules.[1]

The Chinese Staff and Workers' Association (CSWA) has also been utilizing the tactic of grievance filing and arbitration with the NLRB board to
expose garment shops that do not recognize workers' rights to organize,
and evade state labor law by paying wages lower than the prevailing standard or by nonpayment of wages. Complaints are typically filed with investigators at the Wages and Hours Division of the federal and New York State
Departments of Labor, and with prosecutors at the state attorney general's
office and the local district attorney's office. These state agencies and offices are frequently understaffed, and public officials may also lack the de-
termination to aggressively enforce the law. Thus, labor investigations and
legal proceedings may take months and sometimes years. Garment shop
owners who have been subjected to complaints or prosecution frequently
close shop and disappear or open in a new location. CSWA organizers have
responded aggressively in these situations by mobilizing worker pickets
and community protests at the new sweatshop site, or at the owner's home
if they have closed shop altogether. Through these efforts, they have recovered hundreds of thousands of dollars in back pay and withheld wages for
workers and have attempted to create a climate where it is difficult for
sweatshop owners to evade labor law.

Contractors also have organizations representing their interests. As of
1995, there were three organizations representing Chinese American garment contractors: the Greater Blouse, Skirt, and Undergarment Association
(with four hundred to five hundred members), the Metropolitan Area Apparel Association (with some one hundred contractors), and the Sportswear Apparel Association (the smallest association, estimate of membership unavailable). The offices of these associations are in the midtown
Garment District, and they help their members procure bundlework from
Garment District manufacturers. To maximize their bundlework opportunities, some contractors are members of more than one association. The

associations also advise and give seminars to the members on tax issues, garment industry technology, legal issues, and labor law regulations. The president of one association estimated the total number of Chinese American contractors to be from 550 to 600 (located in Chinatown and the outer boroughs). He observed that the number of contractors was still growing, although union shops were experiencing growing competition from independent nonunion shops. In 1995, representatives of these organizations, as well as the ILGWU, estimated that there were twenty thousand to twenty-five thousand people working in Chinese American garment industry establishments, still primarily women. Industry representatives observed that whereas the workforce was more concentrated in the Chinatown production zone in the 1980s, by the 1990s Chinese contractors were becoming more dispersed into the outer boroughs. This observation supports the contention of labor organizers, who noticed that nonunion sweatshops were increasingly moving into clandestine locations in the outer boroughs in order to evade union organizing and labor law.

Nonunion sweatshops predominate in the outer boroughs of Brooklyn and Queens and in New Jersey. In Queens, nonunion contractors work directly with nonunion knitwear designer/manufacturers. Workers in new product lines such as knitwear can be particularly difficult to organize because the product lines often involve jobbers and manufacturers with whom the ILGWU has never had ties.[2] One strategy is for ILGWU organizers to masquerade as rank-and-file workers and check the RN-numbers on garments to determine the contractor's union status.[3] Beginning with the efforts of a Metro Organizing Department operated by ten organizing locals, the ILGWU initiated a Campaign for Justice, which is conducted out of three Garment Workers' Justice Centers, one in the Garment District and the others in the Williamsburg and Sunset Park neighborhoods of Brooklyn (both areas of concentrated sweatshop production). Organizers in this campaign educate garment industry workers about their basic employment rights, including the federally mandated minimum wage of $4.25 (recently raised by the Clinton administration), overtime after working forty hours, and workers' compensation and disability insurance for documented immigrants. Any worker with a wage complaint can file a claim with the New York State Department of Labor, which enforces state labor laws and does not check the immigration status of those filing claims.

In June 1995, the ILGWU and the ACTWU merged operations to become the Union of Needletrades, Industrial and Textile Employees (UNITE!). The ACTWU historically organized workers in the men's clothing sector, which traditionally was more vertically integrated from textile production to garment assembly than the women's and children's garments sector. Recent changes in the men's apparel industry because of growing seasonal variability in men's fashion, however, have reduced vertical integration, leading to a subcontracting structure much like the women's and children's apparel segments. Now comprising some 75,000 members in New York City, and 355,000 members nationwide, the new union hopes that consolidation will assist its efforts overall in the garment industry.

Organized labor's efforts in the New York City garment industry continue to be complicated by the increasing willingness among manufacturers and jobbers to subcontract bundlework to nonunion sweatshops. A good example of nonunion contractors are Korean-owned garment shops. There is now an agglomeration of Korean sweatshops (predominantly nonunion) in the Garment District. This Korean zone has been growing for some ten years, and there are many other shops dispersed throughout the outer boroughs. By one estimate, there are a total of fourteen thousand workers, about two-thirds of them Latino immigrants, in about 460 Korean-owned shops.[4] Many factories recruited workers directly off the street with handbills posted on mailboxes, phone booths, and street signs. The visual clutter created by these handbills led the Fashion Center Business Improvement District to put up four big bulletin boards on a building on the southwest corner of 37th Street, which subsequently removed the boards when this centralization created sidewalk congestion. Even without the boards, prospective workers still congregate around these familiar locations as factory recruiters continue to arrive every morning to take applicants.[5]

The Chinatown Restaurant Industry

The *Chinese Business Guide and Directory* for 1989–90 identified only 192 Chinese-owned restaurants in the four zip code areas (10002, 10007, 10013, 10038) that encompass New York's Chinatown (see Table 3 in chapter 1). I made a more precise enumeration in 1995 by obtaining a list from the New York City Department of Health of eating places in the same zip code areas and adding a fifth zip code area (10012, which includes portions of Little Italy into which Chinese American businesses have been moving in recent years). On this list, I counted 412 Chinese American full-service restaurants (with waiters) and 50 takeout or delicatessen-type eating places (with no waiters). I included restaurants offering Vietnamese cuisine (many Vietnamese are ethnically Chinese) but excluded Thai and Japanese restaurants. I was not able to find a statistical source for a precise enumeration of the number of workers employed in the Chinatown restaurant industry. Based on a street census and an informed extrapolation, Peter Kwong (1987: 26) estimated a workforce of fifteen thousand employed in some 450 restaurants.[6]

It is useful to classify Chinatown restaurants into three categories: (1) smaller noodle shop or dumpling house establishments, which serve low-cost, quickly cooked meals of a simple nature; (2) medium-sized and medium-priced restaurants with more extensive menus, which include more specialized dishes, seafood, and special regional cuisines; and (3) large banquet-style restaurants, which offer many specialized dishes, diverse dim sum offerings, and extravagant meals for special occasions. The smaller noodle and dumpling house restaurants may be described as a type of Chinese fast-food restaurant, although they all feature full waiter service, unlike most American fast-food establishments. These eating places typically hang roasted meats on racks in their windows to attract customers. These roasted meats, along with restaurant dishes, are frequently ordered as takeout food by passing Chinatown pedestrians.

The Silver Palace, which opened in 1976 on the Bowery, was the first major banquet hall to open in Chinatown, with seating for some 820 guests. It was followed by the Golden Unicorn on East Broadway, the Triple Eight Palace beneath the Manhattan Bridge, and, most recently, Jing Fong on Elizabeth Street near the Silver Palace. These restaurants essentially cater to the Chinatown community rather than outsiders. They do a simple lunchtime business on weekdays to office workers and tourists. Large throngs show up for special events such as banquets and weddings on weekday evenings, and for daytime dim sum and nighttime banquets on the weekends. Since the big restaurant day for many Fujianese immigrants is Monday, the weekend traffic extends into the early part of the week at restaurants like Jing Fong. The extended New Year season from January through April is also particularly active.

Jing Fong was financed by a three-million-dollar loan from the Bank of China (Epstein 1993). The chairman of the board is Fujianese. The restaurant was originally on the ground floor underneath the Silver Palace (the entrance faced the opposite direction, toward Elizabeth Street, rather than Canal Street, like Silver Palace), and seated some three hundred guests. The landlord built a much larger space two doors down Elizabeth Street, however, and the expanded Jing Fong, which opened at the end of 1992, now seats eleven hundred guests. One observer (who preferred to remain anonymous) quipped that the old Silver Palace is like a "peanut" next to

Figure 12. The Jing Fong and Silver Palace restaurants, and the Manhattan Savings Bank. Photo by Jan Lin.

the "golf ball" of the new Jing Fong, now Chinatown's largest restaurant (Figure 12).

The workforce in Chinatown's restaurant industry has waged a difficult struggle to unionize in the past twenty years. In the late 1970s, Chinese waiters at a handful of uptown Chinese restaurants successfully won management recognition of a union. These workers affiliated with Local 69 of the Hotel Employees and Restaurant Employees Union (HERE). Somewhat dissatisfied with Local 69, some of these waiters formed their own grassroots, community-based organization in Chinatown, the Chinese Staff and Workers' Association (CSWA). The first campaign of the CSWA was at the Silver Palace, where a labor dispute had erupted when waiters were pressured to share more tips with management. When fifteen waiters refused, they were fired and replaced by management. A picket was organized outside the restaurant with the assistance of the CSWA and drew support from other unionized waiters and many sympathetic members of the Chinatown community (Kwong 1987: 141–43). After a long struggle, management finally rehired the workers and agreed to formation of a union on March 18, 1981. The date became the call letters of their newly established independent union, Local 318.

Following the Silver Palace victory, HERE Local 69 (now renamed Local 100) approached members of independent Local 318 to try to convince them to affiliate with HERE. The president of Local 318, Wing Hoi Chan, accepted a job with HERE, which urged him to change the name of the CSWA to the Chinese Restaurant Workers Association. Wing Hoi Chan felt that the larger membership of HERE (nearly forty thousand) would bring considerable resources to the cause of Chinese restaurant workers. Another CSWA leader, Wing Lam, rejected the affiliation. A crisis of leadership was now engendered within Local 318, and the rank and file eventually voted to stay independent and asked Wing Hoi Chan to resign as president of Local 318. During the turmoil between the two groups, ongoing unionization efforts at Chinese restaurants, such as the Hunan Garden, failed, as bosses spent massively on legal fees to fight unionization and used other tactics like closing and reopening businesses in new locations. A second setback to the restaurant unionization effort occurred when CSWA offices were subject to arson in August 1982. The lack of success at unionizing new restaurants was balanced by some success in the late 1980s in legal campaigns to win back pay for underpaid workers at establishments such as the Peng Teng restaurant (Lii 1993).

On August 20, 1993, in the midst of negotiations periodically conducted for contract renewal, forty-four Silver Palace employees (one-third of the staff) were locked out after refusing to sign a new contract that included "give backs" such as tip sharing with management, elimination of medical insurance, and reduced time off. Richard Chan, executive director of the Silver Palace, in defending the management lockout, cited declining profitability and increased competition from other Chinatown restaurants. He claimed that the Silver Palace was being unfairly held to a "higher standard." Management wanted to apply some of the waiters' tips (mainly men) toward paying dim sum workers (mainly women), whose wages they planned to reduce from the prevailing $6.00 to $8.00 an hour to $2.90 an hour (Palazzo 1994). Management argued that tip sharing, longer work hours with no overtime pay, lower wages, and no benefits were the prevailing standard practices in other Chinatown restaurants.

Unionized workers argued that these "standard practices" were in effect "slave labor" practices and refused to give up their hard-fought union rights, fearing that to give in would be "moving backwards" in Chinatown labor relations. Management offered low prices discounted up to 30 percent in an effort to attract customers to cross the picket line. To encourage the consumer boycott of the Silver Palace, picketing workers successfully employed a coffin (decorated with the message "No More Slavery, Justice for Workers"), a strong omen of bad luck among the Chinese. The vociferous picketing and the campaign to enforce labor law were waged not just to fight oppressive Chinatown bosses but also to enlighten the general public

Figure 13. Silver Palace restaurant workers campaign, 1993. Photo by Corky Lee. Copyright Corky Lee; used by permission of the photographer.

(Figure 13). Jo Ann Lum, an organizer with the Chinese Staff and Workers' Association comments:

> The New York mainstream media tries to paint a picture of the Chinese Americans as a hard working, exploited people who accept slave labor conditions because of something "Chinese." They paint a picture of a willingness to be abused because of the Chinese work ethic. The general public and government officials are led to refrain from interfering in a "Chinatown problem." This picture ignores the importance of labor law enforcement. It allows investigators to be off the hook and be negligent.[7]

After a seven-month standoff, management agreed to end the lockout, rehire workers, and reinstall previous labor standards at the Silver Palace, and four hundred workers and sympathizers gathered for a victory demonstration outside of the restaurant on March 13, 1994. Labor-management relations, however, are still uneasy. To begin with, management only rehired about thirty of the forty locked-out workers. Union representatives had to accept some concessions, including staff reductions and longer working hours. Some of the female dim sum workers were laid off, along with some waiters. Union representatives fought management efforts to completely eliminate the dim sum workers, who management claimed were overpaid compared to other restaurants. Charging management with violation of labor law, the union demanded some $1.5 million in health benefits and back wages in a complaint to the National Labor Relations Board. Management, meanwhile, filed for Chapter 11 bankruptcy protection on January 27, 1995, saying it could not meet debts totaling $3.5 million. The bankruptcy filing reduced to some $160,000 the amount management would be obligated to pay if they were found guilty of labor law violations (Lii 1995a). Some of the workers who were laid off by Silver Palace management were subsequently ostracized by some other Chinatown employers. Former worker May Chang said,

> I was working at Silver Palace restaurant until all nine of us dim
> sum women were illegally fired soon after our 318 Restaurant
> Union had won a fair contract after a grueling seven-month cam-
> paign. I have been in the U.S. for four years and both my husband
> and I have worked in various restaurants in Chinatown. Manage-
> ment has always taken advantage of the workers. Now, I'm afraid
> that my chances of finding another job are slim because I have
> been so active at Silver Palace. Still, I feel I must be involved in this
> campaign so that I can have the rights I am entitled to and a job
> with decent wages and working conditions. (DeAngelis 1995)

In February 1995, organizers at the CSWA were approached by Jing Fong waiters with similar grievances contending that management was forcing them to share up to one-third of their tips and pressuring them to work long hours (sometimes up to seventy hours a week) without overtime compensation. Buoyed by their victory at the Silver Palace, the CSWA formed a new community-wide Committee for Economic Survival of Chinatown and launched a new organizing campaign against Jing Fong. On their second picket of Jing Fong restaurant, the campaign forced the cancellation of a banquet planned for the visit of the daughter of Deng Xiao-ping (leader of the People's Republic of China) and her entourage. In March, picketers reintroduced use of a coffin as a bad omen, a piece of theatrical agitprop that had worked well during the Silver Palace campaign to drive home the issue of "slave labor" and encourage the consumer boycott of the restaurant. During this period of campaign escalation, the number of picketers ranged from 20 to 150. The goals of the campaign were to enforce labor law at Jing Fong in three principal areas: (1) compliance with federal minimum wage law, which was $4.25 per hour in the general labor market but $2.90 per hour for restaurant waiters (since they earn tips); (2) extra compensation for hours worked overtime; (3) guarantees that all tips belonged solely to the waiters and would not be claimed to any degree by management.

In late March, management at Jing Fong began to employ "counter-demonstrators" and successfully assembled the support of other restaurants, the Chinese newspapers, and the police for threatening picketers with "encirclement." The Chinese press threatened to publish close-up photographs of picketing workers to reveal their identities. A large banquet was held at the restaurant attended by management sympathizers. Use of the coffin was criticized as "dirty politics" by restaurant management. Protesters accused the police of pursuing "intimidation tactics" by forcibly making arrests without systematic charges in an effort to break the picket line (the fifth precinct station was directly across the street from the Jing Fong restaurant entrance). Protesters felt that their First Amendment rights were being violated; a legal challenge was subsequently unsuccessful. Jing Fong management built a second, false restaurant entrance in May 1995; police attempted to direct picketers there, but picketers responded by moving their protest to the front of the police station. The picket line was successfully broken as customers could now enter through the first entrance.[8]

During this "encirclement" period, vitriolic personal attacks were made on Wing Lam, director of the CSWA, with posters and public pronouncements labeling him as a "monster," "blood sucker," and "public enemy number one." At the banquet held in support of the management, many chanted "Da dao" (Beat him down). Through his lawyer, Wing Lam professed that he and his family also received death threats (Huang and Robbins 1995). Picketers organized their own poster campaign, charging Chung-Ko Cheng, one of the owners of Jing Fong and a former president of the Fukien-American Association, with having ties to the Fuk Ching gang. Wai Chi Chan, president of the restaurant owners association, was exposed as a top official of the On Leong tong, linked to the Ghost Shadows gang. A photograph of Wai Chi Chan sitting at a restaurant banquet with police captain Thomas Chan was publicized to reveal the alleged collusion that existed between the police, restaurant owners, and organized crime. The campaign for workers' rights at Jing Fong gained sympathetic reporting from the Anglo press, notably the *Daily News* and *New York Newsday*, while the Chinese press leaned toward management. Channel 9, a local television station, devoted a three-part series to the labor dispute that was sympathetic to the workers and raised the issue of alleged collusion between bosses, tongs, and the police.

While management's construction of a false entrance and police collusion had essentially broken the picket by the last week of May, students connected with a group called Students for Workers' Rights moved the campaign into a new stage by starting a hunger strike. Beginning on June 4, 1995, the sixth anniversary of the historic People's Republic of China's government crackdown on student protests at Beijing's Tiananmen Square, five students staged a one-week hunger strike on the pavement outside of Jing Fong to protest the restaurant's "slave labor" policies. One of the student hunger strikers, Susana Joenarti commented:

> I'm a student at Hunter College. My family came here from Indonesia hoping for a better life. But my mother has only found jobs like being a cashier that pay nothing, are unsteady and have irregular hours. She used to come home on the subway at 4 in the morning. She's in her 40's but she has the body of a 70 year old. I worked in a hotel, where you're there to serve the guests and please the management, who have unreasonable, inhumane expectations. In Indonesia, it was much better than this. I got involved in the hunger strike because I felt that being silent means that you're condoning the way things are. I figured that if I didn't endure the seven days of hardship, I would have to endure a whole life of hardship. (De Angelis 1995)

Almost five thousand signatures were collected supporting the hunger strikers and demanding investigations into labor abuses at Chinatown restaurants and garment shops; these petitions were submitted to New York State labor officials. Public support for the student hunger strikers was very high, and reporting was sympathetic in the press. The editors of *New York Newsday* published two student "Viewpoint" columns on the hunger strike and the labor rights campaign.

On July 30, a public hearing was held at Public School 124 in Chinatown at the behest of the CSWA and Students for Workers' Rights on the issue of labor practices in the Chinatown restaurant and garment industries. A panel of officials, which included Maria Echaveste of the U.S. Department of Labor, the New York State assistant attorney general, a New York State Labor Department official, representatives from the offices of U.S. Representative Nydia M. Velazquez (who represents Chinatown), Manhattan borough president Ruth W. Messinger, and state senator Franz S. Leichter, were on hand to hear testimony from several workers, including former employees of Jing Fong who had been dismissed, about labor abuses in Chinatown. Conceding that the efforts of her office to enforce labor law were insufficient, Echaveste pledged her commitment to improve on that record (Williams 1995).

Shortly thereafter came the establishment of The Apparel and Restaurant Guidance and Enforcement Team (TARGET) by the U.S. Department of Labor, a special task force of both federal and New York State Wage and Hour Division investigators, who will closely monitor labor law compliance in the community. Chinese-speaking investigators will be brought in to implement the effort. In September 1995, after a lengthy investigation following a complaint by the CSWA, the New York State attorney general, Dennis Vacco, found that Jing Fong was guilty of labor law violations, and ordered management to pay its employees more than one million dollars in back wages (Gordy 1995).

Chinatown Street Traders

Street traders and vendors are a hallmark of traditional society and were commonplace in turn-of-the-century New York and are familiar in third-world cities. Street trading offers perhaps the easiest mode of entry to the job market for the new immigrant. There are relatively few job-specific skills to be learned; the main requirements are possession of perseverance and what one vendor has described as a "thick skin." Relatively little in the way of capital is required to purchase goods to be hawked and a table or pushcart to display them. For this reason, street traders are mostly self-employed; the exception is vendors who rent pushcarts from a franchised owner. Franchised vendor carts usually offer prepared foods, and this type of vendor is not common in New York's Chinatown. Vendors must register with the New York City Department of Consumer Affairs. Those selling per-ishable items must be licensed with the New York City Health Department. However, many Chinatown vendors operate without licenses.

One of the first street traders to begin operating in New York's China-town was Henry Yung. Mr. Yung says,

> I was born in China, and moved to Hong Kong at the age of nine before finally emigrating to the U.S. in 1964 at the age of eighteen. I was introduced to the trade by a group of immigrants from Chekiang Province who were experienced peddlers in the midtown area. I believe I was one of the first peddlers to begin working in the streets of Chinatown. Specializing in slippers, I worked with two partners for one or two years; while one partner watched for police, the other guarded the stock. Having the best English and the most outgoing personality, I did the actual hawking of mer-chandise to passing pedestrians. Business was good, we found we could sell $100 to $120 worth of stock during the rush-hour period. When police arrived one day, though, my partners went running, leaving me with a court summons for unlicensed peddling. After paying a penalty of $5 at the municipal courthouse, I began renting a stall on 236 East 28th Street in the midtown area for $85 a month, specializing in gift items. I sold mainly wholesale to retail stores and made periodic trips to flea markets and county fairs in towns surrounding New York City as well as making trips to the South.[9]

Table 4

Profile of Chinatown street traders

Business category	Number	Percentage
Retail trade	114	93.4
Produce	44	36.1
Prepared food	16	13.1
Seafood	5	4.1
Dry food	4	3.3
Clothing/Footwear	21	17.2
Souvenirs/Jewelry	13	10.7
Plants/Flowers	5	4.1
Medicines	3	2.5
Newspaper/Books	3	2.5
Services	8	6.6
Shoe repair	3	2.5
Watch repair	1	0.8
Religious consultation	3	2.5
Palm reading	1	0.8
Total	122	100.0[a]

[a] Total percentage does not add to 100 due to rounding.
Source: Street survey conducted by author on October 17, 1995.

Thirty years later, Yung now presides as chairman of the Yung Kee Group, which operates an import-export wholesaling business between the Far East and the United States from its midtown New York City offices, and a midtown hotel. Yung also owns nearly two dozen properties. He was head of the New York Chinese Businessmen's Association for four years (and remains its honorary president), which represents some twenty-five hundred Chinese businesses (mainly dealing in import-export) in the midtown area. Although regretting his encounter with the law, he recalls with some fondness the independent life he led during his street-peddling days. Yung's Horatio Alger–like rags-to-riches story, however, is no doubt rather exceptional. Street trading is a livelihood of daily toil, and few vendors and peddlers will experience the kind of tremendous upward mobility experienced by Yung.

I did a census of street traders in New York's Chinatown on a sunny afternoon in October 1995 (Table 4) and counted 144 vending establishments. Retail trade activities, as opposed to services, comprised the great majority (over 93 percent) of Chinatown street-trader activities. Produce selling (36 percent) was the most common category of retail trade activity. Vending facilities ranged from small tables, boxes, and buckets placed temporarily on the sidewalk to semipermanent carts and stalls, which remain on the sidewalk at night. Traders worked by themselves or in teams of two or three. Because street-trading activity fluctuates with climate and season, my autumn enumeration was likely lower than one conducted in the summer, though higher than a winter census. Some traders, particularly those in more prominent locations, displayed Bureau of Permits tags on their lapels, but most traders appeared to be unlicensed.

Based on this street count and observations over a number of years, I have found clear indications of clustering. Vendors specializing in services are usually grouped around the former Public School No. 23 on Mulberry Street and Columbus Park, which is adjacent. Produce traders, meanwhile, are clustered in two locations of heavy pedestrian traffic. One location is a vacant triangle of land at the conjunction of three streets just off the busy thoroughfare of Canal Street (there have been perennial proposals for a tourist kiosk at this location). The other is a wide sidewalk in front of Chinatown's largest housing project, Confucius Plaza. Both sites could be described as visual and circulatory gateways into Chinatown. Main arteries such as Canal Street, the Bowery, and East Broadway are popular locations. At one artery where heavy trading activity had been observed in the past, Grand Street, I found little activity at the time of my census, as a result of a clearance campaign by local police. A permanent off-street market at Roosevelt Park held twelve traders at the time of my census.

Some New York City street vendors, particularly those offering prepared foods, lease their stalls from vending corporations. All of the Chinatown street traders that I enumerated, however, are self-employed operators, petty entrepreneurs in their own right. There is thus no history of labor-capital conflict in the Chinatown street-trading sector. Because their business is conducted in the public space of the street, however, street traders are periodically brought into confrontation with the police and the regulatory agencies of the City of New York. These relationships are examined more closely in chapter 6.

3

The Nexus of Transnational and Local Capital: Chinatown Banking and Real Estate

Toward the end of the 1970s and increasingly in the 1980s, journalists' attention was drawn to the phenomenon of overseas Chinese investment capital flowing into banks and real estate development in Chinatown and other districts of New York City (Wang 1979; Gargan 1981a, 1981b; Scardino 1986; Chan 1989). Foreign direct investment seemed to be taking place at an accelerated pace throughout the New York metropolitan region, and inflows of labor and capital were originating from a number of different world regions. Chinatown, unique as an ethnic enclave where both sweatshops and foreign investment were simultaneously occurring in concentrated form, received particular attention. Only a few years after observers had identified Chinatown as a center of revived manufacturing activity, there was talk of the enclave becoming a "mini-finance center."

The appearance of overseas Chinese investment has some parallels with the turn-of-the-century flow of Jewish merchant capital into New York City retailing. The comparison is enhanced when we observe that the Chinese historically served a mercantile role in Southeast Asia similar to that played by Jews in Eastern Europe. A profound divergence arises, however, when we consider the complex global economic dynamics that circumscribe the contemporary insertion of overseas Chinese capital into New York City. These global processes encompass the accumulation of capital and political uncertainty in East Asia, the growing cross-border circulation of capital in the global economy, and the emergence of foreign investment flows into the United States.

These impacts can be discerned in the growing influence of transnational banks in the Chinatown banking industry and the impact of overseas capital on redevelopment in the local property market. Before examining the specific contours of transnational investment and banking activity in Chinatown, I will consider the broader global context of capital outflow from East Asia and the more recent phenomenon of reinvestment in the United States.

Overseas Chinese Capital in Historical Context

A circuit of overseas Chinese (*Nanyang,* literally "southern ocean") capital and labor in Southeast Asia has existed since as early as the third century. Emanating primarily from the mountainous southeast Chinese coastal provinces of Fujian and Guangdong, the Nanyang migrants were already established throughout Southeast Asia as cultivators, laborers, and petty merchants in the "junk trade" with China when Europeans arrived in the sixteenth century. Their mercantile proclivities have led some observers to dub them "Jews of the East" (Pan 1990: 128). Particular dialect groups concentrated in different regions. Fujianese went to Taiwan; Hokkienese to Indonesia, Singapore, and the Philippines; Teochius to Thailand, Laos, and Cambodia; Cantonese to Vietnam; and a mixture of groups to Malaysia (Wu and Wu 1980: 135).

With the growth of European influence in the region, this population grew in importance as a stratum of compradors, or middlemen. By the mid-nineteenth century, some had acquired sufficient capital to become large-scale capitalists in their own right, involved in tin mining in Malaysia, sugar processing in Indonesia, and rice milling in Thailand. After World War I, some branched into rubber production, shipping, and food processing, increasingly bypassing Western merchants. Overseas Chinese banks began to be formed. The Chinese presence in Southeast Asia at this time was beginning to be split into a "superclass" of mercantile and industrial capitalists and the "masses" of petty capitalists and laborers (Yoshihara 1988: 43).

The biggest capitalists got their start through cultivation of political relationships with the governments, military, and royalty in the region (Pan: 137; Yoshihara 1988). Some of them acquired the stature of Rockefellers and Morgans of the East, a coterie of hypercosmopolitan tycoons who regularly traveled to Europe and the United States and sent their children to overseas schools. As the Nanyang capitalists gained regional power and prestige, progressive mandarins of the Qing dynasty in the late nineteenth century began to recruit their capital and know-how for imperial industrial and railway projects. This collaboration was in contrast to the early years of the Qing dynasty, when the mainland empire was at war with an alliance of Nanyang leaders.[1]

Mainland Chinese allegiances with the Nanyang Chinese have historically alternated in synchronicity with periods of dynastic openness and closure vis-à-vis the outside world. This wavering policy is partly responsible for a somewhat split identity among the overseas Chinese. They are ethnic Chinese in origin, but many have intermarried with other Southeast Asian peoples.[2] The populations of Hong Kong and Taiwan are largely refugee and expatriate Chinese with an equivocal identity similar to that of the Nanyang Chinese. Their status remains indeterminate as long as there is uncertainty in their political relationships with the Communist regime on the mainland. A supranational sense of a common Chinese culture and ethnicity among the scattered communities of the "Greater Chinese" diaspora is pervasive (and has been heightened in recent years with economic liberalization in the People's Republic of China and the retrocession of Hong Kong in 1997), but there remains considerable disquiet among the overseas Chinese regarding the ideological rigidity and political repressiveness of the regime on the mainland.

Hong Kong was initially established following the Opium War as a foreign-treaty port for transshipment of goods into and out of China. British and Scottish mercantile interests, along with some Nanyang capital, formed the core of its initial capitalist elite. The Crown Colony absorbed hundreds of thousands of refugees fleeing the ascension of Mao Zedong during the Chinese Communist revolution in 1949. Between 1945 and 1950, Hong Kong's population increased from 600,000 to 2.4 million. The city-state also experienced a substantial inflow of Chinese flight capital investment, particularly from Shanghai elites.

Initially settled by aborigines of Malayo-Polynesian origin, Formosa (now known as Taiwan) was colonized by the Portuguese and then by the Dutch in the sixteenth century before they were evicted by the Chinese in the seventeenth century. The island became a province of China and was sinicized with the settlement of Chinese immigrants, primarily from Fujian Province. Taiwan was colonized between 1895 and 1945 by Japan, which developed the island's initial economic infrastructure. Military and economic elites associated with Chiang Kai-shek's defeated Nationalist (Guomindang) Party fled to the island following the 1949 Communist revolution.[3] They set up a government "in exile" with the ostensible goal of retaking the mainland. The People's Republic of China, meanwhile, regards the island as a "renegade province" that will eventually be reunified with the mainland.

The recent accumulation of overseas Chinese capital begins with the rise of the East Asian newly industrializing countries (NICs) to a semiperipheral position in the world system of states. Economic dynamism since the 1960s in Taiwan and Hong Kong, associated with an export-oriented industrialization program, led to the growth of substantial stocks of surplus capital in central banks and in the private sector. Considerable capital has been reinvested throughout the Pacific Rim, in the People's Republic of China, in Southeast Asian nations such as Malaysia, Vietnam, and Thailand, and in North America. Hong Kong's role as trade entrepôt and financial command center in both the East Asian region and the global economy has also been augmented considerably by the onset of open-door modernization policies in the People's Republic of China beginning in 1979.

Capital outflow is additionally associated with geopolitical change in the region. The announcement of a Joint Declaration between Britain and China in 1984 after two years of negotiations confirmed the retrocession of the Crown Colony lease to the People's Republic of China rule in July 1997. The People's Republic of China asserted that it will operate Hong Kong (which will be renamed Xianggang) for fifty years as a Special Administrative Region under a "One Country, Two Systems" policy before imposing communism in 2047. The 1989 repression of Chinese student protests in Tiananmen Square and subsequent ascendance of hard-liner factions in Beijing redoubled expectations that both emigration and capital flight would continue to accelerate out of Hong Kong. Canada, which in 1986 began granting quick immigration status to foreigners willing and able to invest at least $250,000 in projects deemed beneficial to the economy, has been a popular destination for Hong Kong expatriates. Vancouver and Toronto have been especially popular as destinations; the more affluent immigrants are a hypercosmopolitan elite of millionaires dubbed "yacht people" and "Oriental Rothschilds."[4]

While Hong Kong represents a historical fusion of Nanyang, British mercantile, and refugee Shanghai Chinese, the accumulation of capital in Taiwan reflects the cumulative effects of Japanese imperialism, followed by Guomindang flight capital, and finally substantial U.S. military and economic aid following the Korean War as part of an American Cold War strategy of regional containment of communist China. Taiwan's rapid economic development in the postwar era has been attributed largely to export-oriented industrialization policies (Lin 1973). One significant measure of its ascent is foreign currency reserves, which reached US$76.7 billion at the end of 1987, second in the world only to Japan's $95 billion. The general policy of Taiwan's central bank has been to invest its reserves in short-term, dollar-denominated deposits in foreign banks in the United States, Singapore, and Europe. There were tight government restrictions, however, on private capital outflow, though wealthy Taiwanese could circumvent the laws by underinvoicing exports to the United States, often channeling funds into real estate investment, as a possible step toward immigration (Seth and McCauley 1987).

Progressive political liberalization and the lifting of martial law in July 1987 led to the lifting of official restrictions on outward capital flow from Taiwan. Aside from the United States, China and traditional centers of Nanyang activity in Southeast Asia are popular areas for investment. Economic integration between the People's Republic of China and Taiwan proceeds with gradual economic liberalization in both nations. Taiwan is the major foreign investor in China's Fujian Province, which is the ancestral home of most Taiwanese. These moves toward economic integration are balanced, however, by considerable uncertainty in the political realm. Political disquiet in Taiwan was heightened in 1995 when China conducted threatening military exercises in the Taiwan Strait prior to Taiwan's first-ever democratic presidential election. Ongoing concern about the tenuous political relationship between Taiwan and China fuels some flight capital to destinations such as the United States, though political uncertainty is generally a greater concern among Hong Kong investors than those from Taiwan.

Foreign Investment in the United States

Recent capital flow to the United States is an outgrowth of recent changes in the global economy and a structural decline in the American economy. After the fall of the Bretton Woods system in 1971 came a new era of capital mobility with devaluations of the U.S. dollar and replacement of the U.S. dollar standard with floating exchange rates in international trade (Thrift 1989). Flows of funds across borders have accelerated both geographically and temporally, supported by the emergence of numerous new monetary instruments and investment markets (such as Eurodollars and Asiadollars) and technological innovations in telecommunications and wire transmissions that facilitate the virtually instantaneous cross-border flow of funds. Linked with the internationalization of finance is growth of transnational corporations with multisite production, administrative, and market facilities. The emergence of a hierarchy of key urban command centers, or global cities, is associated with the growth of the new capitalist global economy. New York and Los Angeles are the main nodal centers in the United States (Sassen 1988).

Foreign investment in the United States after 1971 was also associated with U.S. government moves to finance its Vietnam War deficits via government bond offerings to the international community. The post-1973 period also saw the transfer of surplus petrodollars from many Arab oil states into American portfolio and direct investments.[5] The American economy entered a more pronounced period of decline with the oil shocks of the 1970s. The policies of the Reagan administration after 1981 exacerbated the national debt and accelerated foreign investment in a number of ways. National budget deficits were allowed to soar as tax cuts were implemented and defense spending bolstered. External trade deficits mounted as protective tariffs over imports were reduced. The "New Federalism," which dramatically reduced the amount of federal government funding to states and municipalities (revenue sharing), led many localities to look abroad for investment dollars. Finally, in separate but related developments, the deregulation of U.S. banking produced a crisis with savings and loan associations that threatened the stability of the U.S. economy in the 1980s.

Norman Glickman and Douglas Woodward have assessed the effects of federal trade and finance policies on the changing character of foreign investment in the United States in the 1980s. Under a triple threat of budget deficits, trade deficits, and international debt, the U.S. Federal Reserve Board raised interest rates starting in 1983 to attract foreign capital to the United States. With higher rates available on U.S. securities and bank deposits, a tide of foreign portfolio investment flooded the country. With the resulting demand for U.S. dollars to make these purchases, however, the dollar became inflated, and this had the effect of deepening the trade deficit. In relative terms, U.S. goods became more expensive, and imports cheaper. Thus, although the period from 1982 to 1986 was one of economic recovery, the United States also moved from being the world's biggest creditor nation ($137 billion in the black in 1982) to being the major debtor nation ($263 billion in the red in 1986). This whole process has been called a giant "debt-for-equity swap" (Glickman and Woodward 1989: 112–16). Some observers (Tolchin and Tolchin 1988) more sensationally dubbed the U.S. economy "Brazil North."

There were calls for protectionism during this period, but the Reagan administration was resistant, turning instead to dollar devaluation as a remedy. The Plaza Accord of 1985 joined the central banks of the Group of Seven in coordinated efforts to manage a dollar decline. While any marked effects of this policy on the trade deficit are still to be seen (foreigners did not immediately start buying more U.S. goods), one major unintended consequence was some shifting of foreign investment in the United States from portfolio to direct investment. With other currencies (especially the Japanese yen) appreciating relative to the dollar, American hard assets suddenly became a bargain on the world market. With the downslide in the value of the dollar, and the expectation of continued volatility in foreign exchange markets, the shift to direct assets also marked a hedge against risk.

Thus, foreign investors were not just buying stocks and bonds but U.S. companies and real estate.

Under the New Federalism, state and municipal governments also have been actively involved in encouraging foreign investment. By 1987, at least forty state governments had opened offices in Tokyo to lobby for Japanese investments (Douglass 1988: 346). Mayors, governors, and business development representatives have been making overseas junkets armed with a range of incentives including loans, grants, tax credits, low-interest bond financing, employee training, site and access improvements, and special lease provisions (Glickman and Woodward 1989: 234–38). Foreign corporations are interested because these ventures bring them closer to the American market, particularly in product lines that are subject to strong U.S. import quotas. Some southern states have been especially active in such ventures. Japan had $1.1 billion (U.S. dollars) in total capital and planned investments in Tennessee by 1985, employing some seven thousand workers in thirty companies (Tolchin and Tolchin 1988: appendix F). South Carolina has courted European manufacturers to the extent that some began to call Interstate 85 between Spartanburg and Greenville "the Autobahn" (Glickman and Woodward 1989: 202).

The Japanese were especially active in the late 1980s, making highly visible "trophy" purchases of major downtown office buildings and entertainment conglomerates in Los Angeles and gargantuan, prestigious landmarks such as Rockefeller Center in New York City. The Canadians, British, Dutch, and other Europeans, however, having been involved for many decades in a range of portfolio and direct investments, still top the list in terms of aggregate dollars invested. Middle East investors, usually affluent individual entrepreneurs and oil sheiks, also have been significant participants on a smaller scale since the mid-1970s. Japanese and European investors are primarily institutional actors such as corporations, pension fund companies, and insurance companies, which are also involved in portfolio as well as direct investments. Some European and Canadian individuals of a more predatory nature stood out in the mid-1980s, however; Sir James Goldsmith of Britain and the Campeau brothers and Belzberg brothers of Canada have gained international renown for high-stakes hostile takeovers of American corporations, often leveraged via millions of dollars worth of speculative junk-bond financing. Some companies were restructured and whole subsidiaries sold off or managerial departments closed down within months of purchase.

Overseas Chinese investors have generally operated on a much smaller scale than the Japanese, Europeans, and Middle Eastern investors. Some are nevertheless moving into the big leagues. An example is Hong

Kong billionaire entrepreneur Li Ka-Shing, who made a bid for Columbia Savings and Loan Association of California's $3-billion junk-bond portfolio in October 1990. Gordon Investment, a Canadian concern, was a 50-percent partner with Li's flagship conglomerate, Hutchinson Whampoa, in the offering. Headquartered in Beverly Hills, California, Columbia Savings and Loan lends to more than three hundred large American companies; the purchasers would gain access to inside data of these companies after acquisition of the portfolio (Sterngold 1990). With Japan languishing in the throes of a recession in the early 1990s, some observers predicted the 1990s would be the decade of the overseas Chinese (Kotkin 1993).

A partial enumeration of Hong Kong investment in the United States is possible through statistics provided by the International Trade Commission of the U.S. Department of Commerce. Table 5 presents the sectoral distribution of Hong Kong investment in the United States during the 1974–88 period. Values were reported for 69 of 146 cases. Finance, insurance, real estate, and services (101 of 146 cases) accounted for the bulk of Hong Kong investment in the United States. When broken down more specifically, Hong Kong investment in the areas of real estate, banking, and hotels accounted for 93 cases and $2,683 million, or nearly *two-thirds* of the total of $3,012 million invested in the United States between 1974 and 1988.

Since Taiwanese outward investment was not officially permitted until the lifting of martial law in 1987, a comparable enumeration of Taiwanese investment in the United States cannot be reliably estimated. As figures became available after 1987, estimates from the Republic of China Investment Commission (1989) showed a jump from $70 million in 1987 to $349 million in the first eight months of 1989. A representative of Taiwan's Ministry of Economic Affairs, which issues these numbers suggested, however, that these figures underestimated the size of the actual 1989 flow, which may have been closer to US$1 billion.

Overseas Chinese investment in the United States follows both the geography of Chinese settlement and the hierarchy of finance and banking sites in the U.S. system of cities. Real estate development is closely associated with finance capital activity. Aside from New York City, prominent areas of overseas Chinese investment in the United States include the San Francisco Bay area, Southern California's Monterey Park, Houston, and Denver. San Francisco has seen substantial banking and real estate activity. Monterey Park, a city of 59,000 in the San Gabriel Valley east of downtown Los Angeles, was 40-percent Asian by the mid-1980s, the highest Asian percentage of any U.S. municipality. Sometimes called the "Chinese Beverly Hills," or "Little Taipei," the community boasted some thirty-eight bank

Table 5

Hong Kong investment in the United States by industry sector, 1974–88

Industry sector	Total cases	Cases with reported values	Total reported investments (millions US$)
Mining	3	0	0
Manufacturing	16	8	70.5
Transportation	7	1	2.0
Trade	19	8	63.5
FIRE[a]	78	41	2,053.5
Banking	(30)	(13)	(1,162.7)
Real estate	(45)	(26)	(818.8)
Services	23	11	822.8
Hotels	(18)	(9)	(701.2)
Total	146	69	3,012.3

[a] FIRE is finance, insurance, and real estate.

Source: U.S. Department of Commerce reports on *Foreign Direct Investments in the U.S.: Completed Transactions, 1974–1988.* The only national-level enumeration on foreign investment in the United States, these reports list only the largest investments (amounting to at least $100,000) and only those transactions in which investment was routed directly from the home country. Despite these limitations, the data do give a good picture of the sectoral distribution of foreign investment. Investments not enumerated may have been routed through third countries (such as the case of shell companies domiciled in offshore banking centers) or through local corporate institutions and parties (such as local Chinese companies and investment partnerships). Taiwanese investments in the United States have been mainly through these channels (or sometimes hidden as underinvoiced imports to the United States, since outward investment from Taiwan was officially restricted by the government until 1987).

branches, with $1.5 billion in total assets in the mid-1980s. Local Taiwanese professionals were the first to settle, followed by overseas Taiwanese and Hong Kong real estate investors and trading companies. Mean family income of the Asian population in 1980 was $30,119 per year, as compared to $24,765 among whites (Tanzer 1985).

Taiwanese investment has been moving more slowly into the East Coast. The Evergreen International Company (Evergreen is a Taiwanese conglomerate initially established in shipping container transport), how-

ever, has built a large commercial complex, called Evertrust Plaza, in Jersey City. Taiwanese capital has begun flowing into the satellite Chinatown of Flushing in the New York City borough of Queens. Hong Kong investors, by contrast, have been prominent in Manhattan. World International Holdings of Hong Kong picked up two large properties when it acquired the thirty-nine-hotel chain of the Omni Hotels Group from Aer Lingus. The Hong Kong and Shanghai Banking Corporation paid $10.3 million in 1982 for the opulent Playboy clubhouse at 59th Street and Fifth Avenue. Other properties acquired by Hong Kong investors are the Ramada Renaissance near Times Square, the Peninsula Hotel on Fifth Avenue, and the Grand Bay Hotel on Seventh Avenue.

In the area of banking, New York State and federal legislators and banking interests sought to enhance New York City's position in global finance beginning in the late 1970s. Federal banking acts passed in 1978 and 1981 liberalized the process by which foreign banks could enter the U.S. retail banking market and allowed the establishment of International Banking Facilities (IBFs) in New York City to handle foreign lending, free from U.S. reserve requirements, interest rate ceilings, and city and state taxes. The tax reduction was strategically engineered to drop the total tax liability to 4 percent below the rate in London. The interest was to attract back onshore the billions that were being invested externally in the offshore Euromarket facilities of the Caribbean and Europe. By 1983, the total U.S. market share of all foreign lending reached 33 percent, compared to 28 percent for London. At the end of 1983, there were some 500 IBFs established in the United States, nearly one-half of them holding three-quarters of all the assets in New York State. By the end of 1986, there were 356 foreign-owned banking facilities in New York City, up 46 percent from 1979; London, however, still led with 400 establishments (Lampard 1986; Fry 1980; Port Authority of New York and New Jersey 1987). Many IBF offices are located in the World Trade Center in lower Manhattan.

The Globalization of Banking in Chinatown

It is important to recognize that the growth of Chinese banking and real estate activity in the United States reflects the nexus of overseas capital inflow and locally accumulated capital invested by an immigrant Chinese American population that has generated savings through productive efforts in America. According to my research, the initial accumulation of monetary capital in New York's Chinatown was founded on the savings of individual small depositors, deposited in U.S. savings and loan institutions, which already had a strong presence in the neighborhood. Locally oriented banks owned by Chinese American immigrants began opening, followed by an

expansion into Chinatown by U.S. commercial banks. Overseas Chinese banks finally entered with the deregulation of international retail banking in New York City in 1981. Transnationally oriented banks have captured an increasing share of banking activity in Chinatown since 1981, at the expense of locally oriented banks.

Generally averse to borrowing, individuals in Chinatown predominantly use banks as a savings reservoir, to perform their day-to-day deposit of paychecks, transfers of funds, and cash withdrawals. Certificates of deposit and other notes offering high rates of interest are popular. Foreign exchange and remittance of cash to East Asia are also common. Many Chinese businesses similarly eschew debt financing in their operations; their daily trips to the bank are necessary more for the frequent deposit and cashing of business checks. Chinatown businesses and individuals have increasingly found that transnationally oriented banks better serve their needs than locally oriented banks.

As of 1995, there were thirty-seven bank branches operated by twenty-four different banks in New York's Chinatown. In 1993, these banks held nearly $4 billion in total deposits, according to Federal Deposit Insurance Corporation (FDIC) statistics (see Figure 14). The FDIC statistics do not distinguish whether bank deposits were local or foreign in origin. To gauge the relative influence of global versus local factors in Chinatown's banking industry, then, it is practical to classify banks by country of origin, the geographic scope of their operations, and the character of their banking operations. Banks operating branches in Chinatown may be usefully split into four categories: (1) nine locally oriented Chinese American banks operating eleven branches, (2) seven overseas Chinese commercial banks operating ten branches, (3) three U.S. savings banks operating four branches, and (4) five U.S. commercial banks operating twelve branches.

Table 6 ranks selected banks operating branches in Chinatown by total asset size. Whereas deposits (a bank's working capital) are liabilities, assets (such as loans and portfolio investments) represent the other side of the balance sheet, the bank's actual value. Ranking banks by asset size gives an idea of the institution's relative standing compared to other banking peers. On this basis, it is noteworthy that U.S. commercial banks (which count total assets into hundreds of billions of U.S. dollars) operate on a distinctly higher level than U.S. savings banks and local Chinese American banks, which have total assets generally in the range of millions of U.S. dollars. Overseas Chinese banks have a split profile. Some overseas Chinese banks have assets in amounts similar to the U.S. commercial banks, while others have smaller assets, like the U.S. savings banks and local Chinese American banks. It is also significant that some of the local Chinese banks

(Asia Bank and Great Eastern) have main offices in the satellite Chinatown in Flushing, Queens. The comparison of total asset size in Table 6 reflects only selected banks because data are not publicly available for all the banks considered in this study.

Table 6

Banks with branches in Chinatown ranked by total asset size

Bank	Scope of operations	Total assets (millions $)
U.S. commercial banks		
Citibank	Global	158,535[a]
Chase Manhattan Bank	Global	82,711[a]
Manufacturers Hanover	Global	55,016[a]
Chemical Bank	Global	49,353[a]
National Westminster USA	Global	14,241[a]
Overseas Chinese banks		
Bank of China	Global	150,400[b]
Hong Kong and Shanghai Banking Corporation	Global	113,200[b]
Bank of East Asia	Global	3,700[b]
Bank of Central Asia	Global	1,300[b]
Ka Wah Bank	Global	1,100[b]
U.S. savings and loans		
Bowery Savings Bank	Local	6,519[c]
Manhattan Savings Bank	Local	3,105[c]
Local Chinese American banks		
Chinese American Bank	Local	563[a]
Asia Bank, N.A.	Local	114[c]
Golden City Bank	Local	89[a]
EastBank, N.A.	Local	78[c]
Great Eastern	Local	75[c]
United Orient	Local	57[a]

Note: This is a selected profile of 18 of the 24 banks doing business in Chinatown.
[a] Figures from Sheshunoff Information Services, Inc., 1990.
[b] Figures from "Top 100 Foreign Banks in New York City," *Crain's New York Business* 5, 52, Jan. 1990; *The Banker* 139, 760, June 1989; "Asia's Top 200 Banks," *The Banker* 139, Sept. 1989.
[c] Figures from LACE Financial Corporation, 1988.

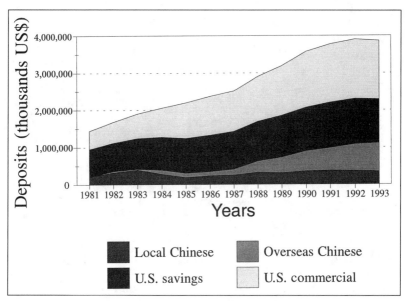

Figure 14. Deposit trends in Chinatown by bank ownership type.

From this standpoint, it is useful to classify U.S. commercial banks together with overseas Chinese banks as being similar in terms of asset size. More importantly, both bank categories are globally dispersed in their operations, and work with clients that include the largest corporations and the wealthiest individuals. U.S. savings and local Chinese American banks, on the other hand, may finance some activity outside of the New York City metropolitan region but are generally much more local or regional in scope. They generally work with smaller corporations and individuals than the globally oriented banks. The locally oriented banks may invest in some nonlocal projects, but these are in the minority; furthermore, they do not maintain affiliated offices outside of the New York City region.

Figure 14 displays deposit trends in Chinatown by bank ownership type between 1981 and 1993. Local Chinese banks experienced the most lackluster growth, increasing their total deposit level by $141 million (from $208 million to $349 million) between 1981 and 1993. Overseas Chinese banks, by contrast, experienced phenomenal growth, from zero deposits in 1981 to $765 million in 1993. U.S. savings banks increased their total deposit level by $420 million during the same period, growing from $747 million to $1.167 billion in total deposits. Finally, U.S. commercial banks experienced the greatest aggregate increase in deposits, growing by $1.092 billion, from $486 million in total deposits in 1981 to $1.578 billion in 1993.

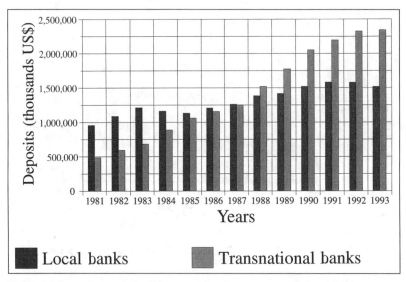

Figure 15. Deposit trends in Chinatown, local versus transnational banks.

Figure 15 presents the data on deposit growth slightly differently. Local Chinese banks are paired with U.S. savings banks as "local banks," while overseas Chinese banks are paired with U.S. commercial banks as "transnational banks." Transnational banks have gained a clear edge over local banks during the course of the study period. In 1981, transnational banks held 34 percent of total deposits in Chinatown; by 1993, they held 61 percent of total deposits. Deposits in transnational banks increased by 382 percent, from $486 million in 1981 to $2.343 billion in 1993. Deposits in local banks, meanwhile, grew by only 59 percent, from $955 million in 1981 to $1.516 billion in 1993.

The Mortgage Activity Reports

On the other side of the balance sheet, I found that transnationally oriented banks gained an increasing share of Chinatown financial activity in lending during the mid-1980s. I conducted this analysis using mortgage activity reports, available to the public at the New York City Commission on Human Rights.[6] Altogether, 309 liens in the amount of nearly $145 million were financed.[7] The trend toward globalization found in the deposit analysis is also unmistakable in the mortgage analysis. Mortgages financed by transnational institutions rose from $5.03 million in 1982 to $58.96 million in 1986. By comparison, annual mortgage activity financed by local banks started at $2.86 million in 1982, rose slightly to $14.74 million in 1985, and dropped to $5.99 million in 1986.

Table 7 compares local and transnational bank involvement in the Chinatown land market by total mortgage activity, total liens, and average lien amount. During the 1982–86 period, transnationally oriented banks authorized larger property transactions than locally situated banks. Local Chinese banks financed the greatest aggregate number of liens (182) but in the smallest average dollar amounts ($193,011), as compared with an average lien amount of $793,317 among transnationally situated Chinese banks and an average of $995,522 among U.S. commercial banks. These differences are not surprising given that transnational banks have much larger total assets than locally situated banks and generally loan to clients with substantially more collateral who are interested in larger-scale projects.

Table 7

Chinatown mortgage activity by bank ownership type, 1982–86

Bank ownership type	Total mortgage activity	Total liens	Average lien amount
Local			
Chinese banks	$35,128,000	182	$193,011
U.S. savings banks	$10,210,000	19	$537,368
Transnational			
Chinese banks	$32,526,000	41	$793,317
U.S. banks	$66,700,000	67	$995,522

Source: New York State Banking Department.

Table 8 examines Chinatown mortgage activity in the same period by building type. A very clear pattern can be discerned. Local banks were more apt to finance residential mortgage activity (32.6 percent of total mortgage activity in the local bank category) than transnational banks, which were more heavily skewed toward financing mortgages of the industrial/commercial variety (90.2 percent of all liens financed by transnational banks). These data indicate that the transnationalization of the banking industry in Chinatown is also linked with a restructuring of land use for nonresidential purposes.

Table 8

Chinatown mortgage activity by building type, local versus transnational banks, 1982–86

	Building type		
Bank ownership type	Residential	Industrial/ Commercial/Other	Total mortgage activity
Local	32.6%	67.4%	$ 42,086,000
Transnational	9.8%	90.2%	$102,478,000

Source: New York State Banking Department.

U.S. Banks Operating in Chinatown

Demand for banking in New York's Chinatown was initially served by local savings and loan institutions such as the Bowery Savings Bank and the Manhattan Savings Bank. These are the two oldest banks in the enclave; both can be traced to the mid-nineteenth century. They have a history as community-oriented institutions that catered to individual depositors (workingmen and -women), small businessmen, merchants, and property owners of the immigrant Lower East Side. Among the oldest financial institutions in the country, U.S. savings banks are concentrated in the northeastern states. They generally pride themselves for their local focus and emphasis on the small depositor and businessperson.[8] The three U.S. savings banks in Chinatown (Manhattan, Bowery, and Lincoln) held about 30 percent of total enclave deposits in 1993.

The Manhattan Savings Bank is the preferred bank for Chinatown depositors. Its predecessor, the Citizens' Savings Bank, was first established in 1860. In 1924, the bank completed a huge dome-topped white granite building on the corner of Canal Street and the Bowery at the entrance to the Manhattan Bridge. It became the Manhattan Savings Bank in 1942 as a result of a merger with Mutual Policy and the Manhattan Institute (Citizens' Savings Bank 1924). The bank's deposit base mushroomed with the arrival of Chinese immigrants, rising from $50 million in the early 1950s to more than $500 million by the early 1990s. Chinese depositors generally do not borrow from the bank; they utilize the branch mainly to invest savings, cash checks, and make day-to-day withdrawals. The bank's management had to increase the number of tellers from six in 1962 to thirty-one as of 1990 to service these operations. An estimated 85 to 90 percent of total deposits are Chinese.

The commercial "money center" banks operating in New York's Chinatown include Citibank, Chase Manhattan, Manufacturers Hanover, Chemical Bank, and National Westminster Bank USA (which is a subsidiary of National Westminster PLC, a British transnational bank). Though domiciled in the United States, these banks are giant institutions with a transnational presence. Recognizing Chinatown's growing deposit base, they began opening retail branches in Chinatown in the 1970s (although some had already been operating on the fringes of the neighborhood).

Being large transnational corporations, large U.S. commercial banks have very structured loan application procedures that require approval by main offices before loans can be disbursed at the branch level. For this reason, they are usually unpopular among Chinatown residents as sources of loan capital. Managers of other banks doing business in Chinatown regarded U.S. commercial banks as interested in using their branches as "deposit feeders," with little interest in providing small-business loans in the area. The U.S. commercial banks are generally appreciated, however, by the Chinatown consumer because they were the first to begin offering technological conveniences such as automatic teller machines (ATMs). Bank managers at the U.S. commercial banks, particularly Chemical Bank, have begun to hire more bilingual staff, translate written materials and ATM instructions into Chinese, and hire community loan officers in order to conform with Community Reinvestment Act prerogatives.

Local Chinese Banks

The first Chinese bank to open its doors in Chinatown was the Bank of China, a Taiwanese financial institution that opened in 1967, mainly dealing with remittances. The bank was reorganized in 1972 with local Chinese capital as a state-chartered institution and renamed the Chinese American Bank of New York. Its main activities in this early stage of growth in the community were small loans (averaging about $10,000) to restaurants, import-export companies, and gift shop owners (Sung 1975: 291).

Other local Chinese institutions opened in the 1970s, including the controversial Golden Pacific Bank, which was eventually closed by federal regulators. Golden Pacific was opened in 1977, its initial stock bought mainly by Taiwanese American investors. The director, Kuang-Hsung (Joseph) Chuang, was an immigrant from Taiwan and a former partner with a Wall Street law firm. Federal officials of the Office of the Comptroller of the Currency (OCC) found deficiencies (inadequate reserves against bad loans) in the bank's activities as early as 1980. Golden Pacific was placed in a "special projects" category for scrutiny, but an official investigation never occurred.

Problems stemmed from what was later called the "Amy Chen account," the transactions of which were never included in bank books. The account was financed through the sale of non-FDIC-insured certificates of deposit (CDs). This account was used to lend $7.8 million to Sandpebbles Realty, a construction firm headed by Huey Mei Chuang (the director's wife) to build the bank's headquarters on Canal Street. The real complications began with a $4.4-million loan to a Taiwanese real estate group that wanted to convert the Regency Hotel in Taipei to condominiums. A legal battle in 1984 over control of the building led to the borrower's desertion of the project. The bank assumed control of the building, which had stopped producing income. Worried about liquidity, Golden Pacific sold more "bogus" CDs, and converted some normal CDs (issued on blue paper) to yellow-paper notes. A legal battle later ensued about the extent to which CD buyers were aware that "yellow" CDs were officially uninsured by the FDIC.

The immediate events leading to federal intervention in the bank's activities stemmed from a customer named Fred Huang, who deposited some third-party checks drawn on Nigerian banks. Some of the checks apparently bounced, and Golden Pacific decided to sue. When Huang's defense lawyers learned of the bank's discrepancies, they notified the OCC. The OCC sent examiners on June 17, 1985, to audit the bank's books. On Friday, June 21, Joseph Chuang met with OCC representatives, who informed him that $14 million in "yellow" certificates were officially deemed liabilities, which meant that Golden Pacific's balance sheet was $5 million in the red. Chuang was not able to readily produce documentation confirming the "Amy Chen" investments (Sandpebbles Realty and the Regency Hotel), which could have been considered assets rebalancing the account. The bank was immediately closed for examination and declared insolvent because of "accounting discrepancies." Two hundred federal examiners from all over the country (including some Chinese-speaking staff from California) descended on the Canal Street bank.

On the following Monday, June 24, Golden Pacific depositors and others congregated outside the bank's headquarters, protesting to the bank as well as the federal government. Speakers contested the bank closing, pointing out that the FDIC usually merged failed banks with healthy ones so that depositors could still have access to funds, rather than closing them. Less drastic measures could have included curtailment of the sale of bogus CDs or ordering a change in management. Meanwhile, important business transactions were being delayed. At one point, demonstrators tried to rush the doors of the bank. The mayor, who attended the rally, tried to calm the crowd and said he was sending a letter supporting depositors to the House

Banking Committee. Representative William Green also promised to send a letter to the FDIC, urging that the bogus certificates be considered insured deposits. Protests continued throughout the week, with community groups and local newspapers accusing the FDIC of racial discrimination.

The FDIC found that $117 million of the bank's total $148.8 million in deposits were officially insured. Of the remainder, some were over the $100,000 ceiling for FDIC-insured certificates of deposit. Another $17 million in bogus certificates were not in legitimate accounts. Fundamental questions were raised about whether clients had been fully informed about these irregularities. Some were sold regulation "blue" certificates that were then converted to "yellow" without their knowledge. Because of these uncertainties, the FDIC said a merger was impractical because long-term litigation was still required for unknown aspects of the bank's balance sheet. Deposit transfer was seen as a better alternative. Also at issue was $15.3 million raised by Golden Pacific representative offices in Boston and Houston, since deposits could not be transferred in such manner under U.S. interstate banking laws.

On Wednesday, June 26, thirty-five banks were invited to submit bids to take over Golden Pacific's $117 million in deposits. Only one bidder, the Hong Kong and Shanghai Banking Corporation, agreed to acquire the deposits, for which it paid a premium of $6.4 million; it also bought about $60 million in loan assets. The FDIC held the remaining assets and paid $117 million for the deposits. The uninsured deposits were still at issue. Hearings in federal court carried on for another year. Finally, in September 1986, bogus CD holders were notified that their deposits were fully insured.

Another local Chinese financial institution, the United Orient Bank, has also been the subject of considerable controversy. The United Orient Bank was established in 1981 with a branch on the Bowery; a second branch was opened in 1983 at On Leong headquarters on Mott Street. In 1984, federal authorities began prosecution hearings against the bank's vice chairman, Eddie Chan (a leader of the On Leong tong), for alleged mob activities. In November, depositors who feared that their bank assets would be frozen staged a run on the bank, withdrawing $5 million in less than a week. They ignored assurances from bank managers that their money was insured by the FDIC. Only after Eddie Chan was officially removed from the board of directors and $6 million was withdrawn did the run stop (Kwong 1987: 117–28).

United Orient Bank continued to experience problems when Ka Chiu Leung, a former president and chairman, was convicted of money laundering in 1989. Finally, bank owners attempted a major turnaround with the hiring of Yungman Lee, a former First Deputy Superintendent of Banks with the New York State Banking Department, as president and chief executive in 1994. Lee has also a record as a Chinatown community advocate. In the 1980s, he served as chairman of the Chinatown health clinic and fought city hall when a jail extension was proposed in the neighborhood (Lii 1994b).

Overseas Chinese Banks

Overseas Chinese banks have had a wholesale banking presence in New York City since the nineteenth century. They did not enter retail banking in Chinatown, however, until the passage of the International Banking Act of 1981. The queen of the overseas Chinese banks is the Hong Kong and Shanghai Banking Corporation (HSBC). The bank was founded in 1865 with offices in Hong Kong, Shanghai, and London by an international group of merchants to finance trade between China, Europe, and the United States. The bank has historically been directed by British expatriates, but now includes a number of Chinese in its lower managerial ranks. The bank owns a 61-percent interest in the Chinese-managed Hang Seng Bank, which is the major retail banker in Hong Kong, accounting for an estimated 50 percent of all deposits and loans on the island. In the 1980s, bank management took HSBC along a campaign of growth and internationalization that pulled it from seventy-fifth largest in the world in 1980 to the twenty-third largest in 1985. Earnings grew at an average of 30 percent in the 1978–82 period (Weberman 1985: 98–99). It now has more than thirteen hundred offices in fifty-five countries all over the world, with its principal strength in Hong Kong, the United States, the Middle East, and, recently, Great Britain. Though impressive in terms of its global reach, the bank is somewhat weak in the world's largest financial centers, such as London, New York, and Tokyo (Rafferty 1991: 291). Unlike the giant transnational U.S. commercial banks, however, it is not heavily exposed in lending to highly indebted, less-developed nations.

International diversification will protect against the political and economic vagaries of what may happen now that Britain has relinquished control of Hong Kong in 1997, but the colony's assets (particularly property) are still the key to HSBC's profitability. Sixty percent of global earnings for HSBC stem from Hong Kong; these represent just one-third of the bank's total assets. Even though the bank has just formed a new holding company with British registration, the bank's headquarters and management remain in Hong Kong (Kristof 1991).

HSBC's American presence was bolstered with the purchase for $262 million (U.S. dollars) in April 1978 of a 51-percent share of ailing Buffalo-based Marine Midland Bank, the world's fifteenth largest bank holding company with total assets of $12 billion (Fry 1980: 79). There was opposition to the acquisition on the part of state banking regulators, who feared asset flight abroad (Glickman and Woodward 1989: 58). The merger was approved only after HSBC chairman, Michael Sandberg, negotiated with New York State Banking Supervisor, Muriel Siebert, and federal Comptroller of the Currency, John Heimann, to switch the bank from a state to a federal charter. Concern about the deal stemmed from concerns that Marine Midland, which was a major force in upstate New York cities, would be neglected by a foreign owner, but there has been no evidence of such discrimination since the purchase (Tolchin and Tolchin 1988: 122). Some bank insiders believed the purchase of the financially unstable Marine Midland was a great mistake (Fry 1980: 88), but recent reports are that Marine Midland has become profitable since HSBC became a 100-percent owner in 1989.[9] In 1987, HSBC acquired a 14.9-percent stake in Midland Bank PLC of Britain, an investment from which it has experienced some losses.

Giant transnationals such as HSBC maintain branch or subsidiary offices in many different regions of the world, but for the other overseas Chinese banks, New York City is the farthest they extend from home operations in East Asia. They specialize in letters of credit to finance import-export trade, money market and treasury activity dealings, buying and selling of foreign currencies, and real estate investments. A New York City location is important because it enables twenty-four-hour trading; Hong Kong businessmen who do not have access to funds after the end of the business day in East Asia can work through a New York City office. The Bank of East Asia is especially involved in the garment import-export trade between New York City and Hong Kong. Smaller than giant institutions such as HSBC and the Bank of China, this bank often participates in loan syndication projects rather than being "market making" loan originators.[10]

Some overseas Chinese banks have had a New York City presence since the nineteenth century. With a total global asset base of $113.2 billion in 1989, HSBC ranks with corporate peers such as Citibank as a transnational banking giant. The Bank of China, though having less of an international network of offices than HSBC, has an even larger asset base. The Bank of China is the foreign exchange arm of the People's Republic of China's central bank, the People's Bank of China. There are no overseas Taiwanese banks with retail branches in Chinatown, though they have recently moved into Flushing, Queens. Their main offices are on Wall Street or at the World Trade Center (Chang Hwa Bank opened an office there in 1989). More significantly, two overseas Hong Kong banks are moving their main offices to Chinatown, joining Hang Seng Bank (which is the only existing overseas Hong Kong bank that currently has its New York City main office in Chinatown). The Bank of East Asia and the Ka Wah Bank of Hong Kong (third largest and seventh largest in Hong Kong, respectively, in terms of asset size in 1990) both built new office buildings in Chinatown in the early 1990s to house their North American headquarters.

The Link between Finance and Rentier Capital

Banks do not just extend credit to rentier capitalists (developers) in order to finance their real estate transactions and construction costs but are rentier capitalists in their own right. The building of headquarters offices in Chinatown facilitates the continued conduct of local economic activity and bilateral trade (the primary circuit of capital) and gives the bank a stake in capitalizing on the proceeds of growth and real estate appreciation in the built environment (the secondary circuit of capital).[11]

The 1980s were a period of heavy land-market activity in New York's Chinatown. In 1981, two high-rise condominium projects involving a combination of overseas Chinese investors and local American developers were announced following the passage of a municipal land-use zoning plan, the Special Manhattan Bridge District. These projects, however, were hotly contested by neighborhood activists (an extended discussion of these events follows in chapter 6). Community-based organizations in New York's Chinatown are generally opposed to upscale residential development in the neighborhood because of concern that rising real estate values will have a displacement effect on the primarily low-income population.

Many upmarket real estate projects went forward in the 1980s, however, such as the Ice House Condominiums, built by Norman Kee, a Chinatown lawyer. Kee assembled a group of local and overseas Chinese investors to build this project of thirty-seven loft-type apartments, which sold for from $300,000 to $450,000. Because of a soft real estate market following the stock market crash of 1987, however, many of the condominium projects just off the pipeline in the greater Chinatown area sold slowly in the early 1990s. Some overseas and local Chinese investors who live in surrounding New York suburbs have bought units as investments, in turn renting the apartments out to more recently arrived immigrants willing to crowd whole families into units to afford the high rents (Bagli 1990).[12] Affluent Chinese Americans are said to prefer prestigious uptown neighborhoods and suburbs. Often, it is the grandparents of the upwardly mobile suburban Chinese who prefer to live in Chinatown. These residents tend to appreciate the familiarity of the Chinese community even while putting up with considerable daily noise and congestion. Meanwhile, the American community has generally not been attracted to the condominium market in the Chinatown area.[13]

In contrast to the aforementioned upmarket projects, medium-sized properties directed more at the interests and needs of less affluent residents have been constructed by Thomas Ip, a garment shop owner and local Chinese investor. Together with four partners, he bought three adjoining three-story buildings at a site on the Bowery near Delancey Street previously owned by an elderly wholesaler of chinaware and restaurant supplies. Zoning permitted Ip and his partners to put up an eight-story residential project, which they called Bowery Court. The thirty-five one- and two-bedroom units, priced from $150,000 to $180,000, were aimed at a more moderate-income population. The investing group (Grand Enterprise, Inc.) negotiated with area banks for special financing, since prospective buyers were expected to be first-time home buyers. Down payments of 15 percent instead of the standard 20 percent were offered, and lawyers' fees were limited to $300. In May 1988, the group purchased the defunct Delancey Theater on Delancey and Eldridge Streets, where it built a similar forty-seven-unit project (Brooks 1988).

It is exceedingly difficult to systematically distinguish between local versus overseas land-market development. One observer from the New York City Office of Business Development has asserted that there is probably a roughly equal dollar amount of local and overseas dollars financing real estate in Chinatown currently, but that the number of *units* financed by local capital slightly exceeds that by overseas capital.[14] Overseas capital, however, was likely more commonly invested in projects of greater luxury and prestige.

On the commercial land market front, there are indications of local and overseas investors pooling their resources to open larger retailing establishments. The first American-style multilevel department store in Chinatown opened on Canal Street and Broadway in 1986, offering a range of medium-priced imported and locally made goods. The Pearl River Mart renovation was capitalized by a group of some twenty local as well as overseas Hong Kong investors. Another large project completed in the late 1980s was the East Broadway Mall, a $4-million project on a rather unusual site, directly under the Manhattan Bridge. Managed by a local Chinese family that started out in the restaurant business and expanded into real estate, this blond marble complex features an upscale range of retail shops as well as a fancy restaurant on the second floor financed by Fujianese investors.

A large mixed-use project financed by local American developers in the early 1990s involved the conversion of a massive records and storage building formerly owned by the utility company Consolidated Edison. The upper floors were transformed into the Royal Elizabeth apartments, an up-market residential offering of eighty condominiums with price tags ranging from $150,000 to $400,000. Vacant lot space was created by demolishing the rear of the building, with the freed "floor-area-ratio" traded to permit the addition of three extra stories on top of the original four. The two bottom floors were converted into the Manhattan Jewelry Center, a space housing several dozen jewelry workshops, a security vault, booths for some two hundred jewelry dealers served by nine entrances at street level, and a res-taurant (Garbarine 1990).

Office development activity in Chinatown has traditionally taken place on the upper floors of tenements and loft buildings (especially along Canal Street, Bayard Street, and East Broadway) and on lots occupied by commercial buildings (which accounted for only 13 percent of the area's total tax lots). Most of the commercial tax lots are one- and two-story build-ings. There are few modern-style office buildings in Chinatown, but this situation is changing.

The first large, modern-style office building built in Chinatown was the Wing Ming (meaning "perpetual brightness") building, a twelve-story structure clad in reflective black glass, which was built in 1978 at Two Mott Street on Chatham Square. It was built at a cost of $6 million by Yip Hon, a Hong Kong businessman who also has investments in Vancouver and Toronto (Wang 1979). Among the occupants are Citibank, Metropolitan Life, import/export firms, and other, small outfits that cater to the Chinese community. Conversions are more common than new construction, how-ever, like the Wing Fat Mansion, at 8 Chatham Square, which was turned into an office condominium by Lawrence Wong, a local developer. The site is occupied by a host of attorneys, doctors, insurance and stock underwrit-ers, and lawyers, including Barst Mukamal, one of the biggest immigration law firms in the country. Another conversion was the Hang Seng Bank's renovation of a century-old manufacturing building at 268 Canal Street into modern offices in the 1980s.

Construction of new office buildings accelerated in the early 1990s with the aforementioned projects of two overseas Hong Kong banks. The Bank of East Asia built a $10-million, seven-story, 50,000-square-foot build-ing at Canal and Mulberry Streets, near the heart of "old Chinatown," which houses its North American headquarters (which were previously located uptown) as well as other offices. The Ka Wah Bank put up a fifteen-story pink-limestone office building (the Glory China Tower) at East Broadway and Catherine Street, the former site of the Pagoda Theater, at a cost of $15 million. Five floors were reserved for their North American headquarters offices, and the rest were leased to other tenants.

Three proposals for Chinatown hotels emerged in the 1980s. Only one was built, a $35-million, 227-room building at the intersection of Broome and Lafayette Streets. The project was initially managed by Danny Li, a former Chinatown garment shop owner, with financing from Maria's Bakery, a Hong Kong–based retail franchise that has several outlets in both Manhattan's core Chinatown and the Flushing satellite Chinatown. The completed hotel was later sold to the Holiday Inn corporation. Two other proposals, one at Centre and Canal Streets, and a 120-room project at Hester and Baxter Streets proposed by Sant Chatwal, an Indian hotel magnate, were eventually abandoned in the soft real estate market of the early 1990s.

Economic Slowdown and Restructuring in the 1990s

By the early 1990s, there were indications that an economic slowdown had taken place in New York's Chinatown. One indicator of the slowdown was a gradual leveling off in the enclave savings rate. A close analysis of the Chinatown banking deposit trends depicted in Figure 14 confirms that total deposits began leveling off in the early 1990s. There was a drop of $43 million in total deposits from 1992 to 1993 (a 1.1 percent decrease), the first decline after twelve years of continual growth. Another indicator of economic slowdown was a decline in the jewelry business. As of 1992, the Manhattan Jewelry Center within the recently completed Royal Elizabeth condominium project was suffering losses and was forced to market space to other retailers (Grant 1992).

During the course of field interviews I conducted in 1990, some banking officials and property managers such as Irving Raber, a long-time neighborhood realtor and property manager, warned that some investment saturation and overbuilding had occurred in Chinatown. In view of the fact that New York City was undergoing a regional recession associated with a dramatic slump on Wall Street in 1987, these predictions did not seem unfounded. Other observers, however, had a more bullish outlook, contending that variables on the level of the global economy insulated Chinatown from regional economic effects. The Chinatown labor and property market, they felt, would remain robust with the continued absorption of flows of labor and capital from prosperous regions of East Asia, some of which boasted the highest growth rates in the global economy in the early 1990s. The impending 1997 retrocession of Hong Kong to the People's Republic of

China also portended a continual flow of flight capital to locations such as New York City.

The moderate economic slowdown that was apparent in New York's Chinatown when I returned for fieldwork in 1995 proved these bullish predictions false. The factors impinging on this economic slowdown were both local and global in origin. First, the regional recession seemed to have finally caught up with the district. The decline in the regional finance, insurance, and real estate (FIRE) industries had severely affected the lower-Manhattan property market, leading to many office and residential property vacancies. The Chinatown FIRE industries and real estate market were similarly affected. Second, an interesting new pattern was developing, that of a flow of capital *back to China*. This reverse capital flight reflected a growing optimism in the international Chinese business community regarding the course of Hong Kong's reunification with the People's Republic of China (interest from American investors and elsewhere in the global investment community was also strong). This interest in investing in China was additionally buoyed by strong growth rates in the People's Republic of China in the early 1990s approaching 14 percent, among the highest in the world during the period.[15]

Chinatown's banking industry was also undergoing a dramatic restructuring, which included bank office closings and major acquisitions or mergers among banks doing business in the district. Bank closings were occurring primarily as an outcome of saturation in the number of banks doing business in the enclave. This restructuring was portended as early as 1989, when Citibank and the Hong Kong and Shanghai Banking Corporation each closed a Chinatown branch office. This pattern continued into the 1990s; the Bank of Central Asia closed its Chinatown branch office at the end of November 1995, transferring the deposits from that branch to the midtown office.

Restructuring in the American banking industry was also having a major impact on banking in Chinatown. Local Chinese banks were being acquired by larger financial institutions. Lincoln Savings Bank was acquired by Anchor Savings Bank in 1994, which was subsequently acquired by Dime Savings Bank in 1995. The Manhattan Savings Bank was acquired by Republic Bank, and the Bowery Savings Bank was acquired by the Greenpoint Savings Bank of Flushing. These dramatic changes among U.S. savings banks doing business in Chinatown do not necessarily mean poorer services for depositors. Greenpoint Savings Bank, in fact, has been very popular among Chinese Americans for the personableness of their loan officers and willingness to grant preferential loan conditions to borrowers with a limited credit record, sometimes without income verification. In addition, the bank is willing to accept large down payments, as much as 25 percent of a mortgage. These terms are ideal for Chinese immigrants who have substantial savings (acquired through frugal spending patterns and pooling of family resources) but low-to-moderate incomes.[16]

Major restructuring trends have also been affecting U.S. commercial banks. Manufacturers Hanover was acquired by Chemical in the early 1990s. National Westminster USA, which has three branches in Chinatown, announced in the summer of 1995 that it would be acquired by Marine Midland Bank at the end of the year. The queen of all mergers, however, was that of Chemical Bank and Chase Manhattan Bank in August 1995, which combined to create the largest bank in the country. The formation of this new megabank marks the climax of a fifty-year trend toward amalgamation since World War II, during which the fifteen largest commercial banks in New York City have merged to form five megabanks. The Chemical-Chase merger was opposed by some groups who feared a reduction in community-based services. Indeed, the closure of seven bank branches in low- and middle-income neighborhoods was announced shortly after the bank merger (Van Gelder 1995). There was running speculation among business observers in New York's Chinatown following the merger regarding the impending closure of a Chinatown branch.

Finally, the decline in banking branches and deposit levels in Manhattan's Chinatown was also an outgrowth of decentralization of the Chinese American population and economic activities to outer boroughs, notably satellite Chinatowns in the Flushing section of Queens and the Sunset Park district of Brooklyn, a phenomenon that is examined in the next chapter. As bank branches open in these locations, especially Flushing, Chinese Americans are increasingly transferring their deposits out of the Chinatown core.

The Growth of Satellite Chinatowns

4

The emergence of satellite Chinatowns in the outer boroughs of New York City is mainly an outcome of congestion in the core Chinatown of Manhattan. The satellites are extensions of both the lower and upper circuit of the enclave economy; restaurants and garment sweatshops can be found in satellite Chinatowns, as well as transnational banks and foreign investors. Residential and economic decentralization on a fundamental level is determined by ecological variables of population density, scarcity of housing, and high land values in the urban core. Residential out-movers are additionally motivated by preferences for privacy and space; their outward geographic mobility, enabled by household savings, also reflects upward social mobility. Economic out-movers follow somewhat in the path of residential decentralization; petty enterprises find that labor is available in the outer boroughs, and banks similarly find that residents there have monetary savings to deposit and invest.

Although satellite Chinatowns initially formed as areas of secondary settlement, they have become gateways for new flows of labor and capital that are leapfrogging the core. This phenomenon conforms with an emerging pattern of neighborhoods in the outer boroughs of New York City becoming areas of primary settlement for new immigrants to the metropolis. Examples are Crown Heights for West Indians (Kasinitz 1992) and "Little Odessa" in Brighton Beach for Russian Jews (Orleck 1987). These trends contrast with classic urban sociological suppositions that inner-ring suburbs (such as New York's outer boroughs) would be areas of secondary settlement for upwardly mobile immigrants (Burgess 1967). In New York City's outer boroughs, many white ethnic outer-borough neighborhoods, such as Flatbush, Bensonhurst, and Canarsie (Rieder 1985), conformed to this pattern during the postwar era. In the past two decades, however, gentrification in the urban core borough of Manhattan has left only two major tenement districts of new immigrant settlement, the Lower East Side/Chinatown and upper Manhattan north of 96th Street.

Table 9, which displays the Chinese population in New York City by borough in 1960 and 1990, clearly shows that the proportion of the population in the core Chinatown has dropped from 35.3 percent to 18.1 percent. The proportion of the Chinese population residing in the two boroughs of Brooklyn and Queens, by contrast, has risen from 28 percent in 1960 to 65 percent in 1990. While Manhattan was the borough with the greatest aggregate number of Chinese in 1960 (with 20,761 persons), Queens had become the borough of choice by 1990 (with 86,885 persons).

Table 9

Chinese population in New York City by borough, 1960 and 1990

	1960		1990	
	Number	Percentage	Number	Percentage
New York City	32,831	100.0	238,919	100.0
Manhattan	20,761	63.2	71,723	30.0
Chinatown[a]	11,578	35.3	43,132	18.1
Greater Chinatown[b]			51,355	
Bronx	2,667	8.1	7,015	2.9
Brooklyn	4,636	14.1	68,191	28.5
Queens	4,585	14.0	86,885	36.4
Staten Island	182	0.6	5,105	2.1

[a] Chinatown is defined as Manhattan census tracts 6, 8, 16, 18, 25, 27, 29, and 41.
[b] Greater Chinatown is defined as the original eight census tracts, plus fourteen adjoining census tracts into which Chinese began moving by 1990: 2.01, 2.02, 10.01, 10.02, 12, 14.01, 14.02, 15.01, 22.01, 30.01, 31, 36.01, 43, and 45.
Sources: Abeles, Schwartz, Haeckel, and Silverblatt 1983; U.S. Census of Population and Housing 1990, Census Tracts, N.Y.-N.J., Standard Metropolitan Statistical Area.

The Formation of Satellite Chinatowns

Map 3 shows the locations of some of the largest new satellite Chinatowns. Flushing and Sunset Park are the major satellite Chinatowns featuring significant Chinese American commercial activity. Other outer-borough satel-

Map 3. Core and satellite Chinatowns in New York City. Credit: Kate Blackmer.

lite Chinatowns are mainly residential concentrations. The formation of satellite Chinatowns has followed the route of the public transportation infrastructure, notably the IRT No. 7 subway line to the Elmhurst, Corona, and Flushing communities of Queens (the F and R trains also lead to some Chinese concentrations in Rego Park and Forest Hills, also in Queens). Bus lines also converge at the Flushing subway terminus. The IRT No. 7 train to Queens is sometimes called the "Orient Express" (Lyons 1986). In Brooklyn, the D, N, and R lines lead to Chinese settlements in Sunset Park and Sheepshead Bay (some Chinese have also settled in Borough Park and Bay Ridge). Eighth Avenue in Sunset Park is the main area of Chinese commercial development in Brooklyn. Many Chinese Americans refer to this satellite Chinatown as "Eighth Avenue" rather than "Sunset Park." The N train stop at Eighth Avenue is called the "blue sky" station by some Chinese because it is the first stop aboveground on the express subway route coming out from Manhattan's Chinatown (Winnick 1990: 66). The D train is taken by some to the Church Avenue/north Flatbush area of Brooklyn. Only the Brooklyn communities offer a direct subway line to Manhattan's Chinatown, increasing the likelihood that Brooklyn residents commute daily to work in the core enclave. The trip from Flushing to Manhattan's Chinatown is longer and involves a subway transfer at the busy Grand Central Station, reducing the incidence of daily commuters coming from Queens.

Providing an alternative to the subway are informal minibus services that shuttle between outer-borough Chinatowns and Manhattan's Chinatown for about the price of a subway token, or slightly more. Usually not officially registered as buses, these large unmarked vans pick up commuters at familiar locations along major Chinatown thoroughfares such as Canal Street and whisk them back to outer-borough locations. Driving above ground, they are somewhat more comfortable than the underground subway ride and will generally deposit riders much closer to their actual place of residence than the subway, saving the rider some commuting time. In the outer boroughs, they pick up commuters at main arteries such as Sunset Park's Eighth Avenue.

The largest and oldest of the satellite Chinatowns is Flushing, which is the main center of Chinese commercial activity in Queens. Flushing has been dubbed "Asiantown" by some observers because of the congregation there of not only Chinese but Korean and Asian Indian businesses, as well as businesses of many other ethnicities, mainly along Roosevelt Avenue, 40th Road, 37th through 39th Avenues, and Main Street. The surrounding residential areas contain many thousands of Chinese families. The first Asians to settle there may have been associated with the United Nations, which was briefly headquartered in Flushing in 1946 (Smith 1995). Enoch Yee Nock Wan (1978: 95) observed that some initial Chinese settlers were expatriates from Cuba and South America and opened restaurants serving Chinese-Spanish cuisine. Chunshing Chow (1984: 146) asserted that the community began to grow in the late 1950s and early 1960s because of out-movement of American-born second-generation Chinese from Manhattan's Chinatown. In addition to out-movers from Manhattan, new immigrants, notably middle-class immigrants from Taiwan, began settling in Flushing following the liberalization of immigration law in 1965. A factor pushing immigrants to settle in Flushing was diminishing availability of adequate and affordable space in Manhattan; a factor pulling them was a desire for home ownership among those that had adequate savings to purchase property in Queens. Another important pull factor was low commercial rents in Flushing. New York City's sixth largest shopping district, Flushing experienced somewhat of a recession in the 1970s, which provided an opportunity for enterprising Chinese businesspeople (Chen 1992).

The Brooklyn population is concentrated mostly around Sunset Park (the second largest satellite Chinatown), Borough Park, and Sheepshead Bay. Sunset Park includes not only some non-Chinese Asian groups such as Koreans and South Asians but also a large quotient of Latino population groups. Chinese became a noticeable population during the 1970s and have continued to expand in the 1980s. A city planning representative recently estimated that about thirty garment factories were in Sunset Park and Bay Ridge, sited in old warehouses and machine shops (Howe 1986). Louis Winnick (1990: 149) counted at least forty Chinese-owned garment factories in operation three years later. Chunshing Chow (1984: 143) reported that Church Avenue in north Flatbush became a popular settlement area in the early 1980s among new, low-income immigrants leapfrogging the core because of lack of affordable housing.

The satellite Chinese settlements found in Queens seem to be generally more prosperous, including middle-class Chinese arrivals who bypass the core Chinatown completely as well as upwardly mobile Chinese moving out from the core. Brooklyn's satellites, on the other hand, seem to attract either the poorest new working-class immigrants who cannot find housing in Manhattan's Chinatown and are leapfrogging the core (Sunset Park), or upwardly mobile core Chinatown residents who have acquired enough savings to purchase outer-borough property (Sheepshead Bay).

In terms of commercial activity, outer-borough Chinese settlements provide an opportunity for petty entrepreneurs to start new businesses out of the competitive milieu of the core. The garment production zone also shows signs of decentralizing with the development of satellite zones, notably in Sunset Park, Brooklyn. Flushing, Queens, the largest outer-borough Chinatown, has become a satellite investment zone with the opening of branches of overseas Chinese banks and construction of real estate projects involving overseas investment capital. These latest developments suggest that satellite Chinatowns may be absorbing not only lower-circuit overflow but some upper-circuit capital flow.

Tables 10 and 11 display statistically some of the distinctive socioeconomic differences between Manhattan's core Chinatown and the outerborough satellite Chinatown populations. Flushing (the largest commercial outer-borough satellite) in Queens and Sunset Park in Brooklyn, the two major centers of outer-borough Chinese commercial activity, and Corona/Elmhurst in Queens and Sheepshead Bay in Brooklyn, two moreresidential, noncommercial settlements, have been selected for comparison. Table 10 shows that the Chinatown core is *generally poorer and more working-class than the outer-borough population.* The Queens settlements of Elmhurst and Flushing contain more residents with occupations in the professional, managerial, and technical categories, and fewer in the semiskilled working-class categories (operators, transportation workers, and laborers) as compared with the Chinatown core. Median annual household income in the two Queens communities ($32,104 in Corona/ Elmhurst, and $29,193 in Flushing) is higher than in the Chinatown core ($17,443).

Table 10

Occupational profile, household income, and poverty status of Chinatown core versus satellite Chinatowns, 1990

	Chinatown core	Corona/ Elmhurst	Flushing	Sunset Park	Sheeps- head Bay
Occupational profile					
Prof./Manag./ Technical	13.3%	26.3%	30.7%	19.0%	27.0%
Sales/Clerical	17.4%	32.0%	33.9%	25.5%	24.6%
Services	25.6%	17.3%	15.5%	18.3%	19.7%
Farm/Fish/Forestry	0.1%	0.3%	0.1%	0.1%	–
Precision production	6.4%	7.2%	6.6%	6.7%	3.0%
Operator/Transp./ Laborer	37.1%	17.0%	13.2%	30.3%	25.6%
Median household income (weighted average)	$17,443	$32,104	$29,193	$27,763	$36,167
Families in poverty	21.6%	13.0%	12.2%	19.6%	12.9%

Source: 1990 Census of Population and Housing, Census and Block Numbering Areas, New York, NY PMSA.

Brooklyn's Sunset Park, on the other hand, has an occupational profile more similar to the Chinatown core (with larger numbers of workers in the semiskilled manual categories, and fewer workers in the professional, managerial, and technical categories). Sunset Park's median annual household income of $27,763 is also the lowest among the four outer-borough satellites. Sheepshead Bay, by comparison, features a larger proportion of workers in the professional, managerial, and technical categories (27 percent as compared with 19 percent in Sunset Park and 13.3 percent in the Chinatown core). Furthermore, the annual median household income in Sheepshead Bay is $36,167, more than twice as high as that in the Chinatown core. Sheepshead Bay is a desirable residential community very near the shore that attracts upwardly mobile Chinese Americans interested in a higher quality of life. Sunset Park, on the other hand, is a location that attracts a greater number of newly arrived lower-class immigrants forced to leapfrog the Chinatown core because of the unavailability of housing.

The housing tenure data in Table 11 provide further evidence of the general differences between the Chinatown core and the satellites. The overwhelming majority of residents in Manhattan's Chinatown (95 percent) are renters. As might be expected, higher home-ownership rates can be found in the Queens settlements of Corona/Elmhurst (29 percent) and Flushing (28 percent). Sunset Park also has a high home-ownership rate (24 percent), and the rate in Sheepshead Bay is even higher (42 percent). There is no Chinese commercial presence in Sheepshead Bay; the area is a residential community for upwardly mobile Chinese Americans interested in an improved quality of life in the outer boroughs.

Table 11

Housing tenure patterns in Chinatown core versus satellite Chinatowns, 1990

	Chinatown core	Corona/ Elmhurst	Flushing	Sunset Park	Sheeps- head Bay
Housing tenure					
Owners (A)	670	3,232	2,869	777	523
Renters (B)	13,717	7,955	7,329	2,432	710
Home-ownership rate					
(A/A+B)	5%	29%	28%	24%	42%
Median value of owner-occupied housing units					
(weighted average)	$168,949	$225,461	$227,924	$176,763	$198,950

Source: 1990 Census of Population and Housing, Census and Block Numbering Areas, New York, NY PMSA.

Congestion in the Chinatown Core

Congestion is not a new phenomenon on the Lower East Side, being particularly marked during the days of pushcart peddlers and tenement homework during the high point of East European immigration from the 1890s to the 1910s. As the tides of East European immigrants diminished starting in the 1920s and Lower East Side immigrants increasingly began moving to New York City's outer boroughs, congestion eased. The white ethnic populations (mainly Italians and Jews) were the main occupants of residential and commercial space surrounding Chinatown when more Chinese immigrants began arriving in the 1960s.

Housing inventory freed by departing white ethnic groups, however, has been far from adequate in keeping up with burgeoning demand from incoming Chinese migrants. Chinatown vacancy rates in 1980 were under 2 percent, compared to 3 percent for Manhattan—both rates are lower than the 5 percent indicative of a "normal" housing market. Chinatown rents are low compared to the rest of New York City but have risen in recent years. Exorbitant "key money" of a few hundred to a few thousand dollars, paid to the landlord, superintendent, or another agent, is commonplace just to secure a lease (Abeles, Schwartz, Haeckel, and Silverblatt 1983: 125–30). A Department of City Planning study (1979: 44–45) found that 75 percent of tenement properties in the oldest part of Chinatown (census tract 29) in 1975 were owned by landlords with Chinese surnames. Chinese ownership was continuing to increase at a dramatic pace: sales data from 1974–75 indicated that 88 percent of new purchasers were Chinese. Commercial establishments were commonly found on the ground floors of tenement properties. Because upper floors were generally residential units subject to city rent controls, building owners made up their profit margins by charging commercial rents of from $10 to $20 per square foot to co-ethnic operators of shops and restaurants.

A study by Abeles, Schwartz, Haeckel, and Silverblatt, Inc. (1983: 161–65) found that sales prices of dwelling units in the greater Chinatown area averaged $4,200 in the 1970–77 period, went up to $8,750 in 1979, and back down to $7,300 in the first part of 1981 (because of recession and rising interest rates). Prices were much higher in the old Chinatown core (census tract 29, approximately)—$9,700 in 1970, $27,000 in 1981—a result of higher demand, a greater concentration of commercial street-level activity, and greater prestige attached to owning property in the core.

With most buildings rent controlled, and operating costs, taxes, and debt servicing a financial burden, Chinatown-area tenement owners often skimp on maintenance and sometimes try to get residents to vacate, which allows greater rent increases under vacancy decontrol statutes. Sometimes they will outright harass tenants to get them to vacate. Local legal services organizations reported increases beginning in 1979 in the numbers of residents seeking assistance in disputes with landlords (Abeles, Schwartz, Haeckel, and Silverblatt 1983: 163). In addition to replacing existing tenants with higher-rent residents, landlords may sometimes rent second-floor space out to commercial tenants. Some fourteen hundred residents were displaced from five hundred old Chinatown apartments in this manner between 1970 and 1980 (Abeles, Schwartz, Haeckel, and Silverblatt 1983: 123).

With demand as it is, Chinatown landlords milk buildings for profits but do not abandon them. Abandonment is much more pervasive in the predominantly Latino-inhabited Lower East Side tenement districts to the north and east of Chinatown, where the percentage of properties in tax arrears of five quarters or more may range from 25 percent to 50 percent. Under Local Law 45, passed in 1976, properties five quarters or more in arrears fall into city ownership through "in rem" vesting procedures. The disposition of these city-owned properties has been the subject of intense negotiations between city officials and the community board for the past seven years. In the Lower East Side, the current plan is to sell vacant city-owned sites to private developers constructing market-rate housing, and to use the proceeds from the land sales to "cross-subsidize" publicly assisted rehabilitation of deteriorated city-owned tenements for low-income and minority residents.

Meanwhile, tenement buildings in Chinatown (still predominantly under private ownership) continue to pass from deteriorated to deplorable condition; code violations are rampant. Federal Section 8 housing subsidies for low- and moderate-income housing rehabilitation were phased out under the Reagan administration. The question of upgrading is problematic; Emanuel Tobier's assessment (1979: 39) is that given the unlikelihood of complete rehabilitation (which would require massive public subsidy), tax abatement or stricter code enforcement might improve levels of maintenance.

Even publicly subsidized tenement rehabilitation is problematic. City-initiated efforts to rehabilitate "in rem" tenement stock (previously abandoned; hence the most deteriorated of tenement buildings) in the late 1970s were plagued by prohibitive cost overruns. The tenements were so full of ill-designed idiosyncrasies and in such an advanced state of decay that bringing them up to contemporary building code requirements was almost (some felt) as expensive as tearing them down and putting up new buildings (Schur 1980: 48).

Flushing as a Satellite Investment Zone

Flushing has become the center of considerable Chinese commercial development because it is the terminus for the only subway line connecting north-central Queens to Manhattan. According to a Chinese newspaper, there were about 120 Chinese stores and businesses located in Flushing in 1982 in a diverse range of industrial categories. In December 1982, the first large project to be built in the district was finished, a mixed-use complex of thirteen low-rise buildings for mixed commercial and residential uses, called New Chinatown or Mini-Chinatown (Chow 1984: 150).

Flushing is beginning to emerge as an alternate finance center to the core Chinatown for New York City's Chinese population. Two local Chinese banks are headquartered in Flushing, the Great Eastern Bank (Taiwanese) and the Asia Bank (Chinese and Taiwanese). Among the overseas Chinese banks with branch offices in Flushing are the Hong Kong and Shanghai Banking Corporation and the China Trust Bank (Taiwanese). The China Trust Bank, which opened an office in Flushing in July 1991, received $6 million in deposits from four hundred depositors within two weeks. A study by the China Trust Bank found that there were thirty-four bank branches in Flushing (of both U.S. and Chinese parentage) in 1990, holding a total of $3.13 billion in deposits, the majority of which were held by American banks (Lorch 1991).

Hotel development has also picked up in Flushing. The eight-story Garden Hotel was built by the Huang Development Group in 1989. A Taiwanese investment group built a Sheraton franchise hotel, the Sheraton LaGuardia East, in Flushing. The fourteen-story hotel also has a linked shopping arcade for stores and restaurants, a four-hundred-seat banquet hall, and meeting rooms. These hotels are aimed at business travelers from Asia but were built primarily with the funds of local Chinese investors (Oser 1990).

Affluent overseas Chinese investors are thus beginning to leapfrog or move out of the congested Chinatown core just like the newest poor immigrants and the upwardly mobile. The establishment of a satellite investment zone in Flushing represents a fusion of overseas upper-circuit interests and the emerging Chinese American middle class. The more working-class population and associated satellite garment production zone in Brooklyn's Sunset Park, however, represents an outward extension of the lower-circuit economy from the Chinatown core.

Asian investment and rapid commercial development are credited by local businessmen as insulating the district from the regional recession experienced in most of New York in the late 1980s and early 1990s. Rampant growth has also had negative side effects, however. Some longtime white and African American residents and small-business owners complain of noise, overcrowding, traffic congestion, and rapidly increasing housing and commercial rents. Some of these established interests criticize the proliferation of Asian signage on Flushing streets brought by these immigrant newcomers. Some local support for slowing growth has been voiced, particularly by white ethnic home owners belonging to neighborhood associations in the peripheral sections of Flushing. These residents have gathered sufficient support to veto some proposals for megascale development projects downtown. An initiative to enact a moratorium on building was countered, however, by a lobby of growth advocates representing white and Asian business interests in downtown Flushing (Smith 1995).

Sweatshops and Labor Organizing in Sunset Park

Brooklyn's Sunset Park has emerged as a satellite garment production area for the Chinese in New York City. Organizers with the International Ladies' Garment Workers' Union (ILGWU) Workers Center in Sunset Park estimate that there are 150 to 200 shops, all nonunion. Garment shops in Manhattan's Chinatown are generally union shops because the workforce is familiar with labor law, and shops are clustered within a centralized area, facilitating communication between workers. Union organizers have found that garment shops in the outer boroughs, by contrast, are more dispersed and hidden. Smaller and more mobile than shops in Chinatown or the Garment District, these shops commonly evade industry standards and labor law, closing quickly so they can easily evade Department of Labor inspectors. This mode of operation was confirmed by reporter Jane Lii, who spent a week working under cover in a Sunset Park garment shop named Chai Feng. The owners of Chai Feng had previously operated a garment shop called Superior Fashions, which had closed suddenly, owing its workers $80,000 in back wages. Nearly all the thirty workers at Chai Feng were recent Fujianese immigrants, some of them illegal aliens (Lii 1995b).

Labor activists have found that traditional shop-floor organizing strategies are ineffective among these surreptitious and evasive Brooklyn sweatshops. Workers experience a high rate of movement between shops during the course of a year, even shuttling alternately between shops in Manhattan's Chinatown and Sunset Park. They do have the common experience, however, of residence in Sunset Park. A variety of family members and community residents may be involved in garment manufacture, including husbands and children, who go after school to help their mothers.

Up to three generations of workers within a family may work in garment sweatshops. Children grow up in a "culture of the garment industry."

Activists associated with the Chinatown Staff and Workers' Association (CSWA) and the ILGWU have thus begun employing a community-based organizing strategy. The CSWA opened a Brooklyn office in 1995, the first organizing office they have opened outside of Manhattan's Chinatown. The much larger ILGWU began implementing such an approach in 1992 through its Campaign for Justice. The ILGWU community-based organizing strategy involves enforcement of National Labor Relations Board (NLRB) rules. Danyun Feng, director of the ILGWU Campaign for Justice, says,

> If 50 percent of the workers in a sweatshop sign a union authorization card, then an application can be made to the NLRB to hold an election and legally form a union, which then must be recognized by the sweatshop owner. Organizing is difficult in a volatile industry, however, since sweatshops frequently experience turnover depending on the availability of bundlework from the midtown Garment Center jobbers and manufacturers. Sweatshop contractors may work sequentially with a series of different jobbers and manufacturers during the course of a year. With industrial rents very low in Brooklyn, sweatshop owners will frequently close shops to fight labor organizing and legal campaigns. They may open a new shop "around the corner" and rehire previously fired workers.[1]

The ILGWU Campaign for Justice nevertheless moved forward, beginning with English classes, which were conducted by ILGWU organizers in donated space in local schools and churches and initially attracted about one hundred workers. Social outings to recreational areas in New Jersey were held. By the second year of the campaign, the ILGWU was able to open a workers' center and began forming workers' committees with participants from the English classes. Workshops were held, and skits and mock theater revues about shop-floor politics and labor rights were performed. Workers were encouraged to volunteer in training and organizing themselves. A visit to the Brooklyn district attorney's office was also organized, where a mock court case was held to educate workers about the American legal system. This educational campaign appealed to the district attorney's office because it was an election year.

Eventually, the workers came up with the idea of organizing a demonstration to protest poor working conditions and low wages, and to make demands for union recognition and unpaid back wages. The workers ac-

Figure 16. Brooklyn garment workers demonstration, 1995. Photo credit: UNITE!;
used by permission.

quired the support of the ILGWU Education Department and other union
staff. Plans began to be formulated in May 1995 and were forwarded to the
union leadership for approval. Police permits were procured, and plans
were made for a demonstration of two hundred participants. On June 18,
1995, several hundred (and possibly a thousand) demonstrators turned out
for a march down Eighth Avenue, the main commercial artery of Sunset
Park (Figure 16). This was the largest political demonstration held by Chinese garment workers since the contract dispute of 1982. The majority of
demonstrators were Chinese garment workers and their families, but Latino garment workers from shops in midtown Manhattan, rank-and-file supporters from other labor unions, and nonunion sympathizers also participated (Figure 17). Speakers included workers, ILGWU officials, and local
politicians. The highest-ranking politician to address the rally was Representative Nydia Valezquez (who represents the Lower East Side/Chinatown
district in the U.S. Congress), a Puerto Rican immigrant and a popular de-
fender of labor rights. The event was amply covered by the major Chinatown newspapers, the New York media, and even a television station in
Hong Kong. The ILGWU (now the United Needletrades, Industrial and
Textile Employees [UNITE!]) Campaign for Justice director Danyun Feng
summed up:

Figure 17. Brooklyn garment workers' demonstration, 1995. Photo credit: UNITE!; used by permission.

The idea for the demonstration came from the workers committee out of a feeling of struggle against low wages and fighting for back pay reimbursement. Through this struggle, they turned from being victims to transforming their lives. The overall impact of the successful demonstration was to give the workers confidence. "No Pay No Way" became a popular slogan during the course of the campaign. Some employers paid back wages the night before the demonstration out of fear. In the wake of the demonstration, ILGWU organizers have begun to pressure shop owners with "letters from the Workers Center" without even launching legal proceedings. Collective action may thus be more effective, with results more immediate than time-consuming legal proceedings, which can take one to two years.[2]

The decentralization of population, labor, and capital from the core Chinatown in Manhattan into satellite settlements in Queens and Brooklyn has thus been accompanied by a diffusion of the frontline efforts of labor organizers from center to periphery. Let us now return to the center to consider in detail the dynamics of internal social change beyond the arena of labor action.

5

Solidarity, Community, and Electoral Politics

The dramatic demographic and economic changes in New York's China-town since the end of the exclusion era have been accompanied by equally significant shifts in its social and political structure. The major shift is the emergence of contemporary workplace and community organizations, many led by second-generation Chinese Americans; their growing power has challenged the longtime hegemony of the traditional family and clan associations in the enclave polity. The staff and leaders of these contemporary organizations mediate the relationships of enclave residents with the wider society. These organizational actors essentially broker the provision of resources, many provided by the state, to Chinatown residents. Tangible benefits such as employment and skills training, housing, health, education and other social services, legal aid, and voter education are procured and distributed by these organizers. This system is in contrast to the traditional system, whereby services and benefits were provided through the patronage of a clannish, authoritarian mercantile elite.

The emergence of workplace and community organizations in New York's Chinatown during the post-exclusion era has taken place within a milieu of periodic civil disturbance. Since the 1960s, there has been a dramatic succession of street marches, demonstrations at government office buildings, workplace pickets, and other actions mobilized to contest a number of issues including police brutality, urban development policy, minority employment and federal procurement contracts, and workers' rights. Activists drew their inspiration and tactics from civil rights protests, the Asian American movement, the labor movement, and the community action movement. While these collective actions helped to influence public policy, procure resources, or protect the rights of workers and residents, they also gave participants a sense of community empowerment through the solidarity of their action. Some of these collective actions were the formative incidents in the emergence of new community organizations.

Chinatown social relations in the post-exclusion era have thus been marked by the growing influence of new *organizational solidarities*, which are manifested most visibly through participation in collective action. Experience of political solidarity through periodic bouts of collective action reinforces the more enduring salience of organizational solidarity conferred by membership in new workplace and community organizations.[1] A sense of the contemporary Chinatown community as an urban ethnic enclave and a defended territory is generated, in contrast to the clannish traditional community that existed during the exclusion era. Social relations in traditional Chinatown were governed more by primary ties such as kinship or region of origin, which were sustained through affiliation with family, clan, and district associations. In the new Chinatown, traditional associations have a continuing social and cultural salience, but their social and political influence is increasingly superseded by the contemporary organizations in the everyday life of the community and in its interactions with the wider society. In contrast to the patriarchal profile of the traditional community power structure, the membership and leadership of the contemporary organizations include many women. Furthermore, women have played a prominent role as Chinese Americans have entered local electoral politics.

It would be misleading to assume that traditional associations are backward or obsolescent social institutions. This is a positivist viewpoint that obscures the complexities of social change. Traditional associations had a historical salience in assisting Chinese immigrants in their adjustment to life in a prejudicial American society during the exclusion years, and continue to play a significant role in their cultural lives and familial interactions, especially as there is an ongoing inflow of immigrants. Thus, there has been a continuing growth of new family, clan, and regional associations since the mid-1980s, particularly of the Fujianese variety, as emigration has accelerated out of Fujian Province with the progressive "opening up" of this region of the People's Republic of China. The rise of new Fujianese immigrant associations has somewhat challenged the hegemony of the traditional social order, though from a different social terrain than the contemporary community and workplace organizations, since Fujianese clan associations are institutionally comparable to the older Cantonese clan associations.

This factionalism among the traditional associations is paralleled by considerable factionalism among the contemporary organizations, which somewhat contradicts the manifest facade of solidarity so visibly displayed in public collective action. Contemporary workplace and community organizations are divided by differences of social movement philosophy and tactical methods, competition for constituents and resources, and sometimes vindictive conflict among movement personalities. This personal and organizational factionalism often impedes the common agenda of community mobilization and advancement of the interests of the Chinatown residential rank and file. Divisiveness and factionalism are certainly not uncommon in social and political movements in general, but in the relatively small social and physical space of New York's Chinatown, movement leaders and activists are more regularly brought into confrontation.

Movement factionalism is counterbalanced by periodic bursts of unifying collective action conducted in public arenas. To some extent, community solidarity in political action is achieved through identification of an oppositional enemy, which has been defined by Chinatown activists in various campaigns as oppressive bosses, invasive overseas Chinese investors, obdurate and racist police, and an intrusive redevelopmental state (in its local and federal government forms). Depending on the nature of the campaign and the associated issues or relevant interests, varying degrees of community unity have been achieved through public collective action. In some campaigns, community activists have even been able to rally the leadership of traditional associations to their cause.

The Traditional Political Order

Until the 1960s community power in New York's Chinatown was held by a merchant elite, the leaders of a number of mutual aid associations whose membership was based on surname or region of origin. The surname associations at their largest embraced whole clans from many different districts, and at their smallest linked extended families from just one village. The even larger district associations, called *hui-guan*, were grouped by territory of origin or spoken dialect.[2] These groupings in the United States were analogous to those that existed in mainland China. Immigrants who were outside of the central clans formed their own associations, or *tongs*, which means "chambers" (Kwong 1987: 97). Their antecedents were autonomous local associations and patriotic secret societies (Triads) that flourished in the interdynastic periods of provincial warfare in China. Fraternal organizations linked by belief rather than kinship or geography, their membership was generally suspicious of the prevailing social order.

Chinese immigrants during the exclusion era looked to the traditional associations to secure passage, find employment and housing in the United States, and arrange their legal affairs, since diplomatic outfall after the Opium War led to there being no Chinese consulate in the United States. Rivalry and feuding between the largest hui-guan led to their confederation in the late 1850s into the "Six Companies" in San Francisco (Lyman 1986: 126). The Six Companies officially registered with the Chinese government as *Chung Hua Kung So* (which translates as "the Chinese Public Assembly Hall"), which is known more commonly as the Chinese Consolidated Benevolent Association (CCBA).

Chinatown residents found jobs and housing, gained financial credit, settled disputes, had the social welfare needs of their children and aged cared for, resolved issues with home villages, and resolved issues of American immigration status through the patronage and mediation of their traditional associations and the CCBA. These benevolent manifest functions were accompanied by more malevolent latent ones; the political and economic power of the traditional associations rested on their ability to extract an economic surplus from their constituency via membership dues, business transactional fees, juridical fees, and a community "property tax" system (*po tai*) somewhat like co-ethnic "key money" payments.

Chinese Americans traditionally referred to their CCBA leaders as *kiu ling*, which translates literally as "leader of the overseas Chinese" (Wong 1988: 320). Their relative power reflected the numerical strength of the membership that they represented and their relative status and position in the community's organizational hierarchy. As the "patrons" or "guardians" of the community, the kiu ling were traditionally sought for their perceived access to economic resources and political power. The Chinese kiu ling were similar to the *prominenti*, who were the bankers, merchants, and lawyers of the Italian American community.[3] Because of immigrant exclusion, however, the Chinese immigrant elite was less connected to the host society, remaining internally oriented or concerned with politics in China.

The New York CCBA was first organized and registered with the Beijing Imperial Government in 1881. In 1890, it was legally incorporated in the United States under the Societies Act of New York State. The CCBA was commonly recognized by American observers as the de facto "government" of Chinatown, and the leader of the CCBA was known as the "mayor." Chialing Kuo (1977: 36–37) asserts that the criminal tongs were inserted into the leadership of the CCBA for reasons of protection during the decades of anti-Chinese agitation in the 1870s and 1880s. Stanford Lyman (1974) has a less benign interpretation; he points out that the tongs waged a war to discredit the CCBA at the turn of the century over its failure to overturn the exclusion laws, and eventually gained admission of the tong leadership to the CCBA.

Peter Kwong (1979) has reported that the power of the CCBA began waning as early as the 1930s before recovering somewhat during the 1950s and then diminishing again in the post-exclusion era. According to Kwong, the efforts of the Chinese Hand Laundry Alliance (CHLA) to successfully organize for the rights of Chinese laundry workers in the New York City area in the 1930s effectively broke the control the CCBA had over the industry (the CCBA had previously collected membership dues and transaction "taxes" from all Chinese laundry workers). Along with the smaller Chinese Restaurant Workers Federation, the CHLA then began to link up with militant U.S. labor organizations as well as with more mainstream elements in the U.S. labor movement.

The CCBA had endorsed the Guomindang, or Nationalist Party of China, since 1927, when the Guomindang became the ruling party in China. Through an Overseas Affairs Bureau, the Guomindang actively sought both the political and economic support of the overseas Chinese in maintaining its rule against communist opposition and Japanese invasion on the Chinese mainland (Kwong 1987: 101). In the Cold War climate of the McCarthyite 1950s, the CCBA reasserted its hegemony in the Chinatown polity by strengthening its affiliation with the anticommunist Guomindang (KMT) regime, now exiled to the Republic of China on Taiwan following the Chinese Communist revolution of 1949. The CCBA thus received financial backing from the Taiwanese KMT while legitimizing its dominance in Chinatown with the American government. Renqui Yu (1992) recounts the collusion between the CCBA and KMT agents in New York's Chinatown to red-bait CHLA leaders during FBI investigations in the 1950s. Yu indicates, however, that the historical legacy of the CHLA was primarily more populist-democratic in orientation. As a struggling proletariat who were also small-business owners, the laundry workers of the CHLA promoted a patriotic "people's diplomacy" in the 1940s in New York City to raise relief funds for the Chinese defense effort at home.[4]

The New York City CCBA of the contemporary era includes sixty associations in its total membership. The CCBA president is chosen on a rotating basis every two years from one of the two most influential regional associations, the Ning Yang association and the Ling Sing association. The Ning Yang group includes the largest Toishanese district association; the Ling Sing represents a group of smaller non-Toishanese associations. There is an executive committee of nineteen senators, which includes seven permanent members (representing the most powerful organizations) and twelve nonpermanent members. The seven permanent members are drawn from the two district groups, two merchant associations (the Hip Song tong and the On Leong tong), the New York Chinese Chamber of Commerce, and two political parties (the New York division of the Taiwanese Guomindang, and the Min Chi Tang—the anti-Guomindang Chinese Freemasons Democratic Party). The twelve nonpermanent members are elected by the Community Council, which has eighty-four members, one from each of the sixty member associations, and eight more delegates from the Ning Yang, the Ling Sing, and the Chamber of Commerce (Kuo 1977; Wong 1982).

The traditional hegemony of Guomindang loyalty within the CCBA has eroded since the 1970s with the onset of two related trends. One is the growth of diplomatic relations between the United States and the People's Republic of China following President Richard Nixon's visit to Beijing in 1973, and official U.S. recognition of the People's Republic of China by the Carter administration in 1978 (with an accompanying de-recognition of the Republic of China on Taiwan). The other trend is the revival of emigration from the People's Republic of China (particularly from Fujian province) with the onset of open-door modernization policies in the late 1970s. Many of the newest family and regional associations opening in New York's Chinatown are Fujianese associations. A pro-Beijing position is common among these new associations. The normalization of relations between the United States and the People's Republic of China also led to the breaking away of Fujianese associations, such as the Fukien District Association, formerly aligned with the Guomindang camp.[5] In this vociferous atmosphere of ideological conflict, the remaining Guomindang loyalists set up a new group under the name of the Free Fukien District Association (Chow 1984: 73). A pro-Beijing position among some clan and family associations, however, may sometimes relate more to trade ties with the mainland than communist loyalty. People's Republic of China functionaries, in fact, periodically hold events in Chinatown to encourage Chinese American business investment in mainland China.

As a display of their growing strength, the pro-mainland faction decided to hold their first-ever parade in New York's Chinatown to celebrate the founding of the People's Republic of China. The parade was seen by Guomindang loyalists as a symbolic affront, a rival procession to their own National Day parade for the Republic of China on Taiwan, traditionally held on October 10, or "Double 10," the birth date of Sun Yat-Sen, who led the overthrow of the Qing dynasty and is the father of Chinese nationalism. The pro-Beijing faction, meanwhile, was angered when Fifth Precinct police denied them a parade route down Mott Street through the heart of old Chinatown (which is the route taken by the Nationalist parade). The police suggested an outer route along East Broadway, ostensibly because the date of the proposed Mainland National Day parade, September 25, overlapped with the last day of the San Gennaro Festival in Little Italy, which traditionally created massive traffic jams in the old Chinatown area (Lii 1994a). The outer route along East Broadway was somewhat appropriate since the artery and adjacent blocks are the focus of business and social life for the pro-mainland faction, and many Fujianese traditional association offices, restaurants, grocery stores, and discount retail shops are located there. In any event, the police seemed somewhat more deferential toward the more established Guomindang faction, since they sent official representatives to march only in that procession. The Nationalist parade drew twice the number of marchers (10,000 vs. 5,000) and spectators (15,000 vs. 8,000) as the Mainland parade. There were a handful of pro-democracy demonstrators at the Mainland procession.

There is also political sectarianism among the Chinatown media, although their publishers purport to be neutral. Of the four major Chinese-language daily newspapers, two are perceived to be pro-Taiwan (the *World Journal* and the *United Journal*), one to be pro-mainland (the *China News*, formerly the *China Press*), and one to be politically neutral (the *Sing Tao Daily*). The owners of the *World Journal* also operate a Taiwan-oriented television station, World TV, while the owners of the mainland-oriented *China News* operate a rival television station, Sinovision.

The Emergence of Contemporary Organizations

The growth of the contemporary organizations in New York's Chinatown began with the Asian American movement, which was spearheaded by militant youth and college students, who took on the tactics and political rhetoric of the American antiwar movement, the revolutionary activism of Students for a Democratic Society, and the Black Power movement, and the Maoism of the Chinese Cultural Revolution. Though based primarily on the West Coast, the Asian American movement also has had a significant presence on the East Coast. A radical youth group called the Red Guards in San Francisco was matched by the emergence of a New York City–based group called I Wor Kuen (which means "righteous and harmonious fist" and was the name of a turn-of-the-century anti-imperialist Boxer Rebellion group), led by college students from elite schools on the East Coast. Established in 1969 out of a Chinatown storefront, I Wor Kuen published its own journal, *Getting Together*. The organization sponsored demonstrations against the Vietnam War and the military draft. It also held protests in front of CCBA offices, street demonstrations against Chinatown tourism, and solidarity marches with "third-world peoples." Chinatown was seen as an "internal colony" subject to the oppression of the American state. The established Chinatown social order (signified by the CCBA and the tongs) was seen as feudal, outmoded, and corrupt.

Another militant student group, called the Basement Workshop, composed primarily of working-class students from the City College of New York, was established in 1971.[6] In March 1972, members took part in a thirteen-day takeover of a City College of New York administration building along with a thousand other Asian American students in coalition with black and Latino supporters. They demanded special education for the street youth of Chinatown and creation of relevant programs in research and community services for Asian communities. An Asian studies program was eventually established at the university in response to their demands. Chinatown youth drew some inspiration during this time from Professor C. T. Wu of Hunter College, who wrote the popularly received book *Chinks!* He lectured widely on the significance of the Asian American movement and advocated development of an indigenous leadership by urging students to move to Chinatown and establish the community as a territorial power base (Kuo 1977: 63).

Another organization, the Health Revolutionary Unity Movement, led street protests advocating better health programs for Chinatown residents, who had among the highest rates of tuberculosis in the city. Nearby Gouverneur Hospital had only twenty-five Chinese staff members out of eight hundred. It was alleged that language and culture barriers prevented many Chinatown residents from getting adequate diagnosis and care. A Chinatown Health Fair was held in 1971 in collaboration with the Basement Workshop, where literature was distributed at booths set up for physical examinations, and tests for lead poisoning, diabetes, and tuberculosis were offered during a ten-day "street clinic" (Mark and Chin 1982: 133). City officials eventually responded by installing a Chinatown Health Clinic in the community. Donations eventually totaled $4,000. Chinese medical students and staff joined with Lower East Side health-care activists to pressure for the preservation of Gouverneur Hospital after municipal hospital officials advocated its closing. The New York City Health and Hospital Corporation, however, was constrained by a serious municipal fiscal crisis. In protest, Lower East Side associations staged a mass demonstration on May 7, 1976, and occupied the executive offices of Gouverneur Hospital. Movement leaders were eventually brought onto the board of the hospital (Kuo 1977: 99).

Other militant groups active at this time were the Food Co-op and Workers' Viewpoint. Members of Workers' Viewpoint eventually formed the nucleus of the Asian Americans for Equality, while members of I Wor Kuen eventually founded the Progressive Chinatown People's Association (Kwong 1987: 161–64). Revolutionaries and militants were not the only new social forces in post-exclusion Chinatown. Students and professionals who advocated a more gradualist, reform-oriented approach to social change were also organizing within the community. Some of these activists had previously been involved in radical student action but had toned down their political rhetoric as they settled into working life. Others were more reformist from the beginning. Like the activist militants, reform-oriented professionals felt that the low-income community of Chinatown was plagued by social problems, including poverty, poor housing, and high rates of disease and mental health problems, that had not been sufficiently addressed by the traditional leadership of the CCBA.

One of the first reformist contemporary organizations to be created was the Chinatown Planning Council (CPC). The CPC was founded in the summer of 1964 with a donation of $85, which were the proceeds from the sale of a used car (Wan 1978: 242; Glynn and Wang 1978). In 1965, the CPC started a Head Start education and after-school youth program, both funded by the federal government. Its first federal grant was obtained through a lawsuit against the U.S. Community Development Administration. Many of the first staff members were volunteers, largely reform-minded doctors, nurses, and teachers who had arrived in the postwar era and were raising a second generation. Federal government antipoverty and community development monies continued to be funneled into Chinatown through the CPC. By 1975, the CPC was Chinatown's largest multiservice agency, with an annual budget of $2 million and two hundred staff members working in a variety of areas including employment, housing, youth, the aged, cultural activities, vocational training, and day care. In 1995, as it entered its fourth decade of work in the community, its budget reached nearly $25 million a year, funding forty-five service centers and program offices in twenty-six facilities in Manhattan, Queens, and Brooklyn. Having moved beyond Manhattan's Chinatown to satellite Chinatowns to follow the dispersing population, the organization changed its name to the Chinese-American Planning Council.[7] The largest, most institutionalized contemporary community organization in New York's Chinatown, delivering daily services to the greatest number of individuals, the CPC is also the largest Chinese American community organization in the country. In this position, the CPC has drawn fire and even legal action from more radical community groups who feel it has become a parastatal organization.

Asian Americans for Equality (AAFE) was founded in more militant circumstances during protests surrounding Asian American employment at the Confucius Plaza construction site in 1974. Many AAFE activists were formerly student militants involved in I Wor Kuen or in protests at City College of New York. After its involvement in the Special Manhattan Bridge District community disputes of 1981, AAFE began moving more systematically into the area of tenant organizing and housing preservation. Private and public funding was secured to convert the volunteer organization to a fully staffed professional organization. AAFE leaders and members have sought election to community planning boards, school boards, and public offices. A former AAFE board president, Margaret Chin, made two runs for the New York City Council in the early 1990s. In 1988, AAFE moved into the area of housing development, when ground was broken for construction of Equality House, a fifty-nine-unit, low-income housing cooperative for homeless families and seniors. AAFE also worked with tenant groups to acquire city resources for rehabilitation of fire-damaged buildings. As of 1995, AAFE had three thousand dues-paying members and managed thirteen rehabilitated buildings. It also assists Asian Americans in the legal and financial intricacies of home buying, and lobbies with local officials and policymakers in support of housing programs, about municipal budgetary matters that affect Chinatown neighborhood preservation, and about the community reinvestment policies of banks that do business in Chinatown. Like the CPC, the contemporary AAFE has thus become more institutionalized over the years. Its tradition of activism has somewhat persevered, however; during community meetings surrounding the Special Manhattan Bridge District rezoning in the early 1980s (described in chapter 6), AAFE members led a vociferous protest decrying negotiations with government officials. Other Chinatown community organizations were in turn opposed to AAFE during its efforts to lead the neighborhood in electoral boundary redistricting in the early 1990s.

Another Chinatown contemporary organization is It's Time, founded in 1966 and incorporated in 1970. It began as a multiservice organization working primarily with the low-income white ethnic residents that were the main population in its service area, which includes parts of both the traditional Lower East Side and present-day greater Chinatown. In the twenty years following its founding, its clientele grew increasingly multiethnic, as Latinos and Asians began moving into the area. Asian Americans now constitute the bulk of its clients. The staff has become increasingly Asian American in fitting with these changes. Housing advocacy and tenant assistance are its main activities. It's Time has operated a walk-in housing clinic and housing workshops since 1970. Its staff has helped tenants in deteriorating buildings gain public funds to rehabilitate and convert them to tenant-managed, limited-equity cooperatives. In the late 1970s, the organization led a ten-year law suit to integrate the nearby federally subsidized East River Cooperatives. In 1988, a consent decree was obtained under which 50 percent of vacancies will go to minority group members. It's Time also operates senior and youth programs. Like AAFE, It's Time began moving into the area of housing provision in the early 1990s with the rehabilitation of a six-story Clinton-Henry Housing tenement building as a low-income cooperative for homeless families. As of 1995, however, It's Time was suffering a severe crisis because of diminishing funding sources and was considering a merger with another Lower East Side community organization.

The Progressive Chinese People's Association, which came out of the same radical student origins as AAFE, remained a voluntary organization for a longer period. The group was reorganized in 1977 as the Chinatown Progressive Association (CPA) and has offered a range of services to the community, including English and citizenship classes, a tenants' rights clinic, services for senior citizens, and recreational and cultural activities. The CPA was closely involved with activism surrounding the siting of a city jail on White Street (described in chapter 6) under the Koch administration. Working closely with then Manhattan Borough President David Dinkins, CPA members were eventually brought into his administration when he became New York's mayor. The CPA has recently moved into voter education and registration and has acquired a funding base in the past few years.

The Asian American Legal Defense and Education Fund (AALDEF) provided legal support for Chinatown community organizations in many campaigns for worker and housing rights, focusing primarily on class action suits. Another agency offering legal support is Mobilization for Youth (MFY), which has offices throughout the Lower East Side. MFY concentrates more on individual cases, particularly in the area of housing. Its client base is multiracial, rather than being exclusively Chinese.

Two major workplace organizations active in Chinatown are the International Ladies' Garment Workers' Union (ILGWU, now merged with the ACTWU to form UNITE!) and the Chinese Staff and Workers' Association (CSWA). (Both organizations are described in chapter 2.) As a single-industry union, the ILGWU has had a historical reputation for espousing a brand of social unionism that not only provides for the working rights and health benefits of its members but also provides English classes, voter education, cultural events, and day trips.

The CSWA similarly was initially organized as a social club for workers that provided a space for members to engage in recreation, education, and organizational meetings. Rather than being a single-industry union like the ILGWU-UNITE!, the CSWA has worked for the rights of Chinese restaurant workers and construction workers as well as garment industry workers. While lobbying for the rights of construction workers paid low wages through the Intercity Remodeling and Apartment Repair program, CSWA came into conflict with the CPC, the sponsoring agency in the city-financed program, when it fired all the workers when they tried to form a union local.

I have described only a few of the dozens of contemporary community and workplace organizations that function in New York's Chinatown. However, these organizations have been the most influential in providing services, advocating for rights of workers and residents, and organizing collective action in the community. Among the other organizations that should be mentioned are the Chinatown Manpower Association, which provides job training and education, the Manhattan Neighborhood Renaissance Local Development Corporation (discussed in chapter 6), and the Museum of Chinese in the Americas (discussed in chapter 7).

Factionalism and Solidarity

Conflict between the traditional associations and contemporary organizations has been endemic from the time the newer organizations began to emerge with the student protests of the 1960s, which viewed the Chinese Consolidated Benevolent Association as emblematic of the old feudal order in Chinatown. With the onset of more institutionalized reformist contemporary organizations, this conflict began to reflect an underlying struggle for leadership and resources in the community. An illustrative instance of conflict between traditional and contemporary associations occurred in July 1976, when there was a dispute between the CCBA and the Chinatown Planning Council, which was aligned with other outside community agencies, over the disposition of Public School 23. The relocation of the school from its Mulberry Street location opened up the possibility for replacement with a senior citizens' center and other community facilities. There was common community sentiment that a senior center was desirable, but strong disagreement over which organization would be the lead agency. The CCBA leader denounced the effort of the CPC to work with other, non-Chinatown funding agencies: "Such a strategy is the practice of the 'broker

class' who uses foreign power to suppress their own people. . . . Public
School 23 is located at the center of Chinatown, we cannot tolerate it being
used by foreigners" (*China Post* article of July 19, 1976, quoted by Kuo 1977:
128). The CPC, meanwhile, had indeed assembled support from other contemporary associations as well as outside agencies to support the concept
of a "mini university" in Public School 23 along with other facilities. A CPC-
style plan was the eventual result; a senior center was indeed installed on
the first floor, but the second floor now houses the Museum of Chinese in
the Americas (formerly the Chinatown History Project) and a dance center,
while the third floor contains offices of the Chinatown Manpower Project.

Though generally having a conservative orientation, the leadership of
the CCBA has on occasion included some moderate reformists. M. B. Lee,
president of the CCBA during the mid-1970s, was considered a reformist
"liberal," who led the CCBA during periods of intense community unrest
during protests at the Confucius Plaza construction site in 1974 and police
brutality demonstrations in 1975.[8] This public liberalism may have been
linked with an attempt on his life in 1977, when he fought off a knife-
wielding attacker in his own restaurant. The perpetrator was never brought
to justice; Lee suspected parties seeking control of his family association,
but some Chinatown watchers suspected rightist CCBA elements associated with the criminal tongs.

Factionalism has also been endemic among the contemporary organizations. An early instance of factional conflict because of competition for
resources among the modern associations occurred in 1970 when the CPC
and the Chinatown Foundation applied to the same federal and state agencies for funding. The funding agencies were confused when the CPC lobbied through the district congressperson while the Chinatown Foundation
appealed through the borough president, who then contacted state officials. The conflict intensified when the Chinatown Foundation denounced
the CPC for not having a Chinese American executive director. In response,
the CPC wrote a letter in protest to the New York Commission on Human
Rights, demanding that the president of the Chinatown Foundation, who
was a deputy commissioner, be removed from his post because of charges
of conflicts of interest (Kuo 1977: 58–59). Both the Chinatown Foundation
and another organization, the Chinatown Youth Council, which competed
with the CPC for funding from the U.S. Office of Economic Opportunity,
eventually dissolved or merged with other Chinatown organizations.

The tension between factionalism and solidarity within the community power structure continued to be revealed in two formative political
disputes in the mid-1970s, disputes that led to the first major community-

wide demonstrations of the post-exclusion era in New York's Chinatown. One issue involved hiring policies during the construction of Chinatown's largest housing project, Confucius Plaza. The other concerned the issue of policing policy. In both cases, perception of a common enemy or external threat, the local state, led to some diminishing of community factionalism. Solidarity was engendered through common participation in community-wide collective action.

Confucius Plaza

Confucius Plaza is Chinatown's largest housing project, with 762 mostly moderate-income cooperative units, 10 percent of which are low-income. The $35-million project was mainly funded by the Mitchell-Lama program of New York State, with additional federal, municipal, and private-sector support. Located adjacent to the ramp of the Manhattan Bridge, the forty-four-story building is easily Chinatown's largest built structure. Following the ground breaking in March 1974, however, the construction site became the focus of community protest. Led by a newly created organization called Asian Americans for Equal Employment (AAFEE),[9] picketing demonstrators decried the lack of Chinese or Asian American construction workers. There were demands for an Asian American site supervisor and hiring of forty Asian American construction workers, in accordance with Mayor John Lindsay's Executive Order 71, which specified that 25 percent of workers in government projects should be minority. A continuous picket was held at the site, in other Chinatown locations, and at City Hall. Fifty-seven people were arrested in the first two weeks of protest, some of them community leaders. Chinatown media gave the events wide publicity (Wan 1978: 256). Widespread popular support included the elderly, notably the Chinatown Golden Age Club (Kuo 1977: 133). The CCBA supported AAFEE's position but not the tactics.

The token hiring of two Asian Americans led to the collapse of negotiations, followed by a demonstration on May 16, 1974, at the construction site led by AAFEE and supported by other contemporary Chinatown community organizations, some traditional associations, Chinatown labor organizations, and an assemblage of minority workers' groups such as Harlem Fight Back, Black Economic Survival, and the Black and Puerto Rican Coalition. Hundreds of police were deployed, many on horses. Government officials eventually met with AAFEE, the construction company, M. B. Lee, then president of CCBA, and city councilperson Miriam Friedlander. Other local officials, including the city council president, the vice chair of the National Committee of the Democratic Party, a labor advisor to Mayor Abe Beame, a deputy mayor, and an NAACP representative, were involved in mediation proceedings. Another demonstration was held before the New York City criminal court building, where several demonstrators were jailed. The community dispute was finally resolved with an agreement for the hiring of twelve Asian American journeymen and twenty-seven trainees (Kuo 1977: 103–4). A number of community facilities were also added to the site, including a cultural center, a health clinic, a day-care center, and a senior citizens' center. Shops and a bank are also located at street level.

The community disputes over hiring policies at Confucius Plaza marked the appearance of AAFEE (which later changed its name to Asian Americans for Equality [AAFE]) in the Chinatown enclave power structure. The political resistance that AAFE organized brought diverse segments of the Chinatown community out in solidarist collective action, but the traditional leadership (i.e., the CCBA) was the party that eventually negotiated a settlement with representatives of the local government.

Police Brutality and Anti-Asian Violence

An issue of high emotional impact, police violence against Asians provoked the Chinatown community to vociferous protest a year later. The demonstrations in the weeks following the beating and arrest of Peter Yew, a 27-year-old Chinese American architectural engineer, on April 26, 1975, were among the largest and most militant mobilizations ever to take place in New York's Chinatown. The precipitating incident involved two motorists, a Chinese whose car was double-parked on Bayard Street, and a white driver whose route was blocked; they exchanged angry words and deliberately bumped their cars into each other. The white driver then squeezed his automobile past the parked car, brushing a crowd of Chinese American onlookers. The angered crowd followed the driver, who seeking protection, drove around the corner to the Fifth Precinct police station on Elizabeth Street. According to Peter Yew, who was among the crowd gathered there, police arrested him without provocation while trying to disperse the crowd. He was dragged into the station house, stripped, and beaten. The police, in counter charges, accused Yew of assaulting a police officer and resisting arrest. Yew was eventually taken to Beekman Downtown Hospital and treated for contusions of the forehead and a sprain of the right wrist.

A tense environment of police-community relations had existed in Chinatown since the previous year with the appointment of a new commanding officer who had intensified patrolling under the intent of cracking down on gambling and gang terrorism. Spokesmen for Chinatown youth accused police of aggressive stop-and-frisk searches. In December 1974,

Figure 18. March against police brutality, 1975. Photo by Corky Lee. Copyright Corky Lee; used by permission of the photographer.

two Chinese bystanders were shot (one fatally) by plainclothes police during a scuffle with eight alleged gang members in the Jade Chalet restaurant on Worth Street. That incident sparked protest rallies and complaints by community leaders to the police. A grand jury investigation did not indict the officers, and charges against the suspected gang members, who were unarmed, were dropped. Critics of the police contended the scuffle was touched off by the officers making anti-Chinese remarks.

Charging arrogance and brutality on the part of the police, AAFEE, organized the previous year to protest employment policies at the Confucius Plaza housing project, called for a demonstration on May 12. The elders of CCBA initially endorsed the protest but then wavered in their support. The youthful organizers of AAFEE put on a highly successful demonstration (estimated at twenty-five hundred by police, and much higher by organizers) involving a cross section of Chinatown residents, young and old (Maitland 1975). Surprised by the turnout, the CCBA then launched another demonstration (partially to prove its "leadership" in the community, said some observers) on May 19. This time the merchant elite coordinated the closure of nearly all businesses in Chinatown and drew an even larger crowd (estimated at ten thousand by police, and twenty thousand by organizers). Marching six and eight abreast (Figure 18), the demonstrators completely ringed the five-block triangular City Hall Park. After breaking up the rally as leaders emerged from a meeting with city officials, one thousand younger demonstrators staged a sit-down in the middle of Broadway, and stopped traffic for the remainder of the afternoon (Raab 1975).

Protesters called for the rescinding of charges and payment of damages against Yew, suspension of the police officers who allegedly hit him, and a public apology from the Fifth Precinct police captain. There were further demands for improvement of municipal services for Chinatown in housing, health, and education programs. Fifth Precinct Captain Edward W. McCabe was transferred to a different precinct on May 24. Reassignment of a commanding officer under community pressure was unprecedented in New York City police affairs. In a tense atmosphere within the community, further incidents took place in July, when a crowd of one hundred gathered outside the precinct station to protest a police search of four Chinese Americans stopped in their car on a false weapons charge. A dozen demonstrators were clubbed by police when they blocked passage of a patrol car, though none were arrested. The next day, a grand jury dropped the charges against Yew and indicted the two officers who beat him on charges of official misconduct (Carmody 1975).

Community demonstrations against police brutality in the mid-1970s were among the largest demonstrations ever held in New York's Chinatown. The police are the disciplinary arm of the state, and the people of Chinatown are willing to lay down their differences when confronted by the threat of police violence. The issue of anti-Asian police violence has recurred occasionally since the 1970s, and this issue seems to produce the greatest unity among the diverse Chinatown community power interests.

A Final Note on Factionalism

The broader environment of community conflict between traditional and contemporary associations is balanced somewhat by an emerging environment of cooperation. Some of the more liberal family associations, such as the Lee Family Association, have begun to contribute to the fundraising efforts of contemporary associations. This charitableness is driven by a perception that the contemporary associations can broker resources and services that the family associations have traditionally not been able to deliver. Family association leaders are subsequently drawn into the decision-making leadership of the contemporary associations; the Lee Family Association president, M. B. Lee, for example, is on the board of directors of the Chinatown Manpower Association. Similarly, Richard Chan, executive director of the Silver Palace restaurant and a CCBA leader, has also made ties with the contemporary associations.

Electoral Behavior and Party Politics

In contrast to their ardent involvement in workplace politics and community mobilization, the involvement of Chinatown residents in electoral politics has been slower to develop. According to Chinese Americans involved in voter education and registration, there is a pervasive ignorance of voting procedures and democratic processes, and disbelief that there is any real possibility of reward from political participation. Language is certainly one barrier, and Chinatown political activists have successfully lobbied for the publication of balloting materials in Chinese to help expand the scope of Chinese American participation.

Like that of other immigrant communities, Chinatown's electoral influence is limited because of a large proportion of noncitizens in its populace. As Table 12 details, only 63 percent of the voting-age Asian population of 44,069 in Manhattan Assembly District 62 (which encompasses most of greater Chinatown) were eligible to vote in 1994. This was the lowest eligibility rate among the major racial/ethnic groups. Furthermore, only 38 percent of Asians eligible were registered in 1994, again the lowest percentage among the major minority groups. Finally, voter turnout of Asian voters registered in 1994 was only 40 percent, the lowest rate among the major racial/ethnic groups except the "other" category. As a combined result of these low rates of voter eligibility, registration, and participation, Asian voter turnout in 1994 was only 17 percent of the total turnout, although Asians comprised 41 percent of the total voting-age population in Assembly District 62. The low voter eligibility rate of the Chinatown population will improve over time as immigrants become citizens. Real levels of electoral registration and participation, however, can only improve through active education and registration work in the community.

Voter education and registration efforts in Chinatown are primarily conducted by three organizations, the Chinese Progressive Association (CPA) and the Chinatown Voter Education Alliance (both nonpartisan), and the ILGWU (which openly favors the Democratic Party). The CPA is primarily voluntary but has acquired some government and local funding since 1991, and connects voter registration with citizenship education. The CPA has also been involved with education of senior citizens about electoral issues regarding government social policies that affect them. The ILGWU educates and registers voters through its considerable membership of some twenty-five thousand garment worker women. The Chinatown Voter Education Alliance (CVEA), a large umbrella coalition of twenty-eight community agencies, and cultural, religious, and business organizations, is wholly voluntary. Through this considerable network, the CVEA has registered several hundred voters per year since 1983, commonly at periodic sidewalk tables.[10] The CVEA has worked with the New York City Board of Elections to produce bilingual poll workers, translated and distributed position papers of political candidates to the Chinatown media, promoted electoral participation on the radio, educated children and parents about the electoral process in school and community settings, and sponsored periodic community forums on issues of importance to Chinatown (bringing together community panelists as well as government officials).

Table 12

Voter eligibility and participation in lower Manhattan by race/ethnicity, 1994

Race/ Ethnic group	Voting-age population	Percentage eligible[a]	Percentage registered[b]	Percentage turnout[c]	Percentage of total turnout[d]
Asian	44,069	63	38	40	17
Black	6,918	78	88	53	10
Latino	20,799	75	64	47	18
Non-Hispanic White	33,592	82	85	57	54
Other	1,111	72	95	14	1
Total	106,489	72	64	52	100

[a] Eligible subgroup voter population as proportion of subgroup voting-age population.
[b] Registered subgroup voters as proportion of eligible subgroup voter population.
[c] Turnout of subgroup voters as proportion of registered subgroup voters.
[d] Turnout of subgroup voters as proportion of total voter turnout.
Source: New York City Voter Assistance Commission 1994; Appendix K.

Voter turnout in Chinatown can vary from year to year depending on the type of election and whether a Chinese American is running. Chinese Americans have been candidates in elections for city council, municipal court positions, and the school board (these races are discussed later). Jewish American Democrat Sheldon Silver is the longtime state assembly district representative. After many years of incumbency, he retains immense popularity and as speaker of the New York State House, is now the highest ranking Democrat in the state of New York.[11] Chinatown falls into the U.S. congressional district that has been held for two terms by Democrat Nydia Valezquez, the first Puerto Rican American woman in the U.S. House of Representatives.

Chinatown voters primarily register as Independents. Of the 979 voters registered by the Chinatown Voter Education Alliance in 1994, slightly more than 52 percent registered as Independents, 27.5 percent as Democrats, and a little more than 18 percent as Republicans. The remaining 2 percent registered with lesser parties, such as the Liberal Party, the Conservative Party, and the Right-To-Life Party. The popularity of identifying as an Independent stems from tendencies toward political neutrality, from unfamiliarity with the American political system, and from a strong sentiment among Chinese Americans that party affiliation requires an unusually heavy burden. One price of identifying as an Independent, however, is less influence in the overall political process, because participation in electoral primaries and choice of a broader field of candidates requires registration with an established political party. In municipalities where a single political party dominates, such as the Democratic Party in New York City, elections are often decided at the primary level.

Veterans of voter registration efforts have observed that party affiliation is colored for many immigrant Chinese by their memories of the Communist Party in the People's Republic of China or the Guomindang Party in Taiwan. Party politics generally has a negative connotation linked with authoritarian single-party government in the home country and is associated with heavy responsibility, frequent meeting attendance, and ideological doctrine. Furthermore, the Chinese character for "party" (*dong*) means "clique" or "small group."[12] Many Chinese immigrants consequently do not see the merits of party affiliation in the American political process.

Those Chinese Americans who register as Democrats are attracted to this party's support of the working person, its civil rights orientation, and perceived support of educational and social service funding. Democratic Party affiliation is thus high among Chinatown youth and senior citizens. Those who register with the Republican Party are attracted to its business orientation, anticommunist platform, law-and-order anticrime outlook, and family values perspective.

When it comes to political contributions, Chinatown interests have at times been known to contribute to both political parties, even in the same election. Henry Yang, former head of the Chinese Businessmen's Association, has observed that this tactic is not at all contradictory but is seen as a balanced approach that strategically serves Chinese American interests no matter what the election result.

Political Candidates and Electoral Redistricting

A succession of aspiring political leaders has emerged since the 1970s, notably women. These women have typically emerged from the network of modern organizations that serve Chinatown's educational and community needs. The retarded pace of voter participation among the Chinatown electorate, however, has somewhat impeded the emergence of a popularly elected Chinese American official. Political factionalism among the electorate has also been an obstacle, as a number of competing political clubs and organizations have appeared. Another major barrier has been political district boundaries, which have historically divided Chinatown into separate voting areas. Internal factionalism also plagued Chinatown politics during the course of electoral redistricting proceedings accompanying reforms of New York City's charter in the early 1990s.

Chinese American involvement in local electoral politics began in the early 1970s with the formation of the United Democratic Organization (UDO) by Virginia Kee, a teacher in the Chinatown public schools who was also influential in the formation of the Chinese American Planning Council. The Kee family is well established in Chinatown and has considerable real estate interests. As a member of the local community board (Community Board 3), Kee voted in favor of a Chinatown rezoning plan aimed at stimulating redevelopment and overseas Chinese investment in the early 1980s (see discussion of the Special Manhattan Bridge District in chapter 6). This rezoning was opposed by community interests who favored the retention of affordable housing for the low-income populace. These proceedings hurt Kee when she ran in the Democratic primaries for the New York City Council election in 1985. Chinatown activists instead endorsed Miriam Friedlander, a Jewish American advocate of the adjoining Lower East Side neighborhood, who was seen as friendlier to labor and housing issues affecting the Chinatown community.

Margaret Chin emerged as a Chinatown political contender in the mid-1980s. An immigrant from Hong Kong in 1963 at the age of nine, Chin had a typical upbringing in New York's Chinatown; her father worked in restaurants, and her mother was a garment worker. She became politically conscious while a student at City College of New York in the 1970s, participating in activism surrounding the establishment of Asian American studies there, and volunteering in student-run summer day-care programs operated in Chinatown. She became associated with Asian Americans for

Equality (AAFE) during the Confucius Plaza demonstrations of 1974, and was also involved as an AAFE volunteer during the community campaign against the Special Manhattan Bridge District and the White Street jail in the early 1980s (she eventually served as president of the AAFE board). Her political career began in 1986, when she ran successfully for the Democratic Party State Committee seat in District 61, a position previously held by the departing Virginia Kee.

In 1989, charter reforms were approved, abolishing the Board of Estimate and reducing the power of the borough presidents while strengthening the power of neighborhood interests by expanding the city council from thirty-five to fifty-one seats. Following the enumeration of demographic changes in New York City with the U.S. Census of Population and Housing in 1990, a districting commission was convened in 1991 to draw new city council boundaries to the satisfaction of constituent communities, whose input would be facilitated through the conduct of public hearings in the five boroughs of New York City. The commission's charge was to draw up a plan that would balance the complex needs of honoring (1) the Constitutional standard that population districts be equal in number, (2) the federal Voting Rights Act requirements of fair and effective representation for racial and language minority groups, and (3) the new criteria of the city charter. Similar proceedings were conducted with the redistricting of municipal, state, and federal legislative boundaries across the country.

Charter reform had mandated the creation of new city council districts of about 144,000 in population, or 70,000 fewer than previous districts (note also that city council districts are larger than the state assembly district, as shown in Table 12). Thus, charter reform presented Chinatown interests with a historic opportunity to fashion a district capable of electing a Chinese American. Given that there were just some 43,000 Asian Americans counted by the 1990 census in the eight core census tracts of Chinatown, and some 53,000 in greater Chinatown, it was clear that a Chinatown district would have to include a 60 percent plurality of white, Latino, and black voters in some combination.

AAFE, led by its executive director, Doris Koo, quickly plunged into research and organizational work in drawing up a plan that was broadly similar to the existing state assembly district for which Chin was already Democratic State Committeeperson. AAFE saw this configuration as a successful formula that linked Chinatown with the more-affluent white liberal neighborhoods of lower Manhattan to the south and west, including Battery Park City, TriBeCa, Soho, and portions of Greenwich Village. The proposed district of 137,195 people was 39.3 percent white, 5.4 percent black,

16.6 percent Latino, and 38.4 percent Asian. Longtime AAFE volunteer Chin, who resided on Hanover Street in the Wall Street financial district area, announced her intention to run as a candidate in the proposed district.

The AAFE plan was opposed by a group called Lower East Siders for a Multiracial District, which envisioned a low-income immigrant coalition district that linked Chinatown to the northeast with the Latino and Jewish Lower East Side. The demographic profile of this proposed district was 36 percent Asian, 34 percent Latino, 21 percent white, and 9 percent black. Elaine Chan, a veteran of tenant organizing in Chinatown and the Lower East Side with organizations such as the Joint Planning Council, the Good Old Lower East Side, and It's Time, declared her candidacy in the proposed district. The multiracial district was endorsed by progressive Puerto Rican rights organizations and the Community Service Society of New York, a metropolitan-wide nonprofit research and advocacy organization for the poor.

To further complicate the lower Manhattan redistricting debate, a Latino organization called the Puerto Rican–Hispanic Political Council opposed the multiracial district. Fronted by announced candidate Antonio Pagan, former director of Coalition Housing, Inc. (which builds low-to-moderate income housing), this group favored linking the Latino Lower East Side with white districts to the north. By Pagan's logic, an Asian-Latino district would have pitted the two communities against each other rather than empowering them. He supported the AAFE district in concept, although his group quibbled over some blocks that overlapped with his Latino district. Finally, representatives of the Gay and Lesbian Independent Democrats in Greenwich Village disagreed with the extent to which the AAFE plan extended into the southern reach of their proposed district, which they contended was "one of the gayest neighborhoods in New York" (Lee 1991).

Ultimately, the districting commission followed the basic outlines of the AAFE plan, which linked Chinatown with more-white neighborhoods to its south and west as the new City Council District 1. As an apparent nod to gay interests, the commission detached the southwestern Greenwich Village area from the AAFE district, replacing these census tracts with population areas on the Lower East Side.

In the Democratic primary that followed, Kathryn Freed, a resident of TriBeCa who had run unsuccessfully for the state assembly in 1990, entered the City Council District 1 race against Chin. A tenant attorney and community activist and former chairperson of Community Board 1, Freed was just as familiar to Battery Park City, TriBeCa, and Soho voters as Chin, and had the support of the Downtown Independent Democrats political club. Freed had support from the Village Reform Democrats Club, while Chin had support from the Village Independent Democrats. Elaine Chan of the multiracial district coalition ran briefly but withdrew, and her supporters were split between Chin and Freed. In a four-person Democratic primary race, Freed eventually won with 42 percent of the vote, while Chin came in second with 31 percent.

Persevering, Chin eventually ran on the Liberal Party ticket in the general election. She was able to raise $100,000, qualifying her for another $40,000 in electoral matching funds, the highest amount of any District 1 candidate. She became the victim of divisive politics, however, with the emergence of a Liberal Party opponent, Mei Ying Chan, who publicly red-baited Chin in reference to her earlier days as a militant community activist. Chan was eventually ejected from the Liberal Party following hearings that contested the authenticity of some of her electoral petitions. Her challenge opened the election somewhat, however, and a Chinese American Republican candidate entered the race with strong funding from Chinatown business people. Republican Fred Teng (a former president of the board of the Chinatown Planning Council) had only recently established residence in Chinatown but nevertheless gathered a respectable vote, running third in the 1991 general election behind Freed and Chin. In 1993, Chin unsuccessfully challenged Freed again in the Democratic primaries (Figure 19). This time Teng and the Chinese Republican organization were inactive.

There has been less community divisiveness on the issue of bilingual ballots. Pronounced political and legal lobbying by Chin, as well as the Asian American Legal Defense and Education Fund (AALDEF), pressured the New York City Board of Elections into agreeing to provide Chinese translations for local election ballots beginning in September 1994. The local election board was essentially impelled to comply with federal amendments to section 203 of the Voting Rights Language Assistance Act of 1992, which require localities to provide bilingual ballots in counties with a language minority group population of over ten thousand in any single county. The law, which applies to Latinos, Asian Americans, American Indians, and Alaskan Natives, requires ballots, voter registration forms, and election notices to be published in the appropriate languages of the minority group. Before the amendments to section 203, bilingual ballots were required only if a group with limited English ability made up 5 percent of a county's voting-age population. In dense population centers such as New York City, some language minority population groups, such as Chinese

Figure 19. Election poster for Margaret Chin. Photo credit: Campaign to Elect Margaret Chin; used by permission of Margaret Chin.

Americans (who comprise only about 3 percent of the city's total population), did not qualify for bilingual ballots under the old law.

Community unity helped to carry the bilingual balloting effort, but the volatile and partisan politics of the 1991 redistricting proceedings augurs continued factionalism in Chinatown electoral politics. The kind of collective solidarity that broke down factional divisions in the community during the course of demonstrations against police brutality and municipal redevelopment and hiring policies has not occurred in the electoral arena. Only the voter education and registration efforts of the nonpartisan CVEA received general approval from the diverse interests and rival political clubs that I interviewed. As it currently stands, the workers and residents of Chinatown obtain a greater sense of political effectiveness from collective action than any promise of political reward from electoral participation. In this highly factionalized ethnic enclave, then, community solidarity is engendered by collective action in response to state intrusion, but community conflict is heightened in the electoral process that is directed at political inclusion.

The Enclave and the State

New York's Chinatown is geographically adjacent to the local and federal government complex surrounding City Hall as well as the finance, world trade, and producer services complex of the Wall Street and Battery Park City districts of lower Manhattan. Until the 1970s, the workers and business leaders of the enclave had relatively little impact on urban policy and re-developmental matters taking place in the district. In the past twenty years, however, there has been a series of political conflicts between the enclave and the state over matters of social policy and urban development. These confrontations are partly the by-product of internal social change, that is, a growing outward orientation in Chinatown civil society as the enclave has derived a growing sense of its political power from the emergence of con-temporary workplace and community organizations. These enclave-state contestations are also an outgrowth of external changes in the regional and global economies. As the regional economy has globalized in recent dec-ades, transnational banks and corporations have been increasingly associ-ated with the redevelopment of lower Manhattan. The continued growth of the state has also required the construction of local and federal government facilities, including edifices of municipal security and law such as prisons and courthouses. Thus, in the congested physical space of Chinatown and lower Manhattan, community actors, the state, and global capital have contended perennially over the disposition of space and the pace and scale of its transformation.

Having examined the changing dynamics of community power with-in the enclave, I will now move to an examination of the structure, function, and strategic objectives of the state vis-à-vis Chinatown. Structurally, it is useful to distinguish between the federal government, local government, and regional parastatal organizations (such as the Port Authority and the Urban Development Corporation). The federal government depends large-ly on individual income taxes and corporate capital gains taxes, while local governments are more dependent on property taxes and other local levies. Thus, local governments are more reliant on local economic growth and property development for their revenues, especially since the diminishment and cessation of federal revenue-sharing programs. Quasi-public organiza-tions, meanwhile, which depend on publicly approved bond issues, tolls, and tax surcharges, also benefit from local growth; these organizations have become increasingly influential in municipal growth and politics, es-pecially with the end of revenue sharing.

The federal government has had a broad gatekeeper role in effectively restricting Chinatown's growth during the exclusion era. The liberalization of immigration policy via the Hart-Cellar Immigration Act of 1965 took place alongside an expanded federal presence in urban social policy through fed-eral programs such as the War on Poverty and the Great Society. The imple-mentation of these policies led to the demographic expansion of Chinatown and provided a funding base for emerging community organizations.

Local government policies toward ethnic places have historically been guided by ideologies of slum clearance, cultural assimilation, and law and order. Sanitation and public health, public order, moral uplift, and opposi-tion to the corruption of ethnic machine politics were professed rationales for urban reform and slum clearance during the Progressive Era. Federal and local governments became fuller partners during the post–World War II era under the auspices of urban renewal, as expanded federal housing, urban development, and highway construction monies were made avail-able to localities. This postwar state "directive" stage of urban redevelop-ment was followed by a "concessionary" stage beginning in the mid-1960s, as minority communities protested slum clearance programs (Fainstein and Fainstein 1983).

Since the 1970s, however, the combined effects of deindustrializa-tion, suburbanization, urban fiscal crisis, and the end of federal revenue sharing has forced some central-city managers to pursue new means of growth stimulation and local revenue enhancement. In locales such as New York City, municipal power brokers and local finance and rentier capitalists sustained the regional economy in large part through the solicitation of transnational capital. Lower Manhattan has become a headquarters com-plex for transnational banks and corporations, although initial plans for wholesale redevelopment of the area were reduced after community pro-tests. Globalization contributed to New York City's recovery from the mu-nicipal fiscal crisis of the mid-1970s, while securing the regional economy's position in the global economy in subsequent decades. In Chinatown, city managers also sought to encourage the investment of overseas capital through a special land-use rezoning. This effort was vociferously opposed by community activists concerned with preserving the existing character of the neighborhood, and this state-directed policy was scaled back.

Cities are the centers of jobs and people as much as they are nodal points for the accumulation of capital. Priorities of revenue generation must be balanced by local government managers with strategies of employment retention and investment of capital in productive uses. Chinatown's lower circuit of petty enterprises has thus been of considerable interest. City managers have implemented land-use zoning to protect industrial loft manufacturing space to preserve the livelihood of the Chinatown garment production zone. The restaurants, groceries, and other retail establishments of the lower circuit are also of interest for their utility in supporting urban tourism. An industrial policy and a cultural policy have emerged to stabilize these productive and commercial uses of space in the district.

On the other hand, the local government still perceives Chinatown to be somewhat of a tenement slum of substandard housing, overcrowding, and criminal vice activity. The lower circuit, or informal sector, thus continues to be seen as a nuisance that breeds social pathologies and impedes economic growth and modernization. Tenement housing is to be demolished or upgraded, wherever possible, to upper-class residential space. Public street vendors are viewed as a sanitary and public health hazard to be regulated and controlled. Interests of social control are in fact closely associated with state prerogatives of capital accumulation, industrial production, and social reproduction. The state's institutional apparatuses of public regulation and social control, including the police, courts, and prisons, are in fact headquartered in and around the City Hall area adjacent to Chinatown (there are federal as well as local government office buildings there). Thus, the state itself has as much of a stake in the Chinatown built environment as global capital does. Community conflicts over the disposition of space have arisen in response to state-directed redevelopment plans to invite transnational capital investment and to expand prison and courthouse facilities in the Chinatown vicinity. Municipal schemes to protect local industry and encourage urban tourism, by contrast, have received community support.

Globalization in Lower Manhattan

Governmental and local capital interests worked in concert to stimulate the redevelopment of New York City as an office headquarters center for global capital in the postwar era. The chief product of these intersecting interests is the twin-towered World Trade Center in lower Manhattan, a modernist architectural icon and the principal built domicile for the transnational corporate presence in New York City since its completion in the late 1970s. The World Trade Center was the keystone in a large-scale plan to restructure the built environment of lower Manhattan for a variety of office and upmarket residential uses (including a world trade center) and a cross-island expressway project, which David Rockefeller of Chase Manhattan Bank began engineering as early as 1956. After support was gathered from a group of prominent downtown businessmen (the Downtown–Lower Manhattan Association), consultant studies were commissioned, which recommended the razing of a motley assortment of declining and deteriorated loft manufacturing, warehousing, waterfront pier, and low-income tenement building stock in the districts that surrounded the downtown Wall Street, City Hall, and Battery Park business district area (Robison 1976).

The expressway project and related aspects of the plan were eventually blocked by a diverse anti-redevelopment alliance that included loft-dwelling artists, community-minded middle-class activists, patrician historic preservationists, and Reform Democrats in the Greenwich Village area, including Jane Jacobs (Zukin 1989). The World Trade Center project, however, went forward. Responsibility for the project was assumed in 1964 by the quasi-governmental Port Authority of New York–New Jersey, which financed it through its gigantic capital surplus and additional bond issues. Originally intended to be on the East River shoreline, the project was shifted to the Hudson River to serve New Jersey interests. Port Authority strategists raised the height of the building from the original modest 50 to 70 stories to twin towers of 110 stories. Completed in various stages between 1975 and 1980, the towers immediately displaced the Empire State Building as the world's tallest building.[1] It added some eleven million square feet of office space to lower Manhattan and became the world's largest office complex, beating out the Pentagon, the previous leader (Danielson and Doig 1982: 318–19). Its financial viability was secured for the first several years through the intermediation of then governor of New York Nelson Rockefeller (David Rockefeller's brother), who arranged the temporary rental of much of one tower as offices for New York State employees.

An independent authority was created to oversee development of associated high-income residential projects in Battery Park City, built on Hudson River shoreline landfill created by the World Trade Center excavations. Olympia and York, a huge Canadian development company founded by the Reichmann brothers, was a major investor in the World Financial Center, a related office project.[2] Office construction in the nearby historic

Wall Street area has also undergone rapid growth in the past two decades. The headquarters of many transnational banks are located in the Wall Street area and the World Trade Center.

The escalating redevelopment in the lower Manhattan portion of New York City's poly-nucleated central business district has been paralleled by unprecedented growth in the midtown office market, which is concentrated in a broad swath running from the Empire State Building on 34th Street to the United Nations on the East River. Two quasi-public organizations, New York State's Urban Development Corporation and the city's Public Development Corporation, have assembled land through eminent domain and with the help of $650 million in tax abatements in an attempt to stimulate redevelopment in the west midtown area around Times Square with a giant office and hotel project (Fainstein and Fainstein 1987). Revival in the midtown land market reverses losses suffered for some years with the flight of Fortune 500 headquarters to suburban locations in Connecticut, New Jersey, and other states. Indeed, it could be said that New York City's appeal as a headquarters complex for transnational corporations has essentially involved the replacement of the Fortune 500 with the World 1,000.

The World Trade Center is thus both a material edifice and symbolic landmark for New York City's position as a command center and headquarters complex for global capitalism. This reality was brought home in February 1993, when a massive bomb was exploded at the site, allegedly by international terrorists. After the blast, newly elected Republican governors of both New York (George Pataki) and New Jersey (Christine Todd Whitman) sought to pressure the New York–New Jersey Port Authority into divesting itself of the building complex, arguing that the private sector is better at managing built assets than the government or quasi-governmental organizations such as the Port Authority. In May 1995, Chemical Securities, an investment bank, was contracted to begin a study of the possible sale of the World Trade Center, a move ostensibly aimed at concentrating the agency's activities more on its trade and transportation mandate as manager of New York City's main bridges, tunnels, and airports. The trend toward privatization has been associated with moves to restructure the regional authority by streamlining its operations in order to close a projected budget gap. In September 1995, major layoffs were announced, the first large-scale reductions at the Port Authority since the depression of the 1930s (Lueck 1995).

Zoning the Global City in Chinatown

A study by the New York City Department of City Planning funded by the Rockefeller Family Fund was released in September 1979 as the Manhattan

Bridge Area Study. The issue of street revitalization was raised, and recommendations were issued for street rehabilitation, including repair of street and sidewalk surfaces, new lighting, street signs, creation of pedestrian crosswalks, installation of new traffic signals at key intersections, and some realignments and widening of particularly congested streets. Funding was secured for these improvements through Community Development Program allocations.

The former Public School 23, a city-owned property, was designated for use as a multiservice community facility for meeting halls, recreation areas, day-care and after-school facilities, senior citizens' facilities, and exhibition space. The site was held from public auction so that plans for such facilities could be negotiated through community input and public review. The site currently houses a variety of organizations of the aforementioned nature, including the Chinatown History Museum, a dance studio, and a manpower training project.

Recommendations were also made for improvements to meet housing and social welfare needs, but in view of the scarcity of public resources, no concrete proposals were made aside from increased involvement of other municipal agencies in these areas. Perhaps the most significant proposal of the report, however, was the recommendation to create a "special zoning district" to stimulate new building development while simultaneously seeing to the "preservation of scale" of existing physical design characteristics (New York Department of City Planning 1979: 56). Modification of existing low height limitations were a major part of the proposed encouragements for new development.

The recommendations for rezoning eventually led to the establishment of the Special Manhattan Bridge District (SMBD). New York City's highest planning authority, the Board of Estimate, adopted the SMBD in August 1981 with the stated objective of "upgrading" the mostly vacant twelve-block area bounded by East Broadway, Pike, Monroe, and Oliver Streets proximate to the ramp of the Manhattan Bridge. The rezoning essentially facilitated high-rise development in the generally low-rise area,[3] by granting floor area bonuses to developers who agreed to provide neighborhood amenities, such as community facilities or rehabilitated affordable housing.

Two major high-rise condominium residence projects, which were already in advanced stages of planning and involved overseas investment capital, were announced shortly thereafter. The Henry Street Tower was proposed for a vacant site at 60 Henry Street, a $15-million, 102-unit project of twenty-one stories, with planned selling prices ranging from $170,000 to

$500,000 a unit. Henry Street Partners was a partnership of twenty investors that included three top officers of Helmsley-Spear (a prominent New York City real estate development corporation) and Raymond Wu, a local Chinese investor and insurance broker at New York Life. The Henry Street Partners were led by D. Kenneth Patton, a senior vice president with Helmsley-Spear and a former commissioner of economic development for New York City. The other site, at 87 Madison Street, had been purchased in 1979 by the Overseas Chinese Development Corporation, led by Thomas Lee, a Burmese Chinese, reportedly involving both Hong Kong and Kuwaiti investors. Tenement buildings at the East-West Towers site, owned by the Overseas Chinese Development Corporation, were cleared of tenants and demolished by September 1981. The proposed $21-million, two-towered project of eighteen and seven stories included a total of 143 one-bedroom condominium residences with price tags of up to $150,000 a unit (Wang 1981b). Lee had initially been turned down by City Planning in two requests for a zoning change to allow construction of his building. The Chinatown public, which first gained knowledge of both the rezoning and the condominium projects from a *New York Times* article in the Sunday real estate section, reacted with outrage.[4]

Community Board 3, which encompasses both the Lower East Side and Chinatown, had previously approved the SMBD, and agreed to set up a fact-finding committee after the announcement of the East-West Towers and Henry Street Tower projects. The board held a public hearing on October 5, 1981, (attended by three hundred community residents) on the SMBD. On October 27, the board voted to oppose the special district and called for a public investigation of charges of tenant harassment at the site where tenements had been demolished. In November, the New York City Department of Investigation (DOI) began hearings on these charges. Community organizations formed a Manhattan Bridge Area Coalition to support the tenant defense (*Jin vs. Board of Estimate*) and to investigate alternative strategies for redeveloping the area. In April 1982, the New York DOI released its report, which confirmed that essential services had been cut and tenants had indeed been pressured from the East-West Towers Site, despite the landlord's assertion that relocation monies had been paid. In August 1982, the New York State Supreme Court declared the SMBD null and void on the grounds of inadequate notice for public input as required by Uniform Land-Use Review Procedures (ULURP). The judge ruled that publication of notice in the city record was not sufficient notification, especially in a community where English is not the first language. The City of New York appealed the decision but agreed to revoke the East-West Towers permit, which it did in September 1982. This was the first time in the history of the City Planning Commission that a special permit was revoked.

In March 1983, the city's successful appeal concerning SMBD's legality resulted in its reinstatement by the New York Appellate Division. The community organizations further appealed that decision, however.[5] In April 1983, the Board of Estimate approved the special permit for the Henry Street Tower but instructed the Department of City Planning to meet with community representatives to modify the SMBD to meet the housing needs of low-income residents. As community leaders began meeting with Department of City Planning representatives over prospective modifications to the SMBD, two new law suits were initiated. *Chinese Staff and Workers vs. City of New York,* filed in August 1983, charged that the city violated state environmental laws by failing to consider whether Henry Street Tower and other possible luxury developments in the SMBD would cause gentrification of the neighborhood. *Asian Americans for Equality vs. Koch,* filed in September 1983, charged that the city had a constitutional obligation to use its zoning power to provide a reasonable opportunity for low- and moderate-income housing. This lawsuit cited the Mount Laurel Doctrine, named for a New Jersey town where a 1974 court ruling blocked the implementation of a zoning variance allowing multiple-dwelling unit construction.

In January 1985, the state supreme court overruled the Chinese Staff and Workers' lawsuit, upholding the Henry Street Tower permit. Chinese Staff and Workers' appealed this decision, however, filing an amicus curiae on behalf of twenty housing development corporations; tenant, legal, and community groups; and Councilwoman Miriam Friedlander. In August 1985, the state supreme court ordered the Asian Americans for Equality case to trial, although this lawsuit was eventually unsuccessful. In September 1985, the Manhattan Bridge Area Coalition released their own comprehensive zoning study, prepared by the architectural and urban design firm of Michael Kwartler and Associates and funded by the New York State Council on the Arts, with support from a variety of other Chinatown and metropolitan-wide nonprofit organizations. A public meeting was held in April 1986 at the Transfiguration Church for community review of and reaction to the Kwartler study. This hearing was rocked by a chaotic protest carried out by members of Asian Americans for Equality (AAFE). AAFE opposed any community negotiation whatsoever with municipal officials on the concept of "SMBD modifications," comparing the SMBD to the British and French concession areas created in China after the Opium Wars. They accused the community coalition of being "running dogs" and "traitors."

Finally, in November 1986, New York State's highest court, the court of appeals (in a five to two vote) reversed the findings of two lower courts in the Chinese Staff and Workers' lawsuit, effectively blocking the construction of Henry Street Tower on the grounds of inadequate review of environmental impacts. "Environmental impact" was given a wide latitude in definition, including a range of factors from traffic congestion to "the potential displacement of local residents and business." "Environment," wrote Judge Alexander, means not only natural elements such as land, air, water and noise, but also "population concentration, distribution or growth," and a sense of "community" (Schmalz 1986). This decision was widely interpreted by journalists and legal experts as setting a new precedent in advancing the notion of "secondary displacement" as a form of environmental damage, with wide-ranging legal implications throughout the New York City metropolitan area where community groups sought to preserve neighborhoods from redevelopment.

Meanwhile, the Henry Street Tower site at 60 Market Street had changed hands twice. Henry Street Partners, having purchased the site in 1981 for $900,000, sold the site in May 1985 to Geo Company of Glen Cove, Long Island, for $4 million. The Geo Company president, Barry Marcus, initially wanted to move ahead with an eighty-seven-unit, twenty-one-story structure similar in scale to the original plan (which he called Mencius Plaza), but the project was eventually developed by a group of overseas investors from Hong Kong. The final outcome was a lower, fifteen-story structure built at a cost of $11 million called Honto 88. One hundred luxury condominiums were publicly offered for purchase and occupancy by 1990 (Dao 1990). This lower height more closely conformed to SMBD's suggested compromise modifications.

Thus, development interests, though scaled back, prevailed at the Henry Street Tower site. The original East-West Towers site, on the other hand, remains undeveloped and currently is a parking lot. Thomas Lee, the leading investor in that project, decided to shift his development plans to the western fringe of Chinatown. This area contained fewer residential buildings, raising fewer questions of tenant displacement. His general partner in the new $37-million development was William To, vice president of the HFT Corporation of Hong Kong, and a group of Hong Kong investors were involved as shareholders. The mortgage on the property was initially financed by the Hong Kong and Shanghai Banking Corporation. This project, named Mandarin Plaza, called for 164 luxury condominium units rising twenty-five stories; studios and one- and two-bedroom apartments range from $160,000 to $350,000, and top-floor penthouses, which offered sweeping views of Manhattan, went for up to $582,000. As of April 1990, about 60 percent of the units had been sold, mainly to investors from Hong Kong, where the project has been heavily advertised. Lee was also leading an investment group in a condominium project at 129 Front Street in the Wall Street area.

Representatives of the City of New York, meanwhile, continue to court overseas Chinese investment. In November 1988, the deputy mayor of New York City, Alair Townsend, led a delegation of city representatives and leaders of the Chinese business community to meet with the Hong Kong Development Trade Council to encourage investment. Efforts such as these have encouraged ongoing overseas capital interest in Chinatown land market development.

State-Labor-Capital Cooperation in Garment Industry Planning

Cooperation between capital and labor in the context of industrial relations in the Chinatown production area in the early 1980s set the stage for municipal involvement in garment industry planning. In the early 1980s, Local 23-25 of the ILGWU (the local that represents Chinatown production center workers) and the New York Skirt and Sportswear Association (the organization that represents the manufacturers who send bundlework to the contractors of the Chinatown production zone) jointly sponsored a planning study of the Chinatown garment industry. The results of the research, conducted by consultants, were published in 1983 as the *Chinatown Garment Industry Study*. Statistically exhaustive in scope, the study recognized two primary issues: (1) that the Chinatown agglomeration of contracting shops was the "productive anchor" of New York City in the area of women's apparel and that the continued vitality of the production zone was thus critical to the overall competitive position of the New York City garment industry, and (2) that those same shops were critical to the livelihood of most Chinatown households (Abeles, Schwartz, Haeckel, and Silverblatt 1983).

The principal recommendations of the study were (1) to form a Garment Industry Development Corporation (GIDC) to coordinate policies and provide technical assistance to the Chinatown production zone as well as to the apparel industry as a whole, (2) to formulate land-use policies to preserve the inventory of loft manufacturing space in the Chinatown production zone, (3) to assist garment contractors in acquiring properties and securing long-term leases for industrial space in the Chinatown area and to plan for expansion into outer-borough areas, and (4) to provide training for the Chinatown garment zone workforce and improve social, medical, and residential services for them (Abeles, Schwartz, Haeckel, and Silverblatt 1983: 204–22).

Lower Manhattan land-use policies were the first recommendations to be implemented. Building surveys that had been conducted in 1981 and 1982 during the course of research for the 1983 final report had identified a need to preserve the inventory of loft manufacturing space in the Chinatown area, which was increasingly subject to upmarket residential conversion.[6] Garment shops located in the Soho district were already protected by strict monitoring of residential conversions. A seven-block area, the Walker Street Corridor, was quickly rezoned by the city in December 1982 to prohibit any further residential conversions as a way of protecting the livelihood of some one hundred garment shops operating in the area. Existing illegal conversions were allowed to apply for official permits under a grandfather clause. A proposal was submitted in 1984 to the New York City Department of City Planning for a wider plan controlling future conversions in a larger section of Little Italy, greater Chinatown, and the surrounding commercial Lower East Side. After 1985, residential conversions of loft manufacturing space were possible only through special permit and after careful city review.

Meanwhile, the GIDC was created with the cooperation of the ILGWU, the New York Skirt and Sportswear Association, and the New York City Office of Business Development. They have made progress in four major areas: (1) manpower training, (2) marketing and technology, (3) infrastructure development, and (4) research and planning. In the area of manpower training, workshops for upgrading sewing machine skills (Super Sewers) and workshops in machine repair and maintenance were offered. The GIDC then helped to place course graduates in higher-skilled jobs. A more permanent GIDC Training Center was opened in 1989 to begin offering these courses on a more regular basis. The center is managed by a partnership between GIDC and the Fashion Institute of Technology (which is providing instructors and administrative support) and is housed in space provided by the nearby High School of Fashion Industries. The New York City Office of Business Development contributed $110,000 for the purchase of modern sewing equipment, including computerized marking and grading equipment and software.

In marketing and technology, the GIDC has sought to assist Chinatown firms in competing in the higher end of the industry. Courses have been given in business management and personal computer use for shop owners. An $80,000-study was commissioned in 1990 to identify market segments and niches as well as new technologies and production methods to strengthen the competitiveness of the garment contractors in Chinatown and throughout the New York City region.

In the area of infrastructure development, one of the first projects of the GIDC was the establishment of an industrial condominium for garment shops at 424 Broadway. Affordable commercial space and financing arrangements are provided for garment contractors at the site. Given the difficulties of creating such space on a wider scale in the tight real estate market of lower Manhattan, the GIDC began examining sites in the outer boroughs. Detailed studies eventually led to the selection of the abandoned Brooklyn Army Terminal, which is now managed by the Public Development Corporation (PDC), a not-for-profit organization established by the city to assist in real estate development and to market city-owned property. The PDC has renovated two million square feet of space at the site at a cost of $80 million, and offers long-term, affordable leases with city-subsidized energy costs and low taxes. The loading docks at the Army Terminal allow manufacturers to receive and send out-of-state shipments without the use of trucks.

A consortium of twenty-two Chinese apparel contractors formed a new corporation to set up a satellite production facility, the Metropolitan Fashion Center (MFC), at the Army Terminal. The MFC leased forty thousand square feet at the site in September 1990 and took options on an additional ninety thousand square feet. On-site skills training and classroom instruction were to be provided by GIDC. A shuttle bus would take the workers from the neighboring satellite Chinatown of Sunset Park. A day-care center was planned with the assistance of the ILGWU. The transport advantage of the loading docks was seen as a factor that would make the site competitive with foreign importers. There were twenty-five to thirty workers at the site as of June 1991, with plans to expand to one hundred. All contractors at the site would be union shops. Chinatown banks were not involved in the start-up capitalization of the MFC. The Hang Seng Bank participated as a consultant, conducting a feasibility study during the planning stage of the venture, but did not loan money to the project. In other developments, John Lam, the single biggest Chinatown garment contractor, with some forty shops, had a project "in hibernation" for a cluster of independent contractors in Queens.[7]

The Sanitary State: Street Trader Clearance Campaigns

In the early 1970s, the New York City Department of City Planning undertook a study of Chinatown land use for the New York City Bicentennial Project, which was financed by a "City Options grant" and funding from the National Endowment for the Arts. The results were published in 1976 as the *Chinatown Street Revitalization* study. One of the main conclusions was that the growing concentration of Chinese businesses had created great problems of traffic congestion and street sanitation. Major street improvements and the establishment of pedestrian-only roadways in the heart of old Chinatown were among the recommendations. While there was community consensus around the need for street improvements, Chinatown merchants balked at the idea of pedestrian zoning. The vitality of many ethnic grocers, restaurants, and other retailers, they asserted, depended on daily access by vans and trucks.

The City of New York has historically been antagonistic toward the ethnic street trader. Mobile vendors and peddlers were perceived to cause street congestion and to compete directly with retail stores occupying private property. Sanitation was another problem, caused particularly by vendors of produce, prepared food, and other food products. Some middle- and upper-class residents feared that the appearance of these "backward" signs of the traditional economy disturbed the decorum of the street, would stigmatize neighborhoods, and possibly lead to declining property values. Finally, because many street vendors have traditionally operated in the informal sector outside of municipal regulation, the city had an administrative prerogative in bringing this type of itinerant activity under official control. There were periodic campaigns to clear the various informal street-trading markets (primarily occupied by white European immigrants) of New York City beginning at the turn of the century. The classic popularly known markets were the Jewish Orchard Street market of the Lower East Side and the Irish Paddy's Market of midtown on the West Side. Initial aggressive strategies of market clearance and trader persecution gave way to more liberal efforts to confine street trading to certain municipally designated sites outside areas of existing heavy traffic congestion or established retail activity. These schemes finally culminated in their virtual removal from public streets to enclosed market buildings by the 1930s, under the administration of Fiorello La Guardia (Bluestone 1992).

Public street trading, however, has gradually revived in recent decades. By the 1980s, substantial numbers of African Americans had emerged along 125th Street in Harlem, and Chinese Americans in scattered locations of Chinatown. The midtown area had also become an area of considerable street-vendor activity, with many traders operating carts rented by small to medium-sized business owners and selling, especially, prepared breakfast and lunch foods, ice cream, and other refreshments. There were attempts under Mayors Ed Koch and David Dinkins to clear this activity, especially during the course of election campaigns, under pressure from the established property-owning business community. The Jewish Koch, however, admitted that his father had been a pushcart peddler in his native Poland, and the African American Dinkins also confessed to having been a teenage peddler in his youth, hawking shopping bags and magazines in Harlem (Zukin 1995: 243). These admissions exposed the double-edged quality of street vending: on the one hand, they created congestion and competition for established tax-paying merchants; on the other hand, they provided a route for upward mobility and cultivated entrepreneurial values, values that were held to be part of the national character and were part of the personal history of two of New York's recent leaders. The Dinkins administration's sweep in Harlem in 1992, moreover, was countered by street demonstrations on 125th Street.

A broad crackdown was launched by the new Republican mayor, Rudolph Giuliani (a former U.S. associate attorney general), in 1994. His bold clearance effort was supported by strong detachments of police, some in riot gear, in Harlem and midtown. These forceful evictions were countered by demonstrations in both locations, including a five-hundred-strong march of vendors up Fifth Avenue in April 1994. The Sisyphean task of regulating several thousand unlicensed street traders with a detail of only a few dozen enforcement officers confronts the Giuliani administration.

Clearance of street traders in Chinatown had started earlier and with less hostility. In 1992, recently elected city councilperson Kathryn Freed, who represents Chinatown along with the adjoining lower Manhattan neighborhoods of TriBeCa and Battery Park City, began examining the Chinatown street-trading situation. Established Chinese and Italian American storefront businesspeople organized through the Grand Street Merchants Association had made complaints. Residents of the area had also complained about street congestion, garbage, and smells emanating from the street-trading activity, especially from seafood vendors. The precinct police captain linked a perceived "social problem" of growing street-trader congestion on Grand Street with a problem of drug dealing and vagrancy in the nearby southern part of Sara Delano Roosevelt Park. A homeless encampment near the south end of the park, adjacent to a ramp of the Manhattan Bridge, had already been evicted during the course of construction activity connected with bridge maintenance. A slight economic slowdown and loss of formal-sector employment in Chinatown in the early 1990s was one apparent reason for the spread of street trading. It was also suspected that many unlicensed street traders were illegal immigrants. Councilperson Freed decided to contend with these issues as part of a campaign pledge she had made to improve neighborhood "quality of life."

While vendors were cleared from Grand Street, meetings were held with the Chinatown community, the police, and the New York City Parks Department, Transportation Department, Sanitation Department, Health Department, and Department of Consumer Affairs. A street survey was commissioned with the Hunter College Center for Applied Studies of the Environment. A proposal to relocate vendors to an open-air market in Sara Delano Roosevelt Park was eventually made and implemented. The Parks Department contracted with the University Settlement house to manage the market. At the September 1994 grand opening, the one hundred stalls were nearly full. The market has been less than a success. Vendors initially complained of strict regulations that prohibited sale of wine and liquor, uncooked meats, and seafood. The 7:00 A.M. to 7:00 P.M. hours of opening were not long enough for some vendors. Continuing construction on the Manhattan Bridge led to the closure of the Grand Street subway station, one of Chinatown's two major subway stops. Councilperson Freed managed to obtain a limited reopening of the subway station on weekends. The subway closing and other factors severely hurt the success of the project. During a census of street-trading activity that I conducted in October 1995, I counted only twelve active traders in operation at the site.

The project's apparent failure (for the meantime) provided political fodder for groups opposed to its establishment, such as an organization of vendors known as the Chinatown Vendors Association, which purports to represent some three hundred licensed peddlers. This group was critical of the vendor relocation effort at community board meetings regarding the issue at the end of 1992. They also made appearances at demonstrations held at City Hall regarding vendor clearance. They continue to support the concept of unregulated public street access for Chinatown vendors.

Tourism Initiatives

Use of Chinatown as a tourist district has historical precedents dating back to the turn of the century (see chapter 7), but pronounced efforts by the community and local government to coordinate this use has much more recent roots. In 1988, a community-based voluntary organization called Manhattan Neighborhood Renaissance began to operate a trolley service that picked up tourists in Times Square and drove them to Chinatown/ Lower East Side and neighboring districts of lower Manhattan. Manhattan Neighborhood Renaissance Local Development Corporation (Renaissance) became a funded organization though a grant from the Urban Development Corporation (UDC), a large private nonprofit organization that has been a major player in coordinating the redevelopment of Times Square for tourism. Renaissance was able expand to three vintage trolleys, which were

Figure 20. Chinatown tour bus. Photo by Jan Lin.

gradually phased out after about five years when the business was taken over by the larger midtown tour companies, which operated larger buses or fleets of trolleys. Asian Americans for Equality (AAFE) was instrumental in the organizational development of Renaissance.

Compared to the whistle-stop midtown tour companies such as the Gray Line Tours, New York Apple Tours, and Saddle River Tours (Figure 20), the trolley tour initially operated by Renaissance gave heavy emphasis to the cultural richness, ethnic diversity, and historical significance of the Lower East Side. Renaissance emphasized five neighborhoods, which it called the "five treasures of the Lower East Side" in promotional brochures: Little Italy, Chinatown, the Jewish Orchard–Delancey Street area, Latino Loisaida, and the artist community of the East Village. As Renaissance departed from the business of conducting tours, it moved more forcefully into local economic development, which it fosters primarily through small-business development assistance programs and the organization of a prospective Chinatown business improvement district (BID), a venture that is being funded by the UDC.

BIDs, which originated in the 1970s under the label "special assessment districts," are created in any commercial area by business and property owners who voluntarily pay a tax assessment above and beyond existing municipal levies in order to finance supplemental infrastructure improvements and services that city managers cannot or will not pay for. Common throughout the New York City metropolitan region, the largest BIDs are located in midtown Manhattan locations such as Times Square and the Grand Central station area. As Sharon Zukin suggests, this "privatization of public goods," particularly among the larger BIDs, acquires a conspiratorial logic when neighborhood improvement means the eviction of homeless vagrant populations and the hiring of private security agencies to patrol newly sanitized areas.[8] The overriding logic behind these schemes for urban improvement, she notes, is the continued aggrandizement of property values for local rentier capital (Zukin 1995: 33–37, 66–67).

Neighborhood crime prevention through resident Block Watchers Programs are more the order of the day at the community beat organized by AAFE and Renaissance. Street vendor clearance has not been on the agenda of the Renaissance BID, but sanitation via community awareness has been trumpeted by Renaissance neighborhood clean-up events. The Renaissance BID has more activist origins than the top-down midtown schemes, and is more oriented toward microenterprise development than augmenting the livelihood of large corporations. Larger businesses such as banks interested in improving their neighborhood image vis-à-vis requirements of the Community Reinvestment Act, however, are prominent on the incipient BID board of directors. They may exercise substantial influence in future BID decision making. The real question mark in the prospective formation of a Chinatown BID, however, is the challenge of organizing some kind of developmental consensus in a community that, as we have already recognized, is ridden with conflict and factionalism along lines of national origin and diplomatic orientation among its traditional associations and business elite, and with ideological conflict among its community organizations.

A state-sponsored Chinatown Tourism Council was also created by the Manhattan Borough President's Office under Ruth Messinger (who has a record as a historical preservationist) and publicly launched through a press conference early in 1992.[9] Composed of fifteen leaders of the Chinatown business, arts, and cultural communities, this group's ostensible mission was to promote tourism in Chinatown as an economic development strategy while still preserving its integrity as a community. The group assisted Gray Line Tours in its inauguration of a trolley tour in April 1993, focusing on lower Manhattan neighborhoods. This is one of the uptown tour companies that displaced the Renaissance trolley project. Gray Line Tours, which is more historically and culturally sensitive than New York Apple Tours, takes a continuous daily route past sixteen stops in lower Manhattan, allowing passengers to fashion their personalized tourist experience with the assistance of a walking-tour book. The Chinatown Tourism Council helped to develop the Chinatown section of this walking-tour book.

The Chinatown Tourism Council also promoted local cultural events in the interests of tourism, such as the lower Manhattan Busker's Fair and a Chinatown cultural event involving music and dance in Columbus Park in the summer of 1993. During the 1994 Chinese New Year, they published a calendar of events for distribution to tourists. Partly because of the loss of personnel, the Chinatown Tourism Council was almost defunct by 1995, despite its being selected as a model case study by the University of Colorado Center for Community Studies and the U.S. Tourism and Travel Department (an agency of the U.S. Commerce Department). Christobal Garcia of Renaissance, who remains its titular community chairperson, has increasingly devoted his energies to housing rehabilitation, community stabilization, and microenterprise development.

Tourism was also endorsed by a land-use and planning study conducted by an architecture and urban planning studio class at Hunter College taught by Professor James Jao, who was also a city planning commissioner under the Dinkins administration. The Jao study recommended the construction of visual cues or "gateways" (incorporating elements such as Chinese-style gates, public sculptures, archways, kiosks, banners, murals, and greenery) at appropriate focal street entrances or transition points into Chinatown. Chinese-style gates are common in other Chinatowns but are still noticeably lacking in New York's. The only existing gatewaylike visual devices are a statue of Confucius and a memorial to Chinese American veterans, both located in Chatham Square. The Jao study was never taken seriously by community organizations despite a public meeting held upon its release in November 1992.

The Security State: Prison and Courthouse Expansions

At the time that the SMBD projects were first announced, another large project was proposed on a vacant 1.25-acre site near the core of old Chinatown. The site, bordered by White, Centre, Walker, and Baxter Streets, was purchased on December 2, 1980, by a Chinese shipping magnate, C. Y. Chen, for $6 million. In June 1981, Chen formed a partnership with an American developer, David H. Feinberg, of Feinberg Realty and Construction, a New York–based real estate development firm. The new partnership, China Plaza Company, acquired the site from Chen for $9,750,000. A fifty-two-story, $70-million commercial and residential tower was initially proposed, the largest project ever undertaken by private investors in Chinatown. Nearly half the height of the World Trade Center, the initial proposal was scaled down to two thirty-story towers (Wang 1982). As community opposition to the nearby SMBD projects mounted, these developers quietly began clearing and excavating at the site. Despite repeated requests from community groups for information, the developers refused to release details about the project.

In February 1982, the New York City Department of Corrections announced its intention to acquire the China Plaza Company site in order to build a $71-million, five-hundred-bed detention facility for detainees awaiting or on trial, as an extension to the adjacent Criminal Court Building and the Men's House of Detention (popularly known as "the Tombs"), which was also scheduled for renovation. The Department of Corrections cited a 1981 federal district court order to reduce overcrowding in city jails, particularly at the aging high-security Rikers Island jail. Included in their proposal was a $29-million, 156-bed juvenile center on top of the proposed new jail. As community concern began mounting regarding both the China Plaza Company project and the detention center proposal, Chen pulled out, and the site was subsequently acquired through eminent domain by the Department of Corrections, whose plan was approved by the City Planning Commission; the site was now commonly dubbed the "White Street Jail" project. Talk of providing a community facility was generated by municipal officials in the growing climate of community disquiet surrounding the detention center plan. As the prison plan moved forward, community activists organized under a group called the Coalition for Lower Manhattan. Within the scope of Chinatown community campaigns, this one was particularly successful in unifying diverse elements of the neighborhood, including business and civic leaders as well as community activists and workers. Representatives of the adjacent community of Little Italy also became involved. Periodic protests were held at City Hall, culminating in a large-scale demonstration that turned out a crowd of twelve thousand (this was the official police estimate; organizers claimed twenty thousand) in December 1982. This considerable outpouring led city officials to promise to give up part of the land for use as community space (Gruson 1982).

Opponents of the prison pointed to the plethora of courthouses and detention facilities already in the vicinity of Chinatown and Little Italy. They felt it would harm the cultural and ethnic identity of the neighborhood and attract "undesirable elements." A lawsuit was filed, but a state supreme court judge upheld the detention center plan in an August 1983 decision. Negotiations between community representatives and city officials eventually resulted in an agreement, announced by Mayor Edward Koch on May 1984, for a three-story commercial complex topped by an eleven-story housing tower next to the jail. The community facility was to occupy one-quarter of the fifty-thousand-square-foot block; the jail was scheduled to be completed by July 1988. The Chinatown Planning Council (CPC) had applied for a $12-million federal Housing and Urban Development (HUD) grant to finance the eighty-eight-unit low-income senior citizens' housing tower. The initial agreement was for banks and commercial/retail space on the first floor, and offices on the second and third floors (Carmody 1984).

The CPC and the Chinese Consolidated Benevolent Association (CCBA) controlled the community board overseeing planning for the community site (now called Chung Pak, or "Everlasting Pine"). The CCBA president, Joseph Mei, was the titular chairman of the Chung Pak planning board, but meetings were conducted by the vice chair, CPC deputy director David Chen, who was more versed in English and familiar with dealings with public officials. A group of community organizations excluded from the Chung Pak planning board, called the Committee of Concerned Citizens of Chinatown, objected to the plan for banks on the ground floor, contending that there was a severe lack of small-business commercial space in Chinatown (Kwong 1987: 135). This excluded group, which included organizations such as the Chinese Progressive Association and the Chinese Staff and Workers' Association, also sought representation on the Chung Pak planning board. David Dinkins (then Manhattan Borough president and later mayor of New York), brokered their inclusion, which resulted in one seat on the board. Some of this group opposed negotiation altogether, in disputing the detention center on principles.

In this atmosphere of disquiet among the community organizations, the CCBA seized an opportunity when absences at a board meeting in June 1986 gave it a temporary majority; it expanded the number of board members from fourteen to twenty, adding six more CCBA representatives. This preemptive move drew the wrath of all parties involved, however, including city officials. Objections were based on the knowledge that three of the expanded group of CCBA members represented tong associations (the On Leong tong, the Hip Sing tong, and the Chinese Freemasons) with generally recognized connections to organized crime and youth gangs. A fourth member was a representative of the Eastern Regional Office of the Guomindang Party of Taiwan. City officials moved to oust the six new CCBA board members in September through a lawsuit filed in the state supreme court. Meanwhile, the vice chairman of the Chung Pak planning board, Chen, quietly lobbied for a new vote to reconstitute the board. The CCBA, meanwhile, announced in the Chinese newspapers their intention to boycott the meeting. The CPC thus became the lead community agency with the board reorganization.

As the Chung Pak planning board moved into the building stage of negotiations with the reformist CPC at its helm, the grassroots activist organizations continued to press for community concerns, such as Chinese American involvement in construction contracts and small-business space instead of banking offices on the ground floor. The CPC backed larger businesses, which would allay bankers who were worried about risk. The cash down payment by prospective tenants for the commercial project on the bottom floors was needed as a financial "podium" to back the bridge loan for the senior citizens' housing. Opponents to the CPC plan saw the "seed money" from prospective commercial tenants as more like coerced "key money." The CPC furthermore had found a non-Chinese American private nonprofit developer for the senior citizens' housing, the New York Housing Partnership, which demanded 51-percent control.

A plan for a ground-floor commercial cooperative of eight businesses eventually was accepted, with a sliding scale for the tenants and declining rent on a twenty-five-year lease. The commercial tenants that joined included Fujisan, a Japanese restaurant, and Maria's Bakery, a chain. The nonprofit Chinatown Health Clinic was able to enter the project on the second floor with a thirty-nine-year lease. The third floor became available as space for services because of a drop in interest rates, and eventually was made available for an ILGWU day-care center and the Agency for Child Development. The Chung Pak Development Corporation, led by a community board of directors, manages the project. One recalcitrant commercial tenant pulled out, and that space is currently empty. Managers at Citibank, which supplied the bridge loan, threatened to reduce the mortgage to ten years because of a perceived "risk and instability" problem. Yet the bank cannot foreclose because Chung Pak is a federal project. Furthermore, Citibank was somewhat obliged to have tolerant financial criteria because of Community Reinvestment Act prerogatives, which mandated a certain amount of investment in the neighborhood.

There has also been community opposition to federal government redevelopment projects. In March 1991, the U.S. government authorized $500 million for the construction of two federal office buildings, a federal courthouse on Worth Street facing Columbus Park near the heart of Chinatown, and an office building for the General Services Administration (GSA) nearby in the City Hall area. The Chinatown community was informed of the projects for the first time in August, and in November, a group led by the Chinatown Staff and Workers' Association (CSWA) met with developers and

Figure 21. Foley Square Courthouse demonstration, 1992. Photo by Corky Lee. Copyright Corky Lee; used by permission of the photographer.

federal contractors, demanding that 30 percent of the projects' jobs go to Chinese American workers (nearly 40 percent of the population in the area was Chinese American). The developers and contractors initially promised a special training program and a 40-percent set-aside for Chinese American workers. By February 1992, however, only one Chinese construction worker had been put on the courthouse site, which was the first project to break ground. Councilperson Kathryn Freed, who represents Chinatown, set up a meeting between the carpenters' union and Chinatown labor representatives to discuss Chinese American inclusion, but the union refused to attend the meeting. The CSWA, launching the Campaign for Economic Justice at Foley Square (the courthouse area is called Foley Square) pressed on, however, by trying to pressure government officials to increase Chinese American hiring at the projects (Figure 21).

Chinatown businesspeople begin to get involved with the campaign, extending the issue beyond Chinese American representation in hiring to the inclusion of Chinese American firms in the awarding of construction contracts. The campaign gained endorsements from local bankers, insurance companies, and developers shunned from the bidding process and bond underwriting. Total bids awarded to Chinese developers were about $184,000 out of a total of $48 million. At a meeting of federal representatives, project developers and contractors, and Chinese American leaders set up by Councilperson Freed in June, GSA representative Bill Diamond admitted that the number of Asian workers and contractors was absurdly low. Contractors said this was the union's problem, and Diamond promised to set up more meetings at which the union would be present. The union boycotted these meetings, however, and the CSWA, organizing in a broad unified front with members of Chinatown's traditional and modern associations as well as members of the business community, staged a three-thousand-person demonstration at Foley Square on July 9. A second demonstration was held in August, at which the community called for the resignation of Diamond unless community demands were met. Eventually, eighty Chinese construction workers were hired at the second construction site, the GSA office building. The Campaign for Economic Justice also won a ruling that repealed the requirement that workers at federally funded projects must have a high school diploma and be proficient in English (since these rules discriminate against recent immigrants).

The Place of the State

To conclude, the redevelopmental efforts of the "security state" were driven mainly by administrative priorities of capacity expansion in the built environment, producing place-based struggles over the disposition of Chinatown space in which intervening conflicts over social issues came to the fore. Issues of community control arose regarding municipal plans to expand prison facilities, while matters of civil rights ensued in response to plans to expand the administrative facilities of the federal government. These assertions of state authority and social control intersected with broader strategies of globalization in the regional economy and built environment of lower Manhattan, a process encouraged by a constellation of external interests including the local government, regional parastatal organizations, regional financial interests, and global capital. Strategies of slum clearance and social control served the logic of state interests in producing a friendly investment environment for global capital.

I do not mean to enforce an instrumental view of the state as being hostage to the designs of local financial/rentier elites or the interests of global capital. To clarify, I would offer an urban managerialist point of view that suggests that state/parastatal managers are negotiating between the interests of capital and the demands of community and labor on a sequence of descending levels.[10] At the level of the metropolitan area, banking deregulation and the construction of the World Trade Center since the 1970s has constituted a direct invitation to the transnational business presence in lower Manhattan, although initial plans for widespread redevelopment were scaled back in response to broad community-based opposition. On the level of Chinatown as a metropolitan subarea, state-sanctioned inducements for global capital were similarly corrected following neighborhood conflict; encouragements to industrial capital, by contrast, were a direct acknowledgment by the state of the importance of Chinatown labor to the local economy. On the street level, the state was more restrictive, clearing street traders under priorities of sanitation, tax collection, and the maintenance of an appearance of middle-class decorum. Marginalizing these relatively powerless trader interests, the state delimits the proper uses of public space while "securing" the environment for investment capital and tourism.

7

Encountering Chinatown: Tourism, Voyeurism, and the Cinema

The typical American encounters Chinatown as part of a process of alimentary gratification. Aside from providing a break from normal culinary routine, the prospect of eating Chinese food in association with a journey into the central-city district of Chinatown also affords the diner the opportunity of experiencing the exotic Orient without undertaking transpacific travel. The local cheap amusement substitutes for the cosmopolitan global junket. These pedestrian acts of urban tourism may include a foray into a Chinese grocery, curio shop, martial arts establishment, or herbal medicine store. During the weeks of firecracker excitement leading up to the Chinese New Year, when Chinatown is festooned with decorations and swarming with visitors, these excursions assume an even more extraordinary quality.

Behind the spectacle of the lion dances and nighttime neon, a luster of mystery and surreptitiousness often prevails. Chinatown is, after all, still commonly perceived as a district pervaded with organized crime, vice industries, and depravities associated with illegal immigrant smuggling and sweatshop activity. These images are continually reinforced by tabloid sensationalism, prime-time police and detective television serials such as *NYPD Blue,* and Hollywood films that feed societal demand for lurid sights and violent scenes. This voyeuristic impulse has been sustained by a film industry that has created what Norman Denzin has called our "cinematic society," a cultural landscape that is guided by "[a voyeur's gaze] which each of us has interiorized . . . which I may pay you to perform for me; that gaze which you may ask me to perform for you. This is the gaze of surveillance, the gaze of power, the gaze which unveils the private and makes it public" (1995: 2). Voyeurs are actors who spy on the lives of others, but audiences have become voyeurs that follow these stories as if they were real. Cinematic and television treatments of Chinatown and its Chinese American denizens abound with images of violent criminals engaged in activities such as gambling, prostitution, drug smuggling, and other underground vice activities that are being surveilled by detectives and other servants of the security state. America, then, encounters Chinatown as both tourist and cinematic voyeur.

There has been a succession of films, television shows, dime novels, and reporter's exposés since the turn of the century that have projected representations of Chinatown as a dangerous vice area, tourist spectacle, or enigmatic place. These representations have had a cumulative durability, delimiting and adumbrating subsequent visionings of Chinatown as a voyeuristic object. The protagonists in these popular cultural works are usually white detectives, policemen, or investigative reporters seeking to expose a crime, clean up the vice, or uncover a mystery (such as cynical sleuth Jake Gittes in Roman Polanski's *Chinatown*). The Chinese antagonists may be represented as archenemies of the West (such as the diabolical Fu Manchu) or rising crime bosses (such as Joey Tai in Michael Cimino's *Year of the Dragon*).

Beyond the psychoanalytic perspective, we can comprehend these critical representations of Chinatown and Chinese Americans as having a political construction. Particularly in earlier decades, nativistic and Sinophobic images reinforced state policies of immigration exclusion and foreign policy perceptions of a Chinese geopolitical threat. These representational constructions in the American context have functioned much like the historical discourse of Orientalism, which Edward Said (1979) has described as serving the political, sociological, military, ideological, scientific, and imaginative interests of the West rather than accurately documenting the reality of the East. Orientalism was thus a hegemonic project, constructed to define an oppositional "other" while legitimating the authority and dominance of the West. Orientalist depictions of Chinatown, similarly, divorce Chinatown from the American social context by representing the district as a sinister and malevolent underworld that requires correction and control.

Representational constructions of Chinese Americans and Chinatown have not always been critical. In years of diplomatic alliance with China (during the years of Japanese expansionism), the ideological pendulum reversed, and sympathetic images of Chinese Americans on the side of law and order, such as the detective Charlie Chan, emerged. In the contemporary period, the benevolent "model minority" image of achieving students and successful artists and entrepreneurs has emerged, but negative depictions of Chinese Americans and Chinatown are still pervasive, sustaining local government prerogatives of surveillance and control.

These critical symbolic representations are generally the creation of outsiders to Chinatown and are commonplace throughout the twentieth-century cinematic landscape. White outsiders with some insider knowledge of Chinatown have also periodically sought to capitalize on their familiarity by creating exotic photographic images for affluent armchair voyeurs, or drawing ogling tourists into Chinatown for popular amusement. In the process of retrofitting Chinatown for popular consumption, these outsiders deliberately manipulated reality to suit the imaginary expectations of Western observers. New York's Chinatown has been "staged" in such a fashion since the turn of the century. The Chinese government and Chinese Americans have periodically protested these negative depictions. Chinatown insiders in the contemporary era, meanwhile, have turned from protest to efforts at revising these public images. Chinese Americans authors and artists have been trammeled by existing representations, which like a canon intrude on their own perceptions of themselves. In this chapter, I will examine, in turn, touristic representations of New York's Chinatown since the turn of the century, classic Hollywood depictions of Chinatown and Chinese Americans, and emerging attempts by Chinese Americans to refashion these representations.

Refashioning Chinatown for Armchair Voyeurs

John Kuo Wei Tchen has drawn attention to how Arnold Genthe, an early-twentieth-century photographer, manipulated his photographs of San Francisco's Chinatown to serve the voyeuristic expectations of middle- and upper-class patrons. He deliberately retouched his photographs, sometimes removing white pedestrians and English signage, to heighten the image of Chinatown as an alien and faraway place. Tchen says:

> After looking at his Chinatown books and exhibition prints, the
> viewer gets the distinct impression . . . [of] an exotic, picturesque
> "Canton of the West," a totally Chinese city within San Francisco.
> The truth of the matter is that the ideal "pure" Chinese quarter
> never existed, except in the imagination of its non-Chinese non-
> residents. (1984: 14)

Edward Curtis, a contemporary of Genthe, similarly retouched his photographs of Native Americans by removing incidental items of modern material culture and European influence. Curtis even costumed some of his subjects with a traveling wardrobe of museum props (such as feather head-dresses, beads, and wigs) in order to create a more aesthetically pure "primitive" quality to his portraits (Jackson 1992). Both Genthe and Curtis emerged in Victorian-era America at a time of the end of the frontier and the rise of tourism in American popular culture.

Chinatown as Cheap Amusement:
Rubberneckers and Slummers in Old New York

In the 1880s, it became fashionable for middle-class New Yorkers to go slumming in Chinatown, the Bowery, and other less respectable parts of town to "rub shoulders with the sinners" and see "how the other half lives." Charles Hoyt's musical show *A Trip to Chinatown* opened on November 9, 1891, and ran for 650 nights. The term *rubbernecker* for a gawking tourist entered American parlance during this era. The artist Joan Sloan satirically depicted rubberneckers in a 1917 etching of a horse-drawn cart of geese twisting their necks through the slats of crates in a city scene he called *Seeing New York*. Rubbernecker vehicles, known as "yap wagons" (*yap* was slang for *rustic*), "gape wagons," or "hay wagons," took tourists from Times Square to downtown locations. Some employed decoy tourists to occupy seats to encourage sheepish out-of-towners who were hesitant to enter an empty bus. Entrepreneurial hucksters hooked tourists by touting the awaiting spectacle: "Just starting. See the Chinese opium dens! The Bowery slums! Coney ablaze with light! Last trip of the day. One dollah the round trip" (Allen 1993: 81–84). Typical of these raffish "boulevardiers" in the 1890s was the Irish American impresario George Washington "Chuck" Connors, a white Chinatown insider who held court at various area saloons and was popularly nicknamed the "Mayor of Chinatown," or "lobbygow," a pidgin Chinese term for tour guide. Taking parties of slummers around the Bowery and Chinatown (which he called his "reservation"), Connors spun fables of life in the foreign quarter. A requisite stop in Chinatown was his mock opium den, in which he "exhibited" two addicts, a white woman named Lulu and a half-Chinese man named Georgie Yee. As his fame spread, Connors came into demand among celebrity tourists (including novelists such as Israel Zangwill, theater personalities, and visiting foreign royalty), and he was pulled from his downtown turf to make occasional appearances at uptown theaters, as he brought bawdy Bowery "saloon culture" to the Broadway stage (Sante 1991: 125–29).

A series of streetwise hucksters followed in Connors's wake. Louis Beck's 1898 pulp travelogue on New York's Chinatown describes the exploits of newsman Steve Brodie, who took the visiting General William Booth-Tucker of the Salvation Army on such a tour. The general was fixed up with a pair of huge false whiskers and a Svengali wig. He was taken to Mike Callahan's saloon (where slummers were habitually price gouged and pick-pocketed), the Joss House, and the Chinese restaurant below. The tour was capped off with a mock arrest by a policeman for assuming a disguise.

The word *yen*, which means "craving," came into English use about 1908 from the Cantonese *in yan* (opium craving) (Allen 1993: 155). Although historically typified as an addiction of Chinese men, the novelist Stephen Crane reported that in truth opium smoking was a pastime among both male and female Anglo-Americans. Reports in turn-of-the-century New York City estimated anywhere from twenty-five thousand to five hundred thousand opium smokers, especially among the underworld and show business set of the city. Opium dens were found not just in Chinatown but in the main uptown vice district known as the Tenderloin (Sante 1991: 148). Louis Beck described one visit to a luxuriously appointed "Tenderloin joint" that occupied a whole building on West 46th Street and Seventh Avenue, and appealed to upper-class men as well as women (1898: 167–69).[1]

In the 1920s, elevated sightseeing buses, gaudily decorated with Japanese lanterns and huge signs that announced, "El [Elevated] to See Chinatown" waited periodically on Broadway offering one-dollar tours. These tourist rubberneckers were taken to see the Joss House and the Chinese temple, and told tales of tong murders, traps doors, gambling dens, and "slave girls." Another barker's harangue went: "Fer a dolla an'a ha'f ya ken see Chinatown. Ya don' hafta go to da Josh House—dot's feefty cents ex-trah. Ve'll show ya everytingg voit seeingg" (Leong 1936: 20). Also during this era, waxwork exhibitions of "Underground Chinatown" that depicted the social evils of the Chinese quarter were displayed in Coney Island and other New York City locations (Chen 1941).

At the height of World War II, journalist and author Karl Glick published two books of "writer's diplomacy" that attempted to improve on the negative popular image of Chinatown among the American public. He purported to get behind the lurid sensationalism to uncover the real life of Chinese Americans. In *Shake Hands with the Dragon,* he wrote:

> There are two Chinatowns: one seen from the outside by the tourists and sightseers, the other unseen, the Chinatown that exists behind closed doors and shuttered windows. . . . And the guides, knowing their business, do all they can to help along this fiction, and gather their timid sheep about them, whisper in subdued tones about the murders that have taken place on this corner or in that building. They tell strange tales of mysterious poisonings and sagas of Oriental cruelty and mayhem, and implant in their

> hearers' minds legends of Chinese cunning and revenge. No won-
> der the old lady from Omaha and the young bridal couple from
> Kalamazoo quaver in their boots, cling closer to each other, wind
> their way through the streets in terror, and return home to add a
> detail or two to the stories, spreading the impression. (1941: 81–82)

His attempt is well intentioned, but his perspective is still limited as most of his informants were law enforcement officials. In *Three Times I Bow,* he extended the theme of Chinese and American military goodwill through the introduction of a community insider, Private Kung, a Chinese American who enlists to fight in World War II.

The Cinematic Chinatown

Hollywood has the power to define difference, to reinforce
boundaries, to reproduce an ideology which maintains a certain
status quo.

Gina Marchetti, "Ethnicity, the Cinema, and Cultural Studies"

The earliest cinematic images of Chinese on American screens were decidedly unfavorable. Images of debased and laughable laundrymen were common in the first motion picture shorts, such as *Fun in a Chinese Laundry* (1894), released by the Biograph Company. The "Yellowman" image was commonplace, usually portrayed by white actors who wore Chinese shirts, baggy pants, and Qing-era queue hairpieces. Bumbling and prone to opium addiction, these characters were staged as pagans unable to accept Christianity and Western morality. These films served an ideological aim during the era of Chinese immigrant exclusion; emblematic of this purpose was the 1908 film *Yellow Peril.* Other visual cues such as smoky interiors and figures in the shadows with long fingernails and raised daggers between shaking curtains were employed to convey an image of the mysteries of Chinatown. Chinatown acquired a forbidding quality suffused with overlapping images of white slavery, kidnapping, opium trade, and heathen rites. Tong wars between rival Chinese American criminal syndicates became popular themes in the 1910s and 1920s. These representations evoked fears of a threat to Western civilization, fears that were stirred by distorted associations with the anti-imperialist Boxer Rebellion and Nationalist revolution in China, as well as the chaotic civic unrest propelled by rival warlords in the waning years of the Qing dynasty. These fears reached an iconic height with the emergence of the insidious Doctor Fu Manchu persona.

The Terror of Doctor Fu Manchu

A creation of the British adventure story writer Sax Rohmer in 1913, the persona of Doctor Fu Manchu was based upon a learned mandarin of some scientific inclinations from Kiangsu, China, who became a diabolical madman as a result of the inadvertent killing of his wife and child by a British officer during the Boxer Rebellion. Rohmer's Fu Manchu was characterized as tall, gaunt, feline, and high-shouldered with a brow like Shakespeare, a face like Satan, a closely shaven skull, and cat-green eyes. In some film posters, Fu Manchu's shadow, with clawlike outstretched hands, towered over a cowering white hero and heroine (Jones 1955). The lead role alternately starred Warner Oland and Boris Karloff in successive renditions between 1929 and 1932. Rohmer's novels originally located Doctor Fu Manchu in London's Chinatown, in the Limehouse district of the working-class East End, but the persona enjoyed great popularity when transferred to the American context. Partly because of the popularity of a style of goatee associated with the mysterious antagonist, the Fu Manchu persona remains a part of the American cultural imagination (Figure 22).

The evil Fu Manchu character was ostensibly a representation of Western notions of the global threat posed by the Yellow Peril of educated but vicious Chinese warlords in the interwar period following the collapse of the Manchu (Qing) dynasty. In a historical period when the British were experiencing the decline of their empire, the satanic Fu Manchu persona can be psychoanalytically interpreted as a Freudian projection of a Western ambition to reimpose its colonialist domination of the non-Western world (Weinstein 1984). Rohmer's novels depict detectives of Britain's Scotland Yard confronting this "evil force from the East" who led an international outlaw organization of non-white peoples, the "Si-Fan and the Council of Seven," in their quest to overthrow and dominate the West through conspiratorial means. Fu Manchu's weapons included seduction by voluptuous dark-skinned women and death through nefarious means such as poisoning. His office was underneath an opium den in the Limehouse district, a docking area for British empire ships and a vice district of deviant activity and racial mixing. The Fu Manchu films have been periodically remade in the modern era. In *The Castle of Fu Manchu* (1968), the despotic tyrant establishes himself in a citadel in Anatolia, the Asian half of Turkey, plotting to take over the world with a chemical that will freeze the world's oceans (Moy 1993).

In the 1930s came urban gangster films featuring Italian (*Little Caesar*, 1931; *Scarface*, 1932), Irish (*Public Enemy*, 1931; *Angels with Dirty Faces*,

Figure 22. Fu Manchu movie poster. Used by permission of Jan Lin.

1938) and Chinese (*Chinatown Nights*, 1930; *The Hatchet Man*, 1932) immigrant criminals. Partially in response to the antiracist Hayes Code adopted by Hollywood, the depression-era realism of these films set the violent misdeeds of these characters within a background of impoverished upbringing and the desperate social conditions of their communities, making them more complex and sympathetic icons than the earlier portrayals (Cortes 1993: 61). Geopolitical shifts also began to advance the emergence of more-sympathetic Asian personas.

Master Sleuth Charlie Chan

Charlie Chan, the unflappable "master sleuth," was one of the more favorable Chinese celluloid icons in American popular culture. This persona emerged during the depression years at around the same time as Fu Manchu but had a more durable impression on the American screen, appearing in forty-eight feature films between 1926 and 1950, more than any other motion picture detective character. Charlie Chan has also appeared in books, magazines, theater, radio, television, and comic strips. As the solver of crimes and mysteries rather than the evil perpetrator, Charlie Chan was a much more sympathetic role than Fu Manchu, reflecting Hollywood's attempt to refashion the American image of the Chinese during the years of diplomatic goodwill and the wartime alliance between the two nations against expansionist Japan. These associations were most cogently joined in *Charlie Chan in the Secret Service* (1944), which involved the detective directly in the war effort. It is no coincidence that the last Charlie Chan film was released in 1949, the year of the Chinese Communist revolution.

Detective Chan was the creation of the author Earl Derr Biggers. A midwesterner who grew tired of an early journalistic career, Biggers decided to become a freelance writer, and achieved notoriety with his first Charlie Chan novel, *The House without a Key*, in 1925 (also the first Charlie Chan film, released in 1926). He wrote five more Chan novels before his death in 1933. All the Chan novels were serialized in the *Saturday Evening Post* before being published as books. The character was purportedly based on a Chinese American detective from Honolulu, Hawaii, Chang Apana, whom Biggers had read about while vacationing there. The first ten Chan films featured George Kuwa, a Japanese actor. Warner Oland, a Swedish actor who had earned a reputation depicting Chinese villains in silent serials opposite Pearl White, including Fu Manchu, took over the lead in 1931. The role was passed to Sidney Toler upon Oland's death in 1938 (Figure 23).

A wise, enigmatic, polite, mild-mannered, gracious, and witty figure, the Chan persona had an endless capacity for calling past wisdom to pre-

Figure 23. Charlie Chan movie poster. Used by permission of Museum of Chinese in the Americas.

sent situations, spouting aphorisms like "Theory, like mist on eyeglasses, obscures fact," or "Truth, like oil, will in time rise to surface." Other gems of wisdom included "Chop suey is its own reward!" and "Bad alibi like dead fish—cannot stand test of time." A taciturn figure, Detective Chan was prone to materialize on screen suddenly and noiselessly. He observed crucial events unknown to people involved, his partially hidden face framed in some small round window (Jones 1955). Viewers in China approvingly perceived Chan to be a tribute to the intellect, wisdom, and antiquity of China, while some Chinese Americans viewed the Chan persona as a negative caricature or even a racist insult (Cortes 1993). As Elaine Kim has noted, these critics saw Chan as a "pudgy detective with half-closed, beady eyes held up with scotch tape, wearing baggy pants, and speaking fortune-cookie English" (1986: 107). Others saw the detective as "bovine," the butt of many jokes about his sexuality throughout the series. In the 1970s and 1980s, many Chinese Americans opposed the reintroduction of Charlie Chan in a television serial.

Roman Polanski's *Chinatown* as Representational Cipher

Roman Polanski's classic film noir, *Chinatown* (1974), based on a screenplay by Robert Towne, is ostensibly not even a film about Chinatown. Jack Nicholson is featured in the role of Jake Gittes, a hard-boiled detective who uncovers tragic crimes of familial murder and incest amidst the broader machinations of shady water politics and land speculation in prewar Southern California. Chinatown, however, is insinuated throughout the course of the unfolding whodunit as a mysterious and impenetrable backdrop, a malevolent referent that signifies the duplicity and evil in the emerging modernist wasteland of 1939 Los Angeles. At one point in the film, Noah Cross, the incest-committing, power-broker father warns Gittes regarding his daughter, "You may think you know what you're dealing with but you don't," to which Gittes replies, "That's what the D.A. used to tell me when I worked in Chinatown." Cross's daughter, Evelyn Mulwray (framed by her father for the murder of her husband), is thus associated with Chinatown. Portrayed by Faye Dunaway, Mulwray is effectively Orientalized with arched eyebrows, monochromatic makeup, and full-frontal lighting to flatten her face. Paradoxical allusions to Chinatown are made throughout the film, which finally appears in the last scene as the site of Mulwray's accidental shooting by a policeman.

Although Gittes has discovered the truth about the crimes of Cross in committing incest, murder, and unethical real estate schemes, the detective is finally rendered speechless and powerless to expose him. At the end of the film, Gittes mumbles the phrase "as little as possible," words that refer back to his earlier comment that the D.A. told cops working in Chinatown to "do as little as possible." At the end of the film, Gittes's partner pulls him away from the scene of Mulwray's shooting, advising, "Forget it, Jake. It's Chinatown" (Belton 1991: 948). Chinatown is thus projected as representational proxy for the irrational and the incomprehensible in human nature and the moral decay in the heart of Los Angeles. In the abstract, Chinatown is the scene of unspeakable Oedipal crimes and corruption that undermines justice and eludes law and order.

Furthermore, Asian characters in the film are marginalized, playing stereotypical roles as servants to the upper classes (butler, maid, gardener). These servants eventually attempt to hide Mulwray and her daughter from the clutches of Cross. In the end, however, Chinese bystanders are passive spectators to her killing. Gittes also recounts a racist and sexist "Chinaman" joke to his detective partners with great relish, which plays upon the stereotype of Chinese men as abnormal sexual beings of great inventiveness and endurance. The joke derides Asian men as a sexual threat, while scorning white women for supposedly accepting their depraved advances (Man 1994: 58).

Michael Cimino's *Year of the Dragon*

A new sensationalism has emerged since the 1970s in Hollywood that has revived themes of ethnic involvement in urban gangsterism in milieus of greater violence and brutality than the films of the 1930s. Films have featured Italians (The *Godfather* films, *Goodfellas, The Untouchables, Wise Guys*), Latinos (*Scarface, Code of Silence, License to Kill*), and Asians (*Year of the Dragon, Big Trouble in Little China*) (Cortes 1993: 68–69). *The Year of the Dragon* is a particularly appropriate film to consider because it is set in New York's Chinatown. The screenplay was based on a novel of the same title by Robert Daley, an ex–deputy police commissioner of New York City. The villain of Daley's novel is Mr. Koy, a former Hong Kong police officer who turns to a life of crime organizing youth gangs in New York City's Chinatown, parlaying his former Triad connections into smuggling heroin from Southeast Asia. Mr. Koy seems to be patterned after a real-life character, Eddie Chan, a former Hong Kong police sergeant who moved to New York and rose to a prominent position in the On Leong tong (Kwong 1987). In the novel, an Irish vice squad detective is pitted against this antagonist in a literary parable of good versus evil.

In the film version, Mickey Rourke plays Stanley White, a tough police detective less cynical than Jack Nicholson's Jake Gittes, who charges himself with cleaning up crime and corruption in Chinatown where other cops have turned a blind eye. The screenwriters attempted to make White a more sympathetic character. A Polish American ethnic himself, White professes an interest in learning about Chinese Americans by reading books on the immigrant exclusion experience. White's chief adversary is Joey Tai (played by John Lone), a rising gangster in the Chinatown underworld who is trying to move elder members of the hierarchy into international drug smuggling. White is aided in his endeavors by two "good Asians," the Chinatown beat reporter Tracy Tzu (played by the model Ariane), and Herbert Kuang, a vice squad rookie. Introduced as a brassy and independent career woman who is wary of the occasionally violent detective White, Tzu is reduced by the end of the film to a passive "China doll" who romantically submits to White as somewhat of a reward for his successful feat of domination over the Chinatown threat. Kuang similarly starts out as a guarded figure who at first accuses White of racism: "You make us all die for you. I'm not going to kill myself for you, Captain White. No more 'Chinaman Joe.' Those days are over." Kuang later relents, agreeing to risk his life to gain critical undercover information, which he delivers while bleeding fatally in White's arms, allowing White to complete his mission (Marchetti 1991).

Protests of Orientalist Cinema

The Chinese have not been quiescent in the face of Hollywood's Orientalist depictions of Chinatown and the Chinese. The Fu Manchu films brought protests from the Chinese embassy in America. On July 18, 1932, a virtual riot broke out in New York's Chinatown after detectives of the narcotics squad staged a mock raid on an "opium den" at 4 Doyers Street as one of a series of Fox Movietone shorts on police adventures. The top floor, which offered proper lighting, was chosen for the filming, which had attracted a curious crowd of Chinese numbering in the hundreds. African American performers dressed in Chinese costumes were ceremoniously hauled out of the tenement to a waiting patrol wagon for the camera, and actor detectives displayed a fine collection of opium pipes (furnished by the local police station as supposed evidence). The angry crowd pelted the film team and accompanying police with vegetables and knocked over cameras. The incident reached diplomatic proportions as a Nanjing representative and local Chinese leaders protested the event (Chen 1941).

The filming of Michael Cimino's *Year of the Dragon* also incited Chinese American anger, expressed when community leaders protested to City of New York officials about the use of Chinatown restaurants for the staging of bloody shoot-outs. Unfazed, the film's producers shifted their operations to stage sets in North Carolina and shot some scenes in the Chinatown located in Vancouver, British Columbia. The completed film was released on August 15, 1985, in New York City to the scene of vociferous demonstrations at Times Square theaters. By week's end, hundreds of demonstrators were gathering at theaters in New York and other major American cities protesting the film's negative portrayals of Chinese Americans and Chinatown. Even Robert Daley, whose novel the film is based upon, endorsed the protests. After two weeks, MGM-UA, the film's distributor, issued a disclaimer to be shown before film screenings: "This film does not intend to demean or ignore the many achievements of Asian Americans and in particular, the Chinese Americans."

Representational Rehabilitation by Chinese Americans

Along with opposing Hollywood's filmic images of Chinatown, Chinese Americans have been actively engaged in creative efforts to rehabilitate these mainstream depictions with an authentic representational alternative. Chinese American writers and artists, however, have felt the restrictions of a preexisting Orientalized canon, in which the words and actions they deploy have a "double valence, its meaning already partially predetermined by the dominant culture" (Wong 1994). As Maxine Hong Kingston has written in *Woman Warrior*, "Chinese-Americans, when you try to understand what things in you are Chinese, how do you separate what is peculiar to childhood, to poverty, insanities, one family, your mother who marked your growing with stories, from what is Chinese? What is Chinese tradition and what is the movies?" An effective means of overcoming this barrier is to "fool the demon" and satirize the canon itself, a strategy employed by the filmmaker Wayne Wang.

Wayne Wang's *Chan Is Missing*

Released in 1981, Wayne Wang's *Chan Is Missing* drew critical acclaim the following year (initiated by critic Vincent Canby of the *New York Times*), and is usually cited as the seminal film that blazed the trail for the subsequent emergence of an "Asian American cinema."[2] Filmed in black and white on a shoestring budget of $22,000, the motion picture has been variously described as a gumshoe thriller, film noir, experimental film, and avant-garde cinema with traces of Italian neorealism or Luis Buñuel of the French New Wave. The film deconstructs many filmic and popular cultural stereotypes of Chinese Americans and Chinatown through a parody of the traditional detective story. The story follows two cabdrivers in a circuitous search through Chinatown to find their associate Chan Hung, who has disappeared, owing them $4,000. Middle-aged Jo and his street-jiving, Eddie Murphy–like nephew, Steve, are surrogates for Charlie Chan and Number One Son,[3] in a whodunit that is just as much a "whoisit" (Denzin 1995), as the mystery of Hung's disappearance becomes entwined with contradictions regarding his identity. A series of characters who are questioned about Hung can provide few clues on his whereabouts but proffer plenty of conflicting opinions on his identity.

Chinatown is peopled with an eclectic collection of Chinese American characters, including Chinese "soul brothers," a Chinese cook wearing a "Samurai Night Fever" T-shirt singing "Fry Me to the Moon," street-smart Americanized youngsters, "fresh-off-the-boat" new immigrants, old men and women who look like mainland peasants, young professional Chinese American women in business dress, young Asian men with "GQ looks" and "Loy Fong" girlfriends, and a polarized political spectrum of Chinese who are either pro-Taiwan and assimilationist, or pro–People's Republic of China and anti-American (Denzin 1992). Hung's daughter eventually returns the money, but Hung is never found, confounding the expectations of viewers operating under traditional assumptions that Charlie Chan always solves the mystery. Jo, who is the film's main narrator, is perplexed to the point of questioning his own identity as he comments, "I guess I'm not Chinese enough. I can't accept a mystery without a solution." The various clues suggesting Hung's presence fade into nothingness, like the disappearing Cheshire cat leaving only its grin. Critic William Galperin observes,

> Our release is the realization, conveyed in the disappearance, that presence is in no way authenticated by representation, that representation as we are accustomed to it is inured to us not reality. The helplessness we experience with Chan's departure is an unwillingness more properly to accept helplessness—to accept nothingness as a condition of being, and to accept indeterminacy as something more (and less) than mere absence. (1987: 1165)

Out of this disquiet emerges the film's main point, that Chinatown and Chinese American identity have a kaleidoscopic complexity that cannot be defined by outsider categories or even by those imposed by Chinese Americans themselves. The Chinese American is everyman, and Chinatown is everyplace.

Eat a Bowl of Tea

In 1989, Wayne Wang released a film set entirely in New York's Chinatown, the screenplay adapted from a novel published by Louis Chu in 1961. Unencumbered by outsider tropes and stereotypes, this story has no criminal gangs or crusading police detectives. *Eat a Bowl of Tea* is such a faithful account of real-life bachelor society in postwar New York's Chinatown, in fact, that it exposes all the idiosyncratic profanities of its masculinist inhabitants, the grim dinginess of their apartments, and the hypocrisy of their sexism and patriarchy. An arranged marriage bride, Mei Oi, is brought from China for second-generation bachelor Ben Loy, just returned from wartime service. He becomes sexually impotent under the pressures of his restaurant supervisor job and the stifling expectations of his father, Wang Wah Gay, and other patriarchal Chinatown elders. Playboy immigrant Ah Song pressures Mei Oi into sex, and she bears an illegitimate child. The elders are furious with the scandal, and the couple finally flees to San Francisco, where Loy regains his sexual virility. Sexual impotence is finally overcome by breaking with the authority and ethnocentric traditions of the community patriarchs.

The action is set in the period when New York's Chinatown was beginning its transition from a clannish, insular bachelor society to a family-centered community. The novel and film expose the double standards of the bachelor elders, who flaunt their own loose morality in gambling and visits to American prostitutes but demand purity and fidelity from their wives and the second generation as compensation for their failure as husbands. The elders offer no guidance, and characters such as Ah Song are self-serving and predatory. Weak substitutes for families, the clan associations are more concerned with gossip, decorum, and reputations than giving support to their members.

The Wedding Banquet

Ang Lee's *The Wedding Banquet* (1993), set in contemporary New York City, again conjoins issues of generational conflict with Chinese American sexuality. Yuppie Chinese American property manager Wai-tung conceals his homosexuality from his Taiwanese parents while cohabitating with a Western male partner who is a physical therapist and speaks respectable Chinese. His parents, who still reside in Taiwan, are continually trying to arrange a marriage with a Chinese bride. An opportunity to satisfy his parents is presented when Wei-wei, a woman artist from China and an undocumented alien (a tenant in one of his buildings) seeks marriage for immigration status. A lavish banquet eventually results when his parents travel from Taiwan to New York for the wedding. The wedding is a riotous, exaggerated caricature, a queer amalgamation of traditional Chinese and Western rituals. Wai-tung finally reveals his homosexuality to his parents, who resolve their feelings to an amiable conclusion. Apart from providing a sensitive treatment of alternative sexuality in a Chinese American setting usually known for its traditionalism, *The Wedding Banquet* also highlights differences of class and national origin within the contemporary Chinese American community.

New Cultural Projects in New York's Chinatown

A critical barrier to the efforts of new Chinese American filmmakers is exposure. In New York's Chinatown, the Asian American International Film Festival, held annually since 1978, has given independent filmmakers a chance to gain public attention. The festival is organized by Asian Cine-Vision, a nonprofit video arts center that began as a community cable training organization in 1976. The film festival emerged as a way of both exhibiting contemporary works by Asian American filmmakers and giving shape to emerging themes in the genre. The festival was eventually expanded to include Asian film.

Another new community cultural project is the Chinatown History Project, which was founded in 1980 by John Kuo Wei Tchen and Charles Lai with a focus on salvaging community artifacts (including old storefronts, signs, furniture, photographs, letters, family memorabilia, and other objects of historical value). While traditional museums collect items considered attractive or valuable, the Chinatown History Project sought to collect objects with a "vernacular" focus that were seen as valuable for the history and human stories they represented. Exhibits such as "Salvaging New York Chinatown" recreated the apartment interiors of immigrants from the bachelor society era. Audio/video documentation accompanies museum displays. One of the Chinatown History Project's first major initiatives was "Eight Pound Livelihood," a tribute to the toils of the forgotten Chinese laundry workers of the United States. Oral history interviews with more than one hundred laundrymen were conducted and eventually incorporated into a documentary made for public television, which recounted their lives of quiet struggle and contribution to American life. In the film, Chinatown History Project staffperson and folksinger William (Charlie) Chin sings:

> Eight pound iron, twelve hour day,
> Seven day week, just to make it pay,
> Sort and wash, press and fold,
> Bitter rice on a mountain of gold.

John Tchen recounts how reclaiming of the Chinatown past sometimes involved a process of overcoming deep-seated feelings of community denial and misinformation:

> There was this legend of the clothing store. Some people in southern China with relatives abroad even today believe that the laundry workers actually work in a clothing store. It's a folk myth. The retired laundrymen went back to China and perpetuated the myth,

> because they were too prideful to admit that . . . they washed other
> people's dirty clothes. Now the old bachelor society is literally
> dying away. We hear of seniors who die alone in their apartments,
> and the police have their belongings because there aren't any rela-
> tives. The impression of many, especially the younger ones, is that
> the bachelors are curiosities. One woman I know grew up believing
> they were all dirty old men. (MacFadyen 1983: 74)

History project staff discovered, however, that community members responded positively to their efforts at documenting local history. Tchen re-
members their response to the first Chinatown exhibit, installed in a public
library:

> We had to be in the library while the exhibit was open, and we'd
> see seniors climbing three flights of stairs just to look at the exhib-
> it. Some of them brought little flashlights, to look more closely for
> pictures of mothers or sisters or friends. They'd stand there talking
> for hours. It started to generate a lot of excitement, and that's when
> I realized we could use more exhibits as an organizing tool to get
> more history. That really influenced how this Project was finally
> designed. (MacFadyen 1983: 76)

Among the subsequent projects undertaken was the exhibit "Both Sides of
the Cloth: Chinese American Women in the New York City Garment Industry," which featured oral histories of garment-worker women and the sewing of a communal quilt.

After renaming itself the Chinatown History Museum for a period, in
1995 the museum completely changed its name to the Museum of Chinese
in the Americas. This marked a conscious effort to emulate an emerging
tendency within Asian American historiography to supersede local community and nation-state boundaries while situating New York's Chinatown
as one of many sites throughout the American hemisphere where peoples
of the Chinese diaspora have settled. This new critical approach within
Asian American studies problematizes the use of geographic, cultural, and
gender boundaries in demarcating Asian American places, people, and
identities (Leong 1989; Lowe 1991; Cynthia Sau-Ling Wong 1995).

8

Community Change
in Global Context

Americans are increasingly sensitive to the forces of globalization on the economic livelihood and cultural fabric of their communities and cities. The acceleration of economic and cultural change is pervasive; few localities have not been affected to some degree. It may be observed, however, that globalization has been concentrated in particular "global cities" and other immigration gateway cities that have recently become principal nodes in the cross-border flow of immigrant labor, capital, and commodities.[1] These cities have acquired a multiracial demography and urban ecology that provoke contrasting sentiments of disquiet or approbation in a range of interrelated public discourses and social policy arenas. Public trepidation is evident in public debates over immigration policy, the sweatshop phenomenon, and the issue of foreign investment. Public approval is apparent in public discourses that relate a cultural project of multiculturalism with strategies of urban boosterism and economic globalization.

This book has revealed a community undergoing dramatic economic restructuring, social change, and spatial reconstruction. By situating my analysis of Chinatown community change in regional and global context, I have also sought to clarify the meaning and dynamics of globalization as a macrolevel process by considering its manifold effects within a micro-area of an acknowledged global city, the metropolis of New York City. This project of conceptual clarification seems quite apropos at a time of increasing "globe talk" (King 1995), wherein even firm proponents of global discourse are concerned that the concept of globalization has become increasingly reified, at some risk of becoming a nebulous kind of "global babble" (Abu-Lughod 1991).[2] The need for elucidation is not just academic; the politically charged nature of current public discourses over immigration, foreign investment, trade policy, and urban social policy underscores the need for definitive research that uncovers the subtle nuances and multifarious ramifications of global impacts on American cities and localities.

Bringing the Local Back In

This case study of the process of community change in global context is intended as a contribution to this broader project of conceptual clarification. Particularism is not the aim of this "community study." The manifold complexities of economic and cultural change in Chinatown have been related to broader historical, political, and global forces. I have emphasized how local actors such as municipal government and parastatal organizations are closely implicated in influencing the pace and direction of globalization via policies such as the deregulation of foreign banking, the boosting of foreign investment and world trade functions, and the cultural construction of an "image" of the global city that encourages tourism and investment.

These moves on the part of the local government have elicited varying responses from the residents and workers of the Chinatown community. Foreign investment of the sort that restructures the regional economy and obstructs the capacity of the built environment to support local commerce and industry has been opposed. Local government's moves toward facilitating world trade functions such as tourism drew a popular reception in the community, insofar as these state policies supported the activities of petty entrepreneurs and traders. Local zoning policies and business incubator projects supporting the status of the local garment industry have similarly received general approval from Chinatown garment shop owners and workers. These moves have coupled a sort of developmental protectionism in the land market with a municipal industrial policy that proactively assists local capitalists to flexibly innovate in response to international competition.

Organized labor, similarly, has begun to respond to the vagaries of capital flight by incorporating "global factory" issues into their campaigns. Not merely reviving old organizational localisms, the militant proletariat of Chinatown's sweatshops and tenements are asserting collective solidarities in global context, to wit, "thinking globally while acting locally." Tentative steps toward the actual building of cross-national action have been made by the Union of Needletrades, Industrial, and Textile Employees (UNITE!). In the summer of 1995, UNITE! organized a tour of teenage Central American sweatshop workers in the United States; they gave testimony at union conventions and familiarized the American public with global factory issues through education sessions at union halls and community centers. As UNITE! continues to become increasingly multiracial with the organizing of Latin American, Caribbean, and Asian immigrant textile workers, globalization issues continue to come to the fore.

My focus on local actors affirms Saskia Sassen's recent contention that globalization needs to be thought of as a series of processes that are constituted by people as much as capital (1996b: 188). Discussing the representational implications of such a conceptual project, Sassen also asserts that a focus on the women, immigrants, and peoples of color that comprise the labor force and residential communities of the central city needs to be privileged as an attention to the restructuring dynamics of global capital: "to re-narrate what is now eviction . . . to valorize what has been evicted from the center" (1996b: 183). Finally, she suggests that global cities constitute "analytic borderlands" through which we can uncover instructive narratives on the contours of economic and cultural change in the contemporary world (1996b: 185).

Sweatshop Workers as Agents of Change

The appearance of Chinese immigrant sweatshops may worry some observers who feel they are an indication of American decline, that the United States is looking more and more like a third-world nation. They may also worry that sweatshops are a revival of a phenomenon from an earlier era in our economic history when the huddled masses labored in the shadow of large monopolies and trusts led by capitalist robber barons. Both of these portrayals are somewhat accurate, but their implications can be interpreted differently. Rather than implying that the United States has regressed or degenerated, these comparisons can be read as an indication that the evolving postindustrial future is one of heightened socioeconomic inequality. Thus, advanced capitalism begins to take on some of the features of emerging industrial capitalism, in a new international division of labor in which transnational corporations outsource with a variable geography of manufacturing subcontractors and situate their finance and headquarters offices in a shifting network of sites across both developing and developed nations of the global economy.

In American central cities that earlier experienced the loss of manufacturing activity to lower-wage, lower-tax U.S. Sunbelt states or locations in the third world, the reappearance of the immigrant sweatshop economy has recovered some industrial employment and put a declining loft-manufacturing infrastructure to new use. The business revenue and worker income generated from this industrial activity have been multiplied through the many linkages of the ethnic enclave economy and have augmented the general level of petty retail and service-sector activity throughout the metropolis. Sweatshops and immigrant enclave economies thus provide a net addition of jobs and revenue to metropolitan economies. Rather than displacing U.S. workers, immigrants generally take those low-waged jobs that established residents find socially undesirable or economically unrewarding (such as restaurant and garment work).

By helping to revive the New York City garment industry, Chinese sweatshop workers have boosted rather than hurt the cause of the American worker. Organized labor has been strengthened in an era of long-term industrial decline. The Chinese garment worker rank and file significantly augmented the membership of the International Ladies' Garment Workers' Union (ILGWU). Furthermore, Chinese labor organizers, shop stewards, and business agents have advanced the interests of the labor movement and promoted public awareness through the visibility of their collective action. The Chinese participation also contributed to a unique experiment in state-labor-management cooperation in garment industry planning through the creation of the Garment Industry Development Corporation and projects such as the Metropolitan Fashion Center in Brooklyn.

The workplace militancy displayed by Chinese garment and restaurant workers may be unnerving for some American observers no longer accustomed to such vociferous protests. These proletarian agitations may be seen as indecorous and a disruption of the pace of life in the milieu of the postindustrial city. Through efforts such as the Chinese Staff and Workers' Association (CSWA) Campaign for Economic Survival, however, organizers have sought to expose the reality of "slave labor conditions" in the Chinatown restaurant industry, while destroying the myth of Chinese workers as servile and accepting of these conditions. Rancorous sidewalk pickets and protests were a public pitch for workers' rights and civil rights of political process in the face of paternalistic and abject working conditions. Although labor-organizing efforts in the restaurant industry have not been as successful as garment industry campaigns, they have raised sufficient public attention to induce New York State labor department officials to increase their investigative and regulatory efforts.

In the densely settled enclave of Chinatown, workplace struggles are fought primarily in the context of the community rather than the shop floor. In the historic 1982 ILGWU-sponsored demonstration, garment workers marched through the streets of Chinatown and finally assembled in Columbus Park, sending the message to sweatshop owners that there was community-wide solidarity among workers for a union-endorsed contract. The restaurant industry pickets and demonstrations backed by the CSWA were similarly held in the public space of the street directly in front of the restaurants to draw the attention of the community, the media, and the general public to infringements of labor law. Sympathizers from other community organizations and students joined in the cause. Furthermore, the CSWA, rather than being a single-industry workers' association, is strongly situated in the grass roots of the community. Workplace issues for the CSWA are conceptualized as community-wide issues, and their organizing strategies follow this analytical logic.

Community-based organizing strategies have also been pursued by the ILGWU and the CSWA in the Brooklyn sweatshops, which are more clandestine and less cooperative with organized labor than the Chinatown garment shops. Ties of kinship and ethnic social relations obligate and bind workers to the demands of bosses in the paternalistic working environment of the garment sweatshop. To overcome this status quo in the workplace, labor organizers have built ties of ethnic solidarity in the community. Community-based organizations that integrate workers, community activists, and students in projects of education and labor organizing are common in other Asian American communities throughout the United States, such as the Chinese Progressive Association (CPA) Workers Center in Boston, the Asian Immigrant Women Advocates (AIWA) in Oakland, and the Korean Immigrant Worker Advocates (KIWA) in Los Angeles. AIWA, founded in 1983, works with a diverse array of workers including Chinese garment workers, Vietnamese garment and electronics workers, and Korean hotel maids and electronics assemblers. A 1992 campaign supporting garment workers' attempts to recover back pay owed by an insolvent Chinese contractor reached national proportions when AIWA organizers decided to expose the manufacturer Jessica McClintock for subcontracting with the recalcitrant sweatshop. Pickets and demonstrations were held directly in front of Jessica McClintock boutiques in ten cities. The CPA Workers Center in Boston grew out of an eighteen-month campaign for worker retraining and job replacement following a garment factory closure that laid off 350 Chinese immigrant workers. KIWA was an outgrowth of a 1991 campaign to retain union jobs when the Los Angeles Wilshire Hyatt was acquired by Koreana, a South Korean corporation. KIWA worked closely with a multiethnic coalition of Asian, Latino, and African American workers (Omatsu 1994). Labor-community coalitions are an emerging strategy in many industry sectors throughout the United States (Brecher and Costello 1990).

Group Solidarity and Representational Change

Social change is something that occurs not just in the realm of politics and the economy but also in the intersecting arenas of culture and identity. The wages and health benefits of Chinese women sweatshop workers are a vital contribution to the purchasing power of the immigrant household economy, raising the relative power and authority of the woman as breadwinner and decision maker in Chinatown families. This is an important shift in a community that just three decades ago was still a highly patriarchal bachelor society of immigrant men. The sight of an immigrant Chinese woman on the subway in New York City is to some degree associated with the occupational category "garment worker." This is a stereotype, certainly, but does present a picture of industriousness that supplants earlier images of Chinese women in American popular culture as either subservient, unseen wives, or exoticized sexual objects.

The role of garment sweatshop worker, importantly, would not be a very empowering position in the broader political economy if not for their growing industrial militancy. Sweatshop employment, as we have discussed, is arduous, exploitative work. Since social ties of ethnicity, kinship, and paternalism pervade worker-boss relations in garment sweatshops, workers are usually reluctant to complain about their conditions. Sweatshop owners are prone to suddenly closing factories when threatened by worker organizing campaigns, further hampering unionization. Thus, workers in the sweatshops of both Chinatown and Sunset Park, Brooklyn, have collectively demonstrated in the public space of the community rather than the workplace. Political action has transformed their lives as well as their self-identities. Worker solidarity and identity formation have taken place in the context of community space.

Collective action in workplace struggles for union recognition and improvement of work conditions has thus not only given Chinese sweatshop workers a sense of their own group solidarity and political empowerment but also visibly changed public stereotypes of Chinese American immigrants as servile workers in the debased environment of Chinatown. Chinese women garment workers are at the forefront of this representational revisioning of public images of Chinese Americans and Chinatown. The stereotypes of subservient sweatshop workers and criminal tong hatchetmen recede with the emergence of images of assertive workers, especially women sweatshop workers, in the streets of Chinatown. As figures such as Virginia Kee and Margaret Chin (who both started their careers as educators) have emerged as major political leaders in Chinatown politics, it has become apparent that women are also at the forefront of electoral empowerment in the immigrant enclave.

If women seem to be highly visible in some arenas of Chinatown workplaces and electoral politics, men are certainly not invisible. I do not mean to suggest that labor and community politics in New York's Chinatown are sex segregated. Chinese men are concentrated in the restaurant industry in a fashion comparable to the concentration of women in the garment industry. The political visibility of Chinese immigrant men can be seen in campaigns for labor-law enforcement at the Silver Palace and Jing Fong restaurants. Cooperation among men and women, moreover, is central to the efforts of the many modern community organizations that serve Chinatown and to the many collective actions they have waged toward the improvement of Chinatown housing and social services in the face of the oftentimes invasive redevelopmental bulldozer and the security apparatus of the state.

The working people and residents of New York's Chinatown, thus, are pitted in a daily struggle for existence against the manipulations of capital and the incursions of the redevelopmental state. In establishing their rights as workers and defending the sanctity of their community against state intrusion, they have also been engaged in acts of resistance against conventional stereotypes of Chinatowns as an urban terrain and Chinese Americans as a racial/ethnic category. Through Hollywood films and prime-time detective serials, representations of Chinatown have inscribed it in the American popular imagination as a treacherous urban realm, an exotic criminal underworld that defies easy comprehension and penetration. Chinese Americans are commonly depicted as exploited victims or insolent crime bosses in postures of evasion when confronted by the interrogations of investigative police. Journalistic treatments of Chinatown similarly portray Chinese Americans as an abject labor force cruelly dominated by evasive sweatshop bosses and international smuggling rackets.

There is some truth to these representations in that they allude to the ruthless realities of the sweatshop economy. These cinematic and journalistic framings, however, tend to signify Chinatown through the procedures of investigative disclosure, implying that remedial correction is the responsibility of the state rather than the charge of the people of Chinatown themselves. In the social space of Chinatown, workplace and community politics ultimately converge with the arena of identity politics. Political-economic change is intertwined with cultural change. Chinatown is no secluded, stagnant enclave of powerless sweatshop workers and tenement residents but home and workplace to an assiduous and militant proletariat with a sharp sense of territorial unity, group identity, and community power.

Community Power and Electoral Politics

Urban sociologists traditionally viewed the ethnic community as something that revived ancestral, traditional, cultural, and kinship solidarities as adaptational mechanisms in the process of chain migration to a new country. I see community also as a mobilizing device, something that is emergent in the process of political-economic incorporation into a new society. New group solidarities configured around workplace allegiances and organizational memberships confer political influence and electoral power. The actors that staff and lead these new community-based organizations broker the acquisition and delivery of a range of resources for collective consumption such as employment and skills training, housing, health, education and other social services, and legal aid. These contemporary community-based agencies and social-change organizations constitute an important new political bloc that has challenged the hegemony of the paternalistic bosses and the traditional mercantile elite that dominated the enclave polity through a system of patronage.

Apart from this traditional versus contemporary schism in the Chinatown community power structure, there is considerable competition and factionalism among the contemporary associations. Conflict among the contemporary associations occurs because of differences of social-movement philosophy and tactics, mainly along lines of reformism versus militancy. Factionalism in the community power structure fades, however, in the face of the external threat of state encroachment. Broad unity in the community power structure has occurred in opposition to state incursions such as heavy police surveillance and state-directed slum clearance and redevelopment. Conflict is renewed, however, when the local government incorporates community actors into the policy and planning process. Factionalism among activist organizations in Chinatown civil society vis-à-vis the local government broadly parallels the split between "entrists" and nonreformists that Michael Omi and Howard Winant (1994) find within the broad landscape of American minority power movements in their civil rights disputations with the federal government.

The progress of Chinatown political actors in the terrain of New York City electoral politics has been somewhat weaker than their involvement in workplace and community-based collective action. This is in noticeable contrast to San Francisco and Los Angeles, where Chinese American candidates have made more significant inroads into local political offices. This difference is partly a reflection of historical timing. The Chinese American population on the West Coast is now into its third or fourth generation on American soil, whereas New York's Chinatown has only become a signifi- cant demographic presence since the 1960s. There are also more new middle-class immigrants on the West Coast, whereas New York City contin- ues to absorb a larger proportion of working- and lower-class arrivals. These differences of class background and the timing of immigrant arrival may explain why the denizens of New York City's Chinatown favor collective action to electoral politics.[3]

The Ongoing Influx of Asian Labor and Capital

As the twentieth century draws to a close, there are strong indications that Chinatown will continue to experience dramatic economic, social, and physical transition. Ongoing outward flows of East Asian labor and capital in the 1990s are propelled by a combination of hypereconomic growth, po- litical uncertainty, and social change in the Greater China region. The out- flow of capital has been somewhat reversed as robust growth in the region has stimulated Hong Kong and Taiwanese investment in the People's Re- public of China. Political apprehension continues to be a critical variable, however, particularly in the case of labor outflow. The discovery of streams of undocumented Chinese being carried by smuggling rings into New York City (Chan 1989, 1990; Strom 1991; Fritsch 1993) suggests that there is a ready supply of poor immigrants that will continue to augment New York Chinatown's sweatshop economy. Many of these immigrants emanate from Fujian, a coastal province of southern China and a historical source of mi- grants to the island of Taiwan and other points in Southeast Asia.

Steady economic growth has accompanied the gradual "opening up" of the People's Republic of China since the late 1970s. New modernization policies have promoted foreign investment, linked with a strong export- oriented industrialization program, particularly in coastal provinces. By the early 1990s, annual growth rates had reached phenomenal double-digit levels of 13 to 14 percent (a typical rate of economic growth is 4 percent). This superheated economic growth has been associated with unprecedent- ed social change in the People's Republic of China. The government has loosened strict household registration rules (which during the Communist era had closely tied the Chinese to particular towns and localities), resulting in greater internal migration. As the state-led socialist economy has become increasingly privatized and open to transnational capital, an unregulated informal sector has burgeoned, including arms smuggling, prostitution, and drug running. A growing trade is the smuggling of Chinese emigrants to locales such as the United States through Fujianese ports such as Fuzhou (see Map 1). Poor Chinese emigrants unable to find sufficient employment in the People's Republic of China have begun to look abroad for opportunity, but in some cases are fleeing a strict population control policy that limits families to one child. Violation of the one-child policy can mean fines or forced sterilization. These illegal immigrants may pay fees up to $30,000 (Tefft 1994).

As described at the end of chapter 1, one smuggling route to New York's Chinatown discovered in the late 1980s was through the Canadian border into Niagara Falls, New York. In the early 1990s, sea routes were discovered accompanied by some high-profile interdictions of smuggling ships by the U.S. Coast Guard off both the West and East Coasts. In 1993, the year that the *Golden Venture* ran aground off the borough of Queens in New York, there were some 3,000 Chinese caught attempting illegal entry into the United States. These illegal immigrants commonly seek political asylum, citing the oppressiveness of China's population policy. These appeals are reviewed on a case-by-case basis by the U.S. Immigration and Naturalization Service. Asylum has been most quickly granted to those appellants with direct political ties, such as to the student democracy movement. Meanwhile, many remain incarcerated in prisons and detention centers (Dunn 1994).

Political uncertainty in the Greater China region also motivates the outward flow of capital, which has accumulated considerably with robust regional economic growth. As discussed, Hong Kong outflow began to accelerate following the Joint Declaration of 1984, when Britain announced its intentions to return the island to Chinese sovereignty. The massacre of prodemocracy student demonstrators at Tiananmen Square in 1989 and the subsequent ascension of hard-liner factions in the regime at Beijing have spurred further capital flight. Despite these political apprehensions, Hong Kong capital is increasingly reinvested in China rather than overseas to capitalize on the buoyant growth taking place. Consortiums such as the New China Hongkong Group, a giant group of fifty-four firms and investors (including some of Hong Kong's wealthiest entrepreneurs), seek to integrate economic interests between the two nations prior to reunification. As discussed in chapter 3, this looking back to China as an investment locale was observed to be a growing trend by some businesspeople in New York's Chinatown in the early 1990s, and was regarded as a factor in the economic slowdown of the same period.

Regional political uncertainty continued to heighten in March 1995, as the People's Republic of China staged "war games" including missile tests and mock troop deployments in the Taiwan Strait in the weeks surrounding the first-ever democratic presidential elections on the island, which was ruled by martial law from 1949 to 1987. These moves were meant as a threat to the independence movement on Taiwan, which Beijing still regards as a renegade province that ostensibly could be recovered via a sea invasion. With the retrocession of Hong Kong to the People's Republic of China approaching in 1997, the Chinese government began to speak of Taiwan's inevitable political "reunification" with China. In view of the regional security threat, the United States dispatched two aircraft carriers to the vicinity until the threat had passed and the elections had taken place peacefully. These military exercises produced considerable political disquiet in Taiwan, disturbing bilateral trade links and population movement between the two countries, which have increased in recent years. Taiwanese capital, in fact, has been a major source of foreign investment in Fujian. This is not surprising since many Taiwanese trace their ancestral roots to this region of China.

The recent political instability in the region may disturb this trend toward economic integration and will likely stimulate increased capital flight to the United States. Apprehensive Taiwanese investors of this sort will have a stronger impact on the land market in the Flushing satellite Chinatown than on the core Chinatown of Manhattan. Other locales of Taiwanese activity in the United States, such as Monterey Park, California, are likely to experience growing streams of Taiwanese investment. The East Coast is also already beginning to experience the phenomenon of "parachute kids" (*liuxuesheng,* or "little foreign students"), who are the children of middle-class Asian children sent to U.S. schools, potentially to acquire U.S. permanent residency, while the parents periodically shuttle the transpacific distances on visits. The Chinese sometimes nickname these families *kong-zhong feiren,* or "trapeze artists," and *taikongren,* or "astronauts" (Cynthia Sau-Ling Wong 1995).

In the wake of the Taiwan Strait incidents of March 1995, Taiwanese interests began extending beyond the American economic arena into the realm of electoral politics. In the months leading up to the presidential election of 1996, the Taiwanese government courted Democratic National Committee (DNC) officials with lavish junkets to Taiwan in a successful effort to win language favorable to Taiwanese interests in the Democratic Party platform. The final platform did include language praising "the deployment of an American naval task force to the Taiwan Straits to ensure that China's military exercises did not imperil the security of the region" (Abramson 1996: A16). This effort coincided with moves by Taiwan-born

DNC vice-chairman John Huang to systematically raise campaign monies among the Asian American community, who were perceived to be wary and resentful of growing anti-immigrant sentiment in some ranks of the Republican Party. These coordinated fundraising efforts to "bundle" contributions from Asian Americans (who tended to make individual gifts of a private nature in the past) through highly visible public events emulated the strategy of the Jewish American lobby, which wields great clout through bundling.

Huang eventually came under fire when it came to light that he had illegally solicited campaign contributions from Asians who were not American citizens, including Taiwanese and a high-placed ethnic Chinese Indonesian business interest, the Riady family. In light of these charges, the DNC immediately fired Huang and returned the questionable contributions, as government investigations were launched to review the alleged improprieties. Asian Americans find themselves in an equivocal position in the burgeoning environment of fear and xenophobia over "Asian Money" that accompanies the media-heightened "Asiagate scandal." On one hand, they may be prone to raise the specter of Orientalist media racism and Asia-bashing by pointing out that European consortiums such as Airbus Industries influence U.S. trade policy (Sanger 1997), or that subsidiaries of British tobacco companies contributed generously to the campaign of Republican Bob Dole (Maynes 1996). On the other hand, Asian Americans may perceive that these overseas Asian interests have very little in common with local Asian American interests. As L. Ling-chi Wang, a professor at the University of California at Berkeley, has asserted, it is also possible to argue that overseas Asians use Asian American communities as a cover for advancing their own interests (Sterngold 1996). This case study of New York City's Chinatown has revealed that local industrial capital, small-business interests, local banks, and the low-income residential population have not been well served by the inflow of global capital into the Chinatown banking industry and land market.

The ongoing inflow of Chinese labor also challenges the denizens of New York City's Chinatown. The phenomenon of surreptitious inflows of undocumented aliens, orchestrated by criminal smuggling rackets, nourishes the revival of a public image of Chinatown as a shady and corrupt enclave permeated by underworld interests at a critical period when the agents of social change in the district seek political recognition and legitimacy. Some established residents of Chinatown have tried to disassociate themselves from new Fujianese immigrants. Others have sought to defend the human rights of the incarcerated and incorporate the new arrivals into the community. Their efforts to provide housing, job counseling, and social services to the Fujianese are complicated by dialect differences in the Chinese language, even as the work proceeds apace.

Global Capital, Tourism, and the State

In regard to the matter of urban policy, some implications for city managers may ultimately be drawn from this case study of New York's Chinatown. The city of New York's interest in stimulating overseas investment and redevelopment in Chinatown was guided essentially by an interest in raising land values and tax revenues after a period of severe fiscal crisis suffered in the mid-1970s. On the other hand, the passage of land-use regulations to protect the Chinatown garment production zone demonstrates that the urban and community planning policies of the local government must balance interests of revenue generation with job retention. This relative trade-off between revenues and jobs in New York City's Chinatown is instructive for local officials and urban policymakers to consider in light of current national concerns over foreign investment and immigration. Foreign investment in finance and real estate, though raising revenues and the market value of real property, may displace small businesses and established residents without necessarily creating new jobs.[4]

To return to the matter of comparisons with third-world cities, the city of New York's efforts at street revitalization and trader clearance in Chinatown parallel local government efforts to clear street traders in Jakarta and harbor hawkers in Hong Kong (Jellinek 1988; McGee 1985). In both third- and first-world cities, then, the local government tends to view the lower circuit as an unsanitary nuisance, creating street congestion and impeding the process of "modernization" in a situation where transnational investment is being encouraged.[5]

As observers of the informal sector in the developing world have pointed out, however, the lower circuit is actually an important milieu for the incubation of entrepreneurial values, the employment of otherwise itinerant rural-to-urban migrants, and the sustaining of community self-reliance. Capital-intensive development strategies relying on upper-circuit investment, by contrast, generally do not develop such labor-absorptive capacities, leaving idle labor in need of public assistance (McGee 1985; Santos 1979). When Chinatown small-business owners protested proposed pedestrian-only streets, the city had to relent, recognizing that street-level commerce had a certain desirable self-sustaining livelihood that could be retained while marketing the ethnic enclave for tourists.[6]

Rather than being cleared and redeveloped, ethnic enclaves can be preserved and rehabilitated, and even marketed by city managers for tourism in initiatives that couple neighborhood stabilization with state objectives of economic development. As urban tourism has become an emerging economic development and cultural policy strategy in many American cities, ethnic places have acquired a new historical and sentimental significance in urban civic life. Latino and Southwestern culture permeates the whole of San Antonio's central-city revitalization, anchored around its Riverwalk festival marketplace. Near-city Latino, Asian, and African American neighborhood interests have made proposals in Houston for schemes of redevelopment or community recovery incorporating festival marketplaces with recreational facilities, and promoting minority arts through public history preservation (Lin 1995b). Examples of other minority districts that have been revitalized and successfully marketed for urban tourism include New York City's Little Italy, San Francisco's Chinatown, Boston's Italian North End, and Seattle's International District.

In some locations, these central-city districts may only be vital economic enclaves or residential communities in a vestigial sense within the broader context of the assimilation of minority households and the formation of new ethnic enclaves in the suburbs. "Ethnicity" and "community" in the central city may thus be evoked as symbolic arenas of history, recollection, and sentiment by entrepreneurs marketing ethnic places as retail and entertainment zones in the postindustrial urban "growth machine" (Logan and Molotch 1987). As Sharon Zukin (1995) has observed, economic development in postindustrial cities increasingly revolves around an emerging "symbolic economy" in which culture and entertainment industries are leading sectors.

In New York's Chinatown, emerging schemes of urban tourism take place while the community is still very much an active economic and residential enclave incorporating an ongoing stream of immigrants from East Asia. Informal-sector street commerce is thus carefully monitored. As a "sanitary state," the city of New York continues to view street traders as a threat to public health and middle-class street decorum. Mike Davis (1992) and Don Parson (1993) have found similar state-directed undertakings to evict and marginalize immigrants, the homeless, and urban poor from central-city Los Angeles to make way for massive new redevelopment projects. The forces of the "security state" in both Los Angeles and New York are still guided by generalized fears of the urban minority poor. In both locations, an urban future is portended where the "legitimate uses" of public space are increasingly delimited, and the state continues to marginalize those it sees as antithetical to growth or "public order."

Figure 24. Chinatown postcard. Photo by Corky Lee. Copyright Corky Lee; used by permission of the photographer.

The Place of Chinatown in the Postindustrial City

There is thus a considerable irony that verges on contradiction when we juxtapose the picturesque image of the sanitized ethnic tourist village with the stark reality of the gritty, littered urban district that still functions as a vital residential and employment center for a low-income immigrant prole-tariat (Figure 24). The disjuncture is even more striking when we consider that ethnic place preservation, while a concession by city managers to community insurgency, also assists in projecting an image of a multiethnic investment environment conducive to transnational capital, especially where ethnic places are proximate to central business district locations (and thus subject to displacement) preferred by the finance and advanced cor-porate services complex. There is thus a feedback between cultural and economic globalization processes in the postindustrial city. Globalization should be conceptualized as a problematical phenomenon that produces considerable risks in addition to opportunities for the denizens of ethnic places.

The commercial ethnic tourist village, with its associated tenement residential quarters and its loft manufacturing workplaces, represents a kind of "spatial fix" of an early-twentieth-century building inventory (like a traditional "lower-circuit" economy) in the midst of the still evolving postindustrial city. These gestures of recovery, of preservation of "place," have an apparent antimodern aspect in their reliance upon protectionist land-use rulings and municipal recognition of revived labor solidarities. Community activist Charlie Lai has responded to charges of antidevelopment sentiment:

> We're not advocating squalor, or cold-water flats, or busted-up tenement housing. We just want people to have a place to live and not have to fear the bulldozer or skyhigh rents. Ethnicity has to be viewed as a positive thing, which should be nurtured, other groups before us lost their community and their culture. We wonder if that's really necessary. (Pomfret 1987: 64)

We should recall that preservationist state strategies were responses to community and workplace insurgencies that mobilized ethnic actors through rhetoric, organizing, and public demonstrations in collective campaigns of progressive social change that challenged traditional enclave hierarchies while forming new solidarities. The rhetoric brandished by these community actors has been defensive, yet affirmative and forward-looking in intent. Through the "politics of place" of the past three decades, Chinatown residents, workers, and merchants have acquired a growing confidence in their claim to a central urban space from which they were historically restricted, evicted, or displaced.

This political process has been at times organizationally messy and fragmented, exposing cultural and ideological fault lines in an enclave that is increasingly heterogeneous despite the outward appearance of ethnic homogeneity. Some of these internal cleavages are reflections of external geopolitical dynamics emanating from the still evolving relations between the People's Republic of China, the former Hong Kong (now officially Xianggang), and Taiwan. I reinsert these caveats in order to emphasize that the reassertion of the locality that I describe in New York's Chinatown in response to globalization processes does not necessarily represent the whole enclave, nor is the preservationist tendency necessarily a "permanent fix" that will withstand ongoing economic and cultural change. I recognize community, ethnicity, and "place" as social constructions or contingent solidarities that have the power to mobilize and reinforce networks of association and influence, confer human roles and identities, and grant an affective meaning to physical space in the way that "home" or "turf" implies an emotive or defensive association with territory.

Preservation of Chinatown also has an appeal to the general public, which continues to be drawn to indulge in the sensory, culinary, festive, and acquisitive delights of the ethnic, foreign, or "third-world" bazaar.

More psychoanalytically, these are primal maneuvers of consumption and appropriation, acts of gratification that fulfill human desires and longing for what has been lost in the blasé, routinized, bureaucratic anonymity of the modern metropolis. In the cloistered, sometimes congested quarters of Chinatown, Little Italy, and Little Havana, metropolitan denizens satisfy and celebrate these appetites amidst the sensual immediacy and seasonal pageantry of the urban village. The nostalgic and primal quality of these metropolitan sojourns becomes somewhat diluted with the regularization of urban ethnic tourism as a conventional kind of diversion from the exigencies of the quotidian routine. Regularization does not necessarily detract from the search for authenticity, however, since the habitual tourist may effectively become somewhat of a discriminating cosmopolitan, perpetually on the lookout for new sights and tastes. The epitome of this kind of formulaic criticism is the journalistic epicurean, arts, and lifestyle columns of the metropolitan dailies.[7]

The subtle irony of Chinatown as a touristic presentation is that the creative and culinary activities of ethnic insiders (including artists, preservationists, and restaurant workers) are not just a matter of functional cultural practices internal to the enclave but a *performative* repertoire of cultural displays that increasingly serve the consumptive and spectating demands of outsider audiences. Within the tourist economy, then, ethnicity and community are *dramaturgical* phenomena emanating from daily and seasonal rituals of conduct among enclave participants, self-consciously enacted in the presence of non-enclave observers.

The revalorization of ethnic practices and places in the polyglot environment of the postindustrial city encourages some spirit of optimism. This promising outlook should be tempered by the reminder that pejorative attitudes toward Chinatown and Chinese Americans continue to perennially surface surrounding such issues as illegal immigration, urban social problems, and foreign investment. Local government has been willing to offer some protection to traditional-sector uses but continues to be lured by the revenue-generating potential of developmental upgrading. The residents, workers, and merchants of Chinatown will undoubtedly need to persist in advancing their interests while adapting to ongoing economic and cultural change.

Notes

Preface

1. I should mention that my informants were primarily activists, leaders, and planners rathern than the "rank and file" or the "person on the street." A similar methodology was pursued by Philip Kasinitz in his study of the West Indian community of Crown Heights, Brooklyn. He notes that these kinds of informants provide more access to information on group opinion and political life than the typical layperson (1992:13). This approach seems appropriate since I was more interested in the dynamics of economic and social change than the details of family and religious life, rites of passage, or everyday working life.

Introduction

1. See, for instance, Gwen Kincaid's *Chinatown: Portrait of a Closed Society* (1992), which is a compilation of a series of articles the author previously published in *The New Yorker.* Though rich in human drama, her book is devoted in large part to portraying the underworld of Chinese American organized crime.

2. See, for instance, articles by Chan 1990, 1994; Freitag 1987; and Goldberg 1995.

3. The strength of the associative social and cultural ties in these neighborhoods was seen to be weaker than the equilibrating tendencies of "invasion-succession" in the urban land market, since it was assumed these districts would eventually wither through time with the dominance of rising land market values, which grew in a steady gradient through successive concentric rings outwards from the city center. Racial succession, rather than ethnicity, dominated urban research in the postwar era (particularly in the wake of seminal work by the Duncans and the Taeubers), but an interest in ethnic residential succession revived in the 1970s. In addition to these studies of intergroup residential dynamics in the broad metropolitan context, the "neighborhood life cycle" model has examined social change at the level of the micro-area (Schwirian 1983).

4. Examining Canadian Chinatowns forty years later, David Chuenyan Lai (1988) also employed a human ecology perspective. Moving beyond the free-market

assumptions of the classical human ecologists, he identified state-sponsored expansion of central business districts and urban renewal plans as factors in the "withering" of Canadian Chinatowns. Rather than assimilating into the suburbs, upwardly mobile Chinese, he found, established suburban Chinatowns. He also found evidence of a "revival" stage in many Chinatowns because of the arrival of new entrants with the lifting of Canadian immigration exclusion laws. Revival, he observed, could also be state-sponsored in the incidence of planned "replacement Chinatowns" or "reconstructed historic Chinatowns."

5. A forceful critique of Wirthian urbanism was issued by Gans (1962b), who drew our attention to the persistence of certain *quasi-primary* solidarities in the densely populated metropolis, ordered by relationships of class, ethnicity, or life-cycle stage. The critique was further codified by Claude S. Fischer (1975), who pointed to the incidence of subcultures as an emergent process of urbanization. Subcultural innovation, argued Fischer, was a concomitant process of urbanism; a *critical mass* of population size permitted what would otherwise be only small groups of individuals to become vital, active subcultures. Social network studies, which conceived of territorial solidarities as structures of resource affiliation, also emerged as theoretical alternatives to Wirthian urbanism (Flanagan 1993).

6. Assailing Marxian theory for being generally blind to the significance of *community* or *territory*, Katznelson's analysis of early American urban politics led him to the conclusion that *neighborhood* and *racial/ethnically* affiliated political identities had become more salient than workplace or *class* identities. Spatially rooted political patronage machines, or *city trenches*, had appeared as constitutive elements of the American urban political landscape as early as the Jacksonian era.

7. Manuel Castells's 1983 *The City and the Grassroots* contrasts with his earlier academic formulation (1977, 1979) of "urban social movements" or the "urban crisis" as an emerging structural feature of advanced capitalism, reflecting a point of contradiction between the productive forces and the relations of production, the "post-industrial" service classes being the main proponents of social action. Increasing state (government) intervention in advanced capitalist economies to provide essential services of "collective consumption" (in areas such as housing, education, health, welfare, and transportation) opened up new areas of popular mobilization and contestation. Responding to scholarly criticisms (e.g., Pickvance [1978] and Katznelson [1981], who issued a particularly cogent rejoinder, assaulting Castells's theory of urban social movements as too "automatic," as a "contingent outcome" [211] of a structural-Marxist epistemology that was historically overspecified in its focus on advanced capitalism), Castells reformulated his theory of urban social movements to include a broader historicity, with case studies of historic episodes of urban social change, such as the Paris Commune of 1871 and the Glasgow rent strike of 1915.

8. See, specifically, the findings of Sanders and Nee (1987) and their critique of the initial research of Wilson and Portes (1980), as well as the rejoinder issued by Portes and Jensen (1987).

9. The earliest proponents of the dualistic paradigm came from the fields of anthropology and economics (Boeke 1953; Geertz 1963; Hart 1970, 1973). The International Labor Organization (1972) was sufficiently encouraged by the work of British anthropologist Keith Hart, who coined the appellation *informal sector* in his fieldwork among petty urban traders in West Africa, that they commissioned further

exploration, thus lending tremendous legitimacy to the concept in economic policy and academic circles. Applying the dualistic paradigm to his comparative studies of the developing economies, Milton Santos (1979) introduced the nomenclature of a traditional, locally oriented *lower circuit* and a transnationally oriented *upper circuit* to describe the situation of segmentation in the urban economy. Helen Safa (1982) employed the dual paradigm in her studies of Latin America. T. G. McGee (1979, 1982) applied the concept of *circuits* to his examinations of street hawkers and harbor markets in Hong Kong. Warwick Armstrong and McGee (1985) developed more systematic conceptualizations of dualism and economic circuits via extensive comparative studies of cases in Latin America and Asia. The informal sector concept and the dualist paradigm have not been impervious to criticism. For a forceful critique of the informal sector concept, see Lisa Peattie (1987), who questions the empirical verifiability of the informal sector concept but concedes that it has also opened up new perspectives among development theorists and policymakers on the structural position of the urban poor in the developing world.

10. As applied to New York City, the dualist paradigm and informal sector concept have also been subject to criticism. Roger Waldinger and Michael Lapp (1993), though not contesting the reality of garment sweatshops in Chinatown, have recently questioned the empirical validity of a supposed broader, pervasive informal sector emerging throughout New York City. As a foil to the dualist paradigm, Waldinger has elsewhere (1986–87) advanced the notion (derived from classic mobility theory as propounded by Lieberson [1980]) of an occupational hierarchy or queue of white and nonwhite minority groups in contemporary New York City. Opportunities for minorities and immigrants are provided along a vacancy chain created as whites experience upward mobility. As John Mollenkopf and Manuel Castells (1991: 405) observe, however, the dual city perspective is more prone to emphasize inequality, exploitation, and contradiction, ultimately granting a better understanding of the dynamics of social change. The dualist perspective would thus call into question the current relevance of the vacancy-chain hypothesis, given the dramatic changes in the New York City economy during the shift to postindustrialism.

11. Min Zhou (1992: 14) draws attention to what she calls a "structured duality" between the *protected sector* (Chinese enterprises directed at co-ethnic clientele such as grocery stores) and the *export sector* (Chinese enterprises exporting goods to non-Chinese markets such as garment factories), but she identifies linkages between these two sectors rather than any situation of conflict. She also observes that the ethnic enclave economy may be differentially defined by place of residence, place of work, or industry (Zhou and Logan 1989). She finds some evidence of gender inequality, suggesting that positive returns on human capital in the garment industry for men occur at the expense of negative returns for women. Ultimately, however, she assumes a coherent subeconomy (separate from the white-dominated primary economy as well as the black secondary economy), which is characterized by fundamental unity rather than duality. Despite the reality of co-ethnic exploitation, the socioeconomic potential of the enclave economy confers long-run opportunities to immigrants. The dualist paradigm, on the other hand, problematizes the dynamics of upward social mobility, drawing more attention to matters of persisting inequality, community conflict, and social change, as well as global-level variables. In the final analysis, my perspective can be seen as complementing, rather than conflicting with

Zhou's work, since her "ethnic enclave economy" is essentially like my informal sector, or lower circuit.

12. Joe R. Feagin and Hernan Vera (1995) provide a notable example of a racially incendiary media panic with the Carol Stuart murder case of 1989 in Boston. During the police manhunt that followed her wounded husband's (Charles Stuart) allegation that the murder of his pregnant wife was committed by a black attacker, the local media amplified the racial dynamics of the case by heightening an image of white victimization and black dangerousness. William Bennett, a black man, was eventually apprehended and charged with the crime but was later released when Matthew Stuart (Charles Stuart's brother) confessed to his complicity in an elaborate hoax. Charles Stuart had shot his wife and wounded himself as part of an insurance scam. Charles Stuart committed suicide the day after his brother's confession.

13. Although the idea of the "yellow peril" can ultimately be traced as far back as the Greeks, Gary Okihiro attributes the specific coinage of the term in modern times to Kaiser Wilhelm II of Germany in 1895, who also had a painting commissioned that illustrates the nations of Europe (depicted as women in martial garb) being attacked by demoniac figures of Oriental disposition. He had reproductions of this painting sent to leaders of Europe and to American President William McKinley (1994: 118–19).

14. See Stuart Creighton Miller (1969: 16–37), who asserts that the most positive image of the Chinese was held by Yankee traders during the era of the China trade, roughly 1785 to 1840.

1. From Bachelor Society to Immigrant Enclave

1. This 1790 federal law codified the privilege of naturalized citizenship to "white" immigrants only. The 1882 Chinese Exclusion Act further specified that Chinese would be excluded from citizenship. Because "white" was subject to legislative and judicial interpretation, a number of Japanese and South Asian Indians were able to become naturalized until Supreme Court decisions specifically denied them citizenship. The landmark cases were the 1922 *Takao Ozawa* case for the Japanese, and the 1923 *Bhagat Singh Thind* case for Asian Indians (Takaki 1987: 98–299).

2. Some exceptions were made for government officials, ministers, professors, students, and merchants.

3. Louis Beck (1898) gives this man's name as Quimbo Appo. Bernard Wong (1982: 5) and Calvin Lee (1965) say his name was Lee Ah Bow.

4. Interview by author with representative of Mobilization for Youth (tenant advocacy and legal services).

5. Linkages may also be conceptualized as *vertical* and *horizontal*. Vertical integration refers to the kinds of forward and backward *interindustry* linkages between different industrial categories, as just described. Horizontal integration refers to *intraindustry* cooperation, such as production and pricing strategies aimed at neutralizing competition between co-ethnic enterprises (Wilson and Martin 1982: 137).

6. As discussed in an interview by author with Edmund Yu, representative of the New York City Office of Business Development, January 12, 1990.

7. This earnings outflow has been a problem of interest since the early 1970s. See, for example, Schaffer (1973) and Harrison (1974).

8. These observations were made by M. B. Lee, director of the Lee Family Association, in an interview by author, June 20, 1991.

9. This is Clifford Geertz's definition (1956). Shirley Ardener (1964) distinguishes rotating credit associations from other continuous cooperative devices such as mutual benefit clubs in having the element of "rotation" or "regularity," which implies a term of existence with a distinct beginning and end.

10. See Sassen-Koob (1979) on Dominican and Colombian immigrants, Lovell-Troy (1980) on Greek immigrants, Bonnett (1981) on Caribbean immigrants, Kim (1981) on Korean immigrants, Portes and Bach (1985) on Cuban and Mexican immigrants, and Foner (1987).

2. Labor Struggles

1. According to May Chen of the Union of Needletrades, Industrial and Textile Employees, as reported in an interview by author, October 3, 1995.

2. Katie Quan, representative of ILGWU Metro Organizing Department, interview by author, February 12, 1988.

3. Information based on an interview by author with May Chen, an ILGWU organizer, June 1991.

4. Estimates provided by Sherman Eng, a Chinatown contractor, in an interview by author, June 1991.

5. Another report found that Vietnamese contractors in Philadelphia were acquiring bundlework from the New York City garment center. Italian trucking companies from New York were transporting the bundlework and finished product between the two locations (Petras 1990).

6. Peter Kwong described this methodology in an interview that I conducted with him, January 23, 1990.

7. Jo Ann Lum, interview by author, October 18, 1995.

8. As described by Graham Wong of the Chinese Staff and Workers' Association in an interview by author, October 18, 1995.

9. Henry Yung, interview by author, October 1995.

3. The Nexus of Transnational and Local Capital

1. The Nanyang navies were led by Koxinga, a Ming-dynasty loyalist who sought to evict the more continental Qing dynasty leaders and reinstate Ming power on the mainland from his base in Taiwan (Pan 1990: 7). The Ming dynasty, the most seagoing of the Chinese dynasties, was very friendly to the Nanyang Chinese. Koxinga remains a folk hero in Taiwan.

2. On the other side of the equation, many disgruntled indigenous Southeast Asian peoples have historically looked upon the Nanyang Chinese with a measure of suspicion and distrust because they monopolized many trades and were seen as imperialist comprador "lackeys." Additionally, in the post–World War II period, many Nanyang were branded "cukongs" by anti-imperialist, nationalist Southeast Asians for profiting from close personal relationships with royalty, military elites, and other imperialist-comprador bourgeoisie within their own countries (Pan 1990: 229). Anti-Chinese violence flared in Malaysia and Indonesia in the 1960s, and ethnic Chinese were evicted from Indochina in the 1970s. Singapore, where ethnic Chinese constitute three-quarters of the population, is a noticeable exception to this phenomenon.

3. American military and economic aid was also significant as a source of capital formation in postwar Taiwan. This assistance was heightened beginning in

1951 as part of an anticommunist American strategy of Chinese containment with the onset of the Korean conflict, which initiated the Cold War.

4. The most prominent of the "tycoon" investors is Li Ka-Shing, patriarch of one of Hong Kong's biggest trading families, who bought Vancouver's 204-acre Expo '86 site in 1988 for development as an office/hotel/retail/residential complex. Li also owns 43 percent of the Calgary-based Husky Oil Company and other real estate interests in Canada. With interests still in Hong Kong and the People's Republic of China, Li has not legally emigrated, but his two sons have become Canadian immigrants to guide his empire upon his retirement. Vancouver's University of British Columbia is a popular place for Hong Kong investors to enroll their immigrant children. Affluent bedroom communities such as Kerrisdale, Shaughnessy, and West Vancouver have been popular neighborhoods for residential purchases by Hong Kong investors.

5. A distinction between *portfolio* and *direct* investment should be made here. Portfolio investment involves ownership of bank accounts, securities, and bonds of U.S. companies or governmental bodies. Examples are U.S.-dollar-denominated bank accounts, bellwether government offerings such as thirty-year U.S. Treasury notes, and shares in the financing for speculative, predatory capitalist ventures, such as corporate junk bonds. Junk bonds tend to be highly liquid and are popular for their high rate of return, as a hedge against currency fluctuation, and for diversifying investment portfolios. Direct investments are less liquid and longer term, and involve controlling interest or ownership in a purchased company or real estate, via acquisition, building of a new plant, or joint venture (Glickman and Woodward 1989: 5–6). Overseas Chinese investors tend to be involved in less liquid investments such as bank accounts, securities, and real estate.

6. The mortgage activity reports (MARs) were a special tabulation produced by the Survey Data Security Corporation under contract with the New York State Banking Department from 1979 to 1986. The reports were derived from transaction records in each county clerk's office in New York City. Information was sorted by census tract and included the name of the lender, the dollar amount and number of mortgages, and a profile of building types financed (i.e., 1–6 unit residential, multiple-unit residential, retail-commercial, office-commercial, industrial, and condominiums). Reliable figures on building type were available only for the 1982–86 period. The data are broadly similar to the standard Community Reinvestment Act source on bank mortgage activity, the Home Mortgage Disclosure Act (HMDA) reports. The HMDA reports, however, cover only residential buildings, and since I was interested in Chinatown real estate activity in a greater range of building types, I decided to utilize the MARs.

7. In no way do these data represent *all* the property transactions taking place in New York's Chinatown during this time period. Many transactions were financed by banks that do not have branches in Chinatown, which were outside the scope of my study. I also did not include "purchase money mortgages" in my analysis, which are direct sales handled without a lien, a mortgage broker, or a bank. Included in this category are those sales that may have involved the participation of "an overseas investor with millions of dollars in a briefcase," which are the subjects of popular rumor.

8. There have been some notable cases of fraudulence and instability in the

history of immigrant banking on the Lower East Side, involving banks not considered in this study. The Bowery Savings Bank, the Bowery Bank (taken over by Citibank), and the Chatham and Phoenix Bank (taken over by Manufacturers Hanover and Trust) could be found at the intersection of the Bowery and Grand Street, which was known as "bank corner" in the mid-nineteenth century. The Chatham and Phoenix Bank, known for some unscrupulousness, became insolvent and was closed during the depression. Jarmulousky's Bank, founded in 1873 on the corner of Canal Street and Orchard Street, also was known for some instability, suffering some depositor runs between the panic of 1907 and World War I, when it closed, owing creditors and predominantly immigrant Jewish depositors millions of dollars. Farther north, on the intersection of Delancey Street and Allen Street, the Bank of the United States, a branch of a large Jewish-owned bank, failed in 1932. Attempts to bail it out of insolvency were frustrated by the refusal of short-term credit on the part of other banks, allegedly because of anti-Semitism (Wolfe 1988: 131–48). The two institutions surviving from this era, the Bowery Savings Bank and the Manhattan Savings Bank, have experienced more progressive growth and stability.

9. Comment by Amy Leung, senior vice president of regional banking, Hong Kong and Shanghai Banking Corporation, made during on interview by author, April 14, 1990.

10. For example, Bank of East Asia assembled some of its Far East clients as investors in a $100-million-dollar project that Bankers Trust had syndicated in order to spread the risk.

11. I follow Harvey (1978), Armstrong and McGee (1985), and Feagin (1988) in identifying the *primary circuit of capital* as that pertaining to the appropriation of economic surplus from labor in the arena of production and the work process, encompassing such activities as manufacturing and trade. The *secondary circuit of capital* relates to a situation of overaccumulation, whereby surplus capital derived from the primary circuit is subsequently invested in the built environment (including factories, office buildings, transportation, and housing).

12. This phenomenon was generally corroborated by real estate managers and banking officials in interviews conducted during the course of this study.

13. As reported by Amy Leung, senior vice president of Hong Kong Shanghai Banking Corporation, in an interview by author, April 1990.

14. Edmund Yu, New York City Office of Business Development, interview by author, January 1990.

15. This reinvestment in China is promoted by lobbyists. David Chen, of the Chinese American Planning Council, reported that representatives of the People's Republic of China occasionally hold events in New York's Chinatown encouraging local Chinese investment in China.

16. These positive comments regarding Greenpoint Savings Bank were made by Edmund Yu of the New York City Office of Business Development in an interview by author on January 12, 1990, before Greenpoint's subsequent acquisition of Bowery Savings Bank.

4. The Growth of Satellite Chinatowns

1. Danyun Feng, interview by author, October 1995.

2. Danyun Feng, interview by author, October 1995.

5. Solidarity, Community, and Electoral Politics

1. I derive *organizational solidarity* from the foundational sociological concept of *organic solidarity*, which Emile Durkheim (1933) believed was characteristic of modern industrial society, whereby secondary ties of occupational and associational life supplanted primary ties such as kinship in social life. My notion of organizational solidarity also incorporates Mark Granovetter's (1973) notion that the social relationships produced by contemporary Chinatown workplace and community organizations, though "weaker" than kinship and friendship ties in terms of human sentiment and interpersonal value, are in the final instance stronger in terms of the political or economic influence that they confer. I go beyond both Durkheim and Granovetter, however, in suggesting that the organizational solidarity promoted by Chinatown's workplace and community organizations augments the political and economic empowerment of the Chinese American populace through highly visible bouts of collective action organized around issues of territorial defense or ethnic unity. The historical salience of ethnic collective action in American cities since the nineteenth century is a theme further explored by both Charles Tilly (1990) and Susan Olzak (1985).

2. Stanford Lyman (1974: 18–19) asserts that the district associations, called *hui-guan*, had an ancient genealogy in China, with evidence of their existence back to the Shang dynasty (1766–1123 B.C.).

3. See Mario Maffi (1995).

4. At one point representing some 3,200 laundry workers, the CHLA began in 1933 with a mass meeting of several hundred laundry workers in response to a proposal by the Council of Aldermen of the City of New York to impose an ordinance severely restricting their livelihood. With its populist-democratic orientation, the CHLA was more friendly to Chinese leftists (mainly students in the United States) than the running dogs of the mercantile CCBA. Chinese communists organizing among the laundry workers provoked a communist/populist split in the CHLA in 1936. A secretariat of leftists (the "Quon Shar"), who sympathized with communism, ascended to leadership positions in the late 1930s following the Marco Polo Incident of July 1937, which officially brought China into war with Japan and led to the formation of a temporary united front between the Chinese Communists and the KMT until the Japanese defeat in World War II (Yu 1992).

5. *Fujian* is the newer Mandarin-influenced pinyin romanization. *Fukien* is the older Cantonese-influenced romanization.

6. Basement Workshop later became the core of the community arts, performance, and history documentation projects in Chinatown. Many of their archival materials were eventually transferred to the Chinatown History Project, which was established in 1980.

7. The Chinese-American Planning Council's current executive director, David Chen, acknowledged in an interview by author on September 29, 1995, that the CPC has moved broadly from a militant position of antigovernment "empowerment" to a spirit of "collaboration" with government officials and administrators.

8. One informant noted that Lee's liberalism may partially reflect the influence of his daughters, who were youthful activists.

9. The original acronym for Asian Americans for Equal Employment was AAFEE. When the group's name was later changed to Asian Americans for Equality,

the acronym AAFE came into use and is now the contemporary popular reference within the community.

10. CVEA volunteers set up tables to register voters, especially at the Chemical Bank branch at the intersection of Mott and Canal Streets, a major traffic area for Chinatown residents as well as outer-borough Chinese and a major gateway into the heart of Chinatown. Table registration is also done at other locations in order to capture different Chinatown subpopulations. East Broadway, for instance, is primarily trafficked by Chinatown residents.

11. According to one Chinatown voter registration veteran, Representative Silver's electoral foundation is the Jewish American community anchored in some twenty cooperative housing projects in the Grand Street area of the Lower East Side. This is an eight-thousand-strong voting bloc of primarily senior citizens with consistently high rates of electoral participation. A fierce advocate of social services and other Democratic Party policy principles, House Speaker Silver is currently the third most powerful politician in New York State, behind the Republican governor and lieutenant governor.

12. This important point was made by Peter Cheng of the nonpartisan Chinatown Voter Education Alliance in an interview by author, October 1995.

6. The Enclave and the State

1. The World Trade Center held this honor for only a short time, being surpassed by the Sears Tower of Chicago.

2. The Reichmann brothers were not new players in New York City real estate, having bought eight Manhattan skyscrapers for $400 million in 1977 during the height of the New York City fiscal crisis, valued at more than $3 billion in the early 1990s. Olympia and York is the chief builder of the Docklands/Canary Wharf project in Central London.

3. The noticeable exception is the forty-four-story Confucius Plaza, a 760-unit moderate-income cooperative completed in 1976. Although there were community protests regarding the extent of Asian American employment at the work site, there was widespread approval of the character of the housing constructed, despite its high-rise nature.

4. One Chinese American community board member, Virginia Kee, who was apparently instrumental in lobbying on behalf of Thomas Lee for the zoning change, later viewed the announcement of the three projects with some trepidation. In pointing to the deteriorated state of much of Chinatown's building stock and the high cost of rehabilitation, she commented in an interview, "So the question is whether to let the area to continue to deteriorate or to encourage new private development" (Wang 1981b). The Chinatown Planning Council (CPC) was also implicated in the SMBD approval, since Ms. Kee sat on the CPC board of directors, and Allen Cohen, a managing director of the CPC, also sat on the community board. At Mr. Lee's request, the CPC sent a letter of support for the SMBD to the City Planning Commission. The CPC had furthermore held talks with Mr. Lee on the use of community space within the proposed East-West Towers project. Finally, Ms. Kee's brother-in-law was Norman Lau-Kee, a former board chairman of the Chinatown YMCA. The Chinatown YMCA had been in negotiations with the Henry Street Partners to occupy community space in their project (Wang 1982).

5. The community opposition was argued on two grounds: (1) that the SMBD was implemented with inadequate public input and was therefore unconstitutional, and (2) that the SMBD contradicted city housing policy because it would cause gentrification and "secondary displacement" (via rising land values) of residents in adjacent neighborhoods. The community's March 1983 appeal was struck down, however, by a June 1984 decision by the New York Court of Appeals, which ultimately upheld the legality of the SMBD.

6. The phenomenon of conversion of old manufacturing lofts to upmarket residential space that began in the late 1960s in Soho (see Zukin 1989) is now pervasive throughout the island of Manhattan south of 42nd Street. Motivated by a desire to regulate illegal loft conversions popular among artists while retaining manufacturing space, the city moved first to control residential conversions in Soho loft buildings. In 1981, the Board of Estimate adopted a systematic loft-conversion program and specially designated four large zones where manufacturing uses would be protected: the Garment District, northeast Chelsea, the meat market area (West Village), and an area west of Soho (Wang 1981a).

7. As stated by two representatives of the Garment Industrial Development Corporation in an interview by author, June 1991.

8. Zukin refers particularly to the Bryant Park Restoration Corporation, a subsidiary of the Bryant Park Business Improvement District, which has accomplished the double-edged task of reversing decline in what was a virtually defunct park and making it more accessible to middle-class area residents and office workers while displacing homeless loiterers and vagrants. Newly sited cafes and restaurants mark this successful scheme of "domestication (gentrification) by cappuccino," she quips (1995: xiv).

9. Cristobal Garcia, the current executive director of the Manhattan Neighborhood Renaissance Local Development Corporation, was initially drawn into Chinatown affairs through employment with the Manhattan Borough President's Office.

10. These points are made in response to comments and queries raised by Charles Tilly in a personal communication written September 27, 1990.

7. Encountering Chinatown

1. Ivan Light (1977) informs us that the nightclubs and brothels of Harlem, as well as the speakeasies of Irish and Italian Americans of New York City during Prohibition, depended in large part on demand from a white clientele.

2. Wayne Wang was born in Hong Kong in 1949 and named after American actor John Wayne. After moving to the United States at the age of 18, he received a master's degree in film in 1973, after which he returned to Hong Kong to direct films. He returned to the United States in 1975, working in community programs assisting new immigrants before returning to film (Sakamoto 1991).

3. Jo and Steve at one point jokingly introduce themselves as "Charlie Chan and Number One Son." At another point, Jo derides the Chan mystery series: "Those old films are a source of cheap laughs" (Denzin 1995).

8. Community Change in Global Context

1. The principal American global cities, which are command centers of the global economy, are Los Angeles and New York (Sassen 1988). Other U.S. immigra-

tion gateway cities (which are lower-order centers of global economic command functions) of the past three decades include San Francisco, San Diego, Houston, Miami, Washington, D.C., and Chicago (Muller 1993).

2. At a session of the 1996 American Sociological Association Annual Meetings held in New York City on "World Cities: New York in the American and Global Context," Janet Abu-Lughod reiterated her concerns, fretting jocularly that the globalization concept was becoming labeled as "globaloney" by some observers.

3. These points were made by Peter Cheng of the Chinatown Voter Education Alliance in an interview by author, October 1995.

4. The noticeable exceptions are "greenfield" investments, or foreign investment in manufacturing, such as in the "Waterbelt" region of the American Midwest (Japanese automobile companies have built assembly plants here, particularly in Tennessee) and the "Euroville" region of South Carolina (where many European manufacturers have located factories). Not only have jobs been created in these regions, but local officials have commonly negotiated for local subcontracting in associated industries such as auto parts and industrial hardware (Tolchin and Tolchin 1988; Glickman and Woodward 1989).

5. McGee suggests (1985), based on research in Hong Kong beginning in the late 1960s on government efforts to clear and resettle hawkers (at public expense), that conflicts between the two circuits tend to emerge when the upper circuit is in a period of expansion. He disparages the loss of picturesque central-city bazaars of the lower circuit, which by contrast have been successfully retained for tourism in Singapore and Bangkok (198–200).

6. Chinatown restaurants draw lunchtime clientele from nearby government offices and Wall Street businesses as well as out-of-town tourists.

7. The cosmopolitan tourist or epicurean should be distinguished from the lowbrow tourist or creature of habit whose savoring of ethnic difference may be equal to that of the aesthete, but whose satisfaction may be obtained through the familiarity of a certain plate, restaurant, proprietor, or street corner rather than the perpetual quest of newness. Anne Tyler's novel, *The Accidental Tourist* (1985), parodies the adventure of tourism with its depiction of a protagonist who writes travel books for anti-cosmopolitans (such as world-weary businessmen) who seek familiar American products and restaurants in their sojourns abroad.

Bibliography

Abeles, Schwartz, Haeckel and Silverblatt, Inc. 1983. *The Chinatown Garment Industry Study.* New York: Local 23-25, International Ladies' Garment Workers' Union and New York Skirt and Sportswear Association.

Abramson, Jill. 1996. "Taiwan Won Platform Terms with Democrats." *Wall Street Journal,* Oct. 25, p. A16.

Abu-Lughod, Janet. 1991. "Going beyond Global Babble." In *Culture, Globalization and the World-System,* ed. Anthony D. King, 131–37. London: MacMillan.

———. 1994. *From Urban Village to East Village: The Battle for New York's Lower East Side.* Cambridge, Mass.: Blackwell Publishers.

Abu-Lughod, Janet, and Richard Hay Jr., eds. 1979. *Third World Urbanization.* New York: Methuen.

Allen, Irving L. 1993. *The City in Slang: New York Life and Popular Speech.* New York: Oxford University Press.

Anderson, Kay J. 1987. "The Idea of Chinatown: The Power of Place and Institutional Practice in the Making of a Racial Category." *Annals of the Association of American Geographers* 77 (4): 580–98.

———. 1991. *Vancouver's Chinatown: Racial Discourse in Canada, 1875–1980.* Montreal: McGill-Queen's University Press.

Anderson, Kay J., and Fay Gale. 1992. *Inventing Places: Studies in Cultural Geography.* Melbourne: Longman Cheshire.

Appelbaum, Richard. 1996. "Multiculturalism and Flexibility: Some New Directions in Global Capitalism." In *Mapping Multiculturalism,* ed. Avery F. Gordon and Christopher Newfield, 297–316. Minneapolis: University of Minnesota Press.

Ardener, Shirley. 1964. "The Comparative Study of Rotating Credit Associations." *Journal of the Royal Anthropological Institute of Great Britain and Ireland* 94: 201–29.

Armstrong, Warwick, and T. G. McGee. 1985. *Theatres of Accumulation.* New York: Methuen and Company.

Bagli, Charles V. 1990. "The Bowery's Boozy Image Undergoes a Transformation." *New York Observer,* Aug. 27.

Bahr, Howard M., and Theodore Caplow. 1991. "Middletown as an Urban Case Study." In *A Case for the Case Study*, ed. Joe R. Feagin, Anthony M. Orum, and Gideon Sjoberg, 80–120. Chapel Hill: University of North Carolina Press.

Bailey, Thomas R. 1987. *Immigrant and Native Workers: Contrasts and Competition.* Boulder, Colo: Westview Press.

Barth, Gunther Paul. 1964. *Bitter Strength: A History of the Chinese in the United States, 1850–1870.* Cambridge: Harvard University Press.

Beck, Louis J. 1898. *New York's Chinatown.* New York: Bohemia Publishing Co.

Belton, John. 1991. "Language, Oedipus and Chinatown." *MLN* 106, 5 (Dec.): 933–50.

Blauner, Robert. 1972. *Racial Oppression in America.* New York: Harper and Row.

Bluestone, Barry, and Bennett Harrison. 1982. *The Deindustrialization of America.* New York: Basic Books.

Bluestone, Daniel. 1992. "The Pushcart Evil: Peddlers, Merchants and New York City's Streets, 1890–1940." In *The Landscape of Modernity*, ed. David Ward and Olivier Zunz, 287–312. New York: Russell Sage Foundation.

Boeke, J. H. 1953. *Economics and Economic Policy of Dual Societies as Exemplified by Indonesia.* Haarlem: H. D. Tjeenk Willink and Zoon N.V.

Bonacich, Edna. 1973. "A Theory of Middleman Minorities." *American Sociological Review* 35: 583–94.

Bonnett, Aubrey W. 1981. "Structural Adaptation of Black Migrants from the Caribbean: An Examination of an Indigenous Banking System in Brooklyn." *Phylon* 4 (Dec.): 346–55.

Brackman, Harold, and Steven P. Erie. 1995. "Beyond 'Politics by Other Means'? Empowerment Strategies for Los Angeles' Asian Pacific Community." In *The Bubbling Cauldron: Race, Ethnicity, and the Urban Crisis*, ed. Michael Peter Smith and Joe R. Feagin, 282–303. Minneapolis: University of Minnesota Press.

Brecher, Jeremy, and Tim Costello. 1990. *Building Bridges: The Emerging Grassroots Coalition of Labor and Community.* New York: Monthly Review Press.

Bressi, Todd. 1987. "Chinatowns Stand Their Ground." *Planning* (American Planners Association) 53, 12, 6 (Nov.): 12–16.

Brooks, Andree. 1988. "New Bowery Housing: A Rare Sight in Chinatown." *New York Times,* July 29, p. B14.

Buder, Leonard. 1989. "Biggest Heroin Distributor Seized, U.S. Agents Say." *New York Times,* Oct. 20, p. B3.

Burawoy, Michael, et al. 1991. *Ethnography Unbound: Power and Resistance in the Modern Metropolis.* Berkeley: University of California Press.

Burgess, Ernest. 1967. "The Growth of the City: An Introduction to a Research Project." In *The City*, ed. Robert E. Park, Ernest W. Burgess, and Roderick D. McKenzie, 47–62. Chicago: University of Chicago Press.

Buttenweiser, Ann L. 1987. *Manhattan Water-Bound: Planning and Developing Manhattan's Waterfront from the Seventeenth Century to the Present.* New York: New York University Press.

Carmody, Deirdre. 1975. "The Case That Stirred Chinatown Is Dropped." *New York Times,* July 2, p. 37.

———. 1984. "Pact Announced on Housing Next to Planned Chinatown Jail." *New York Times,* May 10, p. B7.

Caro, Robert. 1975. *The Power Broker: Robert Moses and the Fall of New York*. New York: Vintage Books.

Carson, Diane. "Cultural Screens: Teaching Asian and Asian American Images." In *Shared Differences: Multicultural Media and Practical Ideology*, ed. Diane Carson and Lester D. Friedman, 165–83. Urbana: University of Illinois Press.

Castells, Manuel. 1977. *The Urban Question: A Marxist Approach*. Cambridge: MIT Press. English translation of French edition first published 1972.

———. 1979. *City, Class, and Power*. New York: St. Martin's Press.

———. 1983. *The City and the Grassroots*. Berkeley: University of California Press.

Chan, Yuen Ying. 1989. "Riding the Dragon." *Village Voice*, Oct. 31, pp. 33–35.

———. 1990. "Merchants of Misery." *New York Daily News*, Sept. 24, p. 7.

———. 1994. "Chinatown Dungeons." *New York Daily News*, Dec. 21, p. 7.

Chen, Hsiang-shui. 1992. *Chinatown No More: Taiwan Immigrants in Contemporary New York*. Ithaca, N.Y.: Cornell University Press.

Chen, Jack. 1980. *The Chinese of America*. San Francisco: Harper and Row.

Chen, Julia I. Hsuan. 1941. "The Chinese Community in New York: A Study in Their Cultural Adjustment, 1920–1940." Ph.D. diss., American University.

Chin, Ko-Lin, Robert J. Kelly, and Jeffrey Fagan. 1994. "Chinese Organized Crime in America." In *Handbook of Organized Crime in the United States*, ed. Robert J. Kelly, Ko-Lin Chin, and Rufus Schatzberg. Westport, Conn.: Greenwood Press.

Chin, Stephen A. 1986. "Silent Shadows on the Silver Screen." Unpublished master's seminar paper, History Department, New York University.

Chow, Chunshing. 1984. "Immigration and Immigrant Settlements: The Chinese in New York City." Ph.D. diss., University of Hawaii.

Citizens' Savings Bank. 1924. *Citizens' Savings Bank: Its Founders, History and Homes*. New York.

Cohen, Robert. 1981. "The New International Division of Labor, Multinational Corporations and Urban Hierarchy." In *Urbanization and Urban Planning in Capitalist Society*, ed. Michael Dear and Allen Scott, 287–315. New York: Methuen.

Cortes, Carlos E. 1990. "The Immigrant in Film: Evolution of an Illuminating Icon." In *Beyond the Stars*, ed. Paul Loukides and Linda K. Fuller, 23–34. Bowling Green, Ohio: Bowling Green University Press.

———. 1993. "Them and Us: Immigration as Societal Barometer and Social Educator in American Film." In *Hollywood as Mirror: Changing Views of "Outsider" and "Enemies" in American Movies*, ed. Robert B. Toplin, 53–73. Westport, Conn.: Greenwood Press.

Daly, Michael. 1983. "The War in Chinatown." *New York*, Feb. 14.

Danielson, Michael N., and Jameson W. Doig. 1982. *New York: The Politics of Urban Regional Development*. Berkeley: University of California Press.

Dao, James. 1990. "The Hong Kong Connection." *Daily News*, Apr. 29, business section, p. 1.

Davis, Mike. 1990. *City of Quartz*. London: Verso.

DeAngelis, Pat. 1995. "The Jing Fong End Slave Labor Campaign: Why I Am Fighting Back." Informational flyer printed by Chinese Staff and Workers' Association, New York City.

Denzin, Norman. 1995. *The Cinematic Society: The Voyeur's Gaze*. London: Sage Publications.

DeStefano, Anthony M. 1990. "On the Street, Fear of Violence and Bad Blood." *New York Newsday*, Oct. 16, p. 4.

Douglass, Mike. 1988. "Transnational Capital and Urbanization on the Pacific Rim: An Introduction." *International Journal of Urban and Regional Research* 12, 3 (Sept.): 343–55.

Duncan, James, and David Ley. 1993. *Place/Culture/Representation*. New York: Routledge.

Dunn, Ashley. 1994. "Golden Venture's Tarnished Hopes." *New York Times*, June 5, p. 39.

Durkheim, Emile. 1933. *The Division of Labor in Society*. Trans. George Simpson. New York: The Free Press.

Elliot, John. 1989. "Corporate Net Spreads Overseas." *Financial Times*, Oct. 10. Part of a special Financial Times Survey on Taiwan.

Epstein, Jason. 1993. "A Taste of Success." *The New Yorker* 69, 9: 50–56.

Erie, Steven P. 1985. "Rainbow's End: From the Old to the New Urban Ethnic Politics." In *Urban Ethnicity in the United States* (Urban Affairs Annual Reviews, vol. 29), 249–275. Beverly Hills, Calif.: Sage Publications.

Espiritu, Yen Le. 1992. *Asian American Panethnicity*. Philadelphia: Temple University Press.

Fainstein, Norman, and Susan Fainstein. 1983. "Regime Strategies, Communal Resistance, and Economic Forces." In *Restructuring the City: The Political Economy of Urban Redevelopment*, ed. Susan S. Fainstein, et al., 245–82. New York: Longman, Inc.

Fainstein, Susan. 1987. "Local Mobilization and Economic Discontent." In *The Capitalist City*, ed. Michael Peter Smith and Joe R. Feagin, 323–42. New York: Basil Blackwell.

Feagin, Joe R. 1988. *Free Enterprise City: Houston in Political and Economic Perspective*. New Brunswick, N.J.: Rutgers University Press.

Feagin, Joe R., and Michael Peter Smith. 1987. "Cities and the New International Division of Labor: An Overview." In *The Capitalist City*, ed. Michael Peter Smith and Joe R. Feagin, 3–34. New York: Basil Blackwell.

Feagin, Joe R., and Hernan Vera. 1995. *White Racism: The Basics*. New York: Routledge.

Fischer, Claude S. 1975. "Toward a Subcultural Theory of Urbanism." *American Sociological Review* 80, 1: 319–41.

Flanagan, William G. 1993. *Contemporary Urban Sociology*. Cambridge: Cambridge University Press.

Foner, Nancy. 1987. *New Immigrants in New York*. New York: Columbia University Press.

Freitag, Michael. 1987. "New York Is Fighting Spread of Sweatshops." *New York Times*, Nov. 16, p. B1.

Friedmann, John, and Goetz Wolff. 1982. "World City Formation: An Agenda for Research and Action." *International Journal of Urban and Regional Research* 6, 3 (Sept.): 309–44.

Fritsch, Jane. 1993. "Seven Die as Immigrant Ship Grounds off New York City." *New York Times*, June 7, p. A1.

Frobel, Folker, Jurgen Heinrichs, and Otto Kreye. 1980. *The New International Division of Labor.* London: Cambridge University Press.

Fry, Earl H. 1980. *Financial Invasion of the U.S.A.* New York: McGraw-Hill.

Galperin, William. 1987. "'Bad for the Glass': Representation and Filmic Deconstruction in *Chinatown* and *Chan Is Missing.*" *MLN* 102, 5 (Dec.): 1151–70.

Gans, Herbert. 1962a. *The Urban Villagers.* New York: The Free Press.

———. 1962b. "Urbanism and Suburbanism as Ways of Life: A Reevaluation of Definitions." In *Human Behavior and Social Processes: An Interactionist Approach,* 625–48. Boston: Houghton Mifflin.

Garbarine, Rachel. 1990. "An Expanding Chinatown Is Now Getting Condos." *New York Times,* Nov. 16, p. A36.

Gargan, Edward A. 1981a. "New Money, People and Ideas Alter Chinatown of Tradition." *New York Times,* Feb. 28, p. A1.

———. 1981b. "Asian Investors Battle for Footholds in Chinatown." *New York Times,* Dec. 29, p. A1.

Geertz, Clifford. 1956. *The Rotating Credit Association: An Instrument for Development.* Cambridge, Mass.: Center for International Studies.

———. 1963. *Peddlers and Princes.* Chicago: University of Chicago Press.

Gelman, Mitch. 1990. "Chinatown Gang Execution." *New York Newsday,* Oct. 16, p. 5.

Glazer, Nathan, and Daniel Patrick Moynihan. 1963. *Beyond the Melting Pot.* Cambridge: MIT Press.

Glick, Karl. 1941. *Shake Hands with the Dragon.* New York: McGraw-Hill.

———. 1943. *Three Times I Bow.* New York: McGraw-Hill.

Glickman, Norman. 1987. "Cities and the International Division of Labor." In *The Capitalist City,* ed. Michael Peter Smith and Joe R. Feagin, 66–86. New York: Basil Blackwell.

Glickman, Norman J., and Douglas P. Woodward. 1989. *The New Competitors: How Foreign Investors Are Changing the U.S. Economy.* New York: Basic Books.

Glynn, Thomas, and John Wang. 1978. "Chinatown." *Neighborhood: A Journal for City Preservation* 1, 3 (Dec.): 9–23.

Goldberg, Carey. 1995. "Sex Slavery, Thailand to New York." *New York Times,* Sept. 11, p. B1.

Goldberg, Michael A. 1985. *The Chinese Connection: Getting Plugged into Pacific Rim Real Estate, Trade, and Capital Markets.* Vancouver: University of British Columbia Press.

Gordy, Molly. 1995. "Fork over 1M, Eatery Told." *New York Daily News,* Sept. 22.

Gottdiener, Mark, and Joe R. Feagin. 1988. "The Paradigm Shift in Urban Sociology." *Urban Affairs Quarterly* 24, 2 (Dec.): 163–87.

Granovetter, Mark. 1973. "The Strength of Weak Ties." *American Journal of Sociology* 78, 6: 1360–80.

Grant, Peter. 1992. "Chinatown Fortune Reads: No Crash Here." *Crain's New York Business,* Mar. 2, p. 13.

Gruson, Lindsey. 1982. "City's Plan on New Jail Is Assailed." *New York Times,* Sept. 3.

Gurr, Ted R., and Desmond S. King. 1987. *The State and the City.* Chicago: University of Chicago Press.

Hall, Peter. 1966. *The World Cities.* New York: McGraw-Hill.

Harrison, Bennett. 1974. "Ghetto Economic Development, A Strategy." *Journal of Economic Literature* 12 (Mar.): 1–37.

Hart, Keith. 1970. "Small-Scale Entrepreneurs in Ghana and Development Planning." *Journal of Development Studies* 6, 4: 104–20.

———. 1973. "Informal Income Opportunities and Urban Employment in Ghana." *Journal of Modern African Studies* 11, 1: 61–89.

Hartman, Chester. 1974. *Yerba Buena: Land Grab and Community Resistance in San Francisco.* San Francisco: Glide Publications.

Harvey, David. 1978. "The Urban Process under Capitalism: A Framework for Analysis." *International Journal of Urban and Regional Research* 2, 1 (Mar.): 101–31.

———. 1989. *The Condition of Postmodernity.* Cambridge, Mass.: Basil Blackwell.

Hayden, Dolores. 1995. *The Power of Place: Urban Landscapes as Public History.* Cambridge: MIT Press.

Hays, Constance L. 1989. "Man Admits Drug Trafficking." *New York Times,* Aug. 19, p. A27.

Helfgott, Roy B. 1959. "Women's and Children's Apparel." In *Made in New York: Case Studies in Metropolitan Manufacturing,* ed. Max Hall. Cambridge: Harvard University Press.

Heyer, Virginia. 1953. "Patterns of Social Organization in New York City's Chinatown." Ph.D. diss., Columbia University. Ann Arbor: University Microfilms.

Holmes, John. 1986. "The Organization and Locational Structure of Production Subcontracting." In *Production, Work, Territory,* ed. Allen J. Scott and Michael Storper. Boston: Allen and Unwin.

Hoover, Edgar M., and Raymond Vernon. 1959. *Anatomy of a Metropolis.* Cambridge: Harvard University Press.

Howe, Marvine. 1986. "Chinatown Plan Is Key to Dispute." *New York Times,* July 20, p. 22.

Huang, Vivian, and Tom Robbins. 1995. "Chinatown Wage War." *New York Daily News,* Apr. 20, p. 10.

Hummon, David M. 1988. "Tourist Worlds: Tourist Advertising, Ritual, and American Culture." *Sociological Quarterly* 29, 2 (July): 179–202.

Hunter, Albert J., and Gerald D. Suttles. 1972. "The Expanding Community of Limited Liability." In *The Social Construction of Communities,* ed. Gerald D. Suttles, 44–31. Chicago: University of Chicago Press.

International Labor Organization. 1972. *Employment, Incomes, and Equality: A Strategy for Increasing Productive Employment in Kenya.* Geneva: International Labor Organization.

Jackson, Peter. 1978. "Ethnic Turf: Competition on the Canal Street Divide." *New York Affairs* 7, 4: 149–58.

———. 1992. "Constructions of Culture, Representations of Race: Edward Curtis's 'Way of Seeing.' " In *Inventing Places: Studies in Cultural Geography,* ed. Kay Anderson and Fay Gale, 89–106. Melbourne: Longman Cheshire.

Jackson, Peter, and Jan Penrose. 1994. *Constructions of Race, Place, and Nation.* Minneapolis: University of Minneapolis Press.

Jacobs, Jane. 1961. *The Death and Life of Great American Cities.* New York: Vintage.

Jellinek, Lea. 1988. "The Changing Fortunes of a Jakarta Street Trader." In *The Urbanization of the Third World,* ed. Josef Gugler, 204–23. Oxford: Oxford University Press.

Jones, Dorothy B. 1955. "The Portrayal of China and India on the American Screen, 1896–1955: The Evolution of Chinese and Indian Themes, Locales, and Characters." Paper for Communications Program, Center for International Studies, Massachusetts Institute of Technology.

Kasinitz, Philip. 1992. *Caribbean New York: Black Immigrants and the Politics of Race.* Ithaca, N.Y.: Cornell University Press.

Katznelson, Ira. 1981. *City Trenches.* New York: Pantheon.

Kennedy, Lawrence W. 1992. *Planning the City upon a Hill: Boston since 1630.* Amherst: University of Massachusetts Press.

Key Publications, Inc. 1990. *Chinese Business Guide and Directory.* New York.

Kifner, John. 1991. "New Immigrant Wave from Asia Gives the Underworld New Faces." *New York Times,* Jan. 6, p. A1.

Kim, Elaine. 1986. "Asian Americans and American Popular Culture." In *Dictionary of Asian American History,* ed. Hyung-Chan Kim. New York: Greenwood Press.

Kim, Illsoo. 1981. *New Urban Immigrants: The Korean Community in New York.* Princeton, N.J.: Princeton University Press.

Kincaid, Gwen. 1992. *Chinatown: Portrait of a Closed Society.* New York: Harper-Collins.

King, Anthony D. 1995. "Re-presenting World Cities: Cultural Theory/Social Practice." In *World Cities in a World-System,* ed. Paul L. Knox and Peter J. Taylor, 215–31. New York: Cambridge University Press.

Kirby, Andrew. 1993. *Power/Resistance: Local Politics and the Chaotic State.* Bloomington: Indiana University Press.

Kotkin, Joel. 1993. *Tribes: How Race, Religion, and Identity Determine Success in the New Global Economy.* New York: Random House.

Kreye, Otto, Jurgen Heinrichs, and Folker Frobel. 1986. "Export Processing Zones in Developing Countries: Results of a New Survey." Working Paper No. 43. Geneva: International Labor Organization Multinational Enterprises Programme.

Kristof, Nicholas D. 1991. "Bank Looks beyond Hong Kong." *New York Times,* Jan. 7, p. D1.

Kung, Shien-woo. 1962. *Chinese in American Life.* Seattle: University of Washington Press.

Kuo, Chia-ling. 1977. *Social and Political Change in New York's Chinatown: The Role of Voluntary Organizations.* New York: Praeger Publishers.

Kwong, Peter. 1979. *Chinatown, New York: Labor and Politics, 1930–1950.* New York: Monthly Review Press.

———. 1987. *The New Chinatown.* New York: Noonday Press.

LACE Financial Corporation. 1988. *The Bank Rating Service for Funds Managers and Investors.* McLean, Va.

Lai, David Chuenyan. 1988. *Chinatowns: Towns within Cities in Canada.* Vancouver: University of British Columbia Press.

Lampard, Eric. E. 1986. "The New York Metropolis in Transformation: History and Prospect. A Study in Historical Particularity." In *The Future of the Metropolis,* ed. Hans Jurgen Ewers et al. Berlin: Walter de Gruyter and Co.

Lamphere, Louise. 1992. *Structuring Diversity: Ethnographic Perspectives on the New Immigration.* Chicago: University of Chicago Press.

Lee, Calvin. 1965. *Chinatown, U.S.A.* Garden City, N.Y.: Doubleday and Co.

Lee, Felicia R. 1991. "Blocs Battle to Draw Chinatown's New Council Map." *New York Times,* Apr. 30, p. B1.

Lee, Rose Hum. 1949. "The Decline of Chinatowns in the United States." *American Journal of Sociology* 54, 5 (Mar.): 422–32.

Leichter, Franz S., et al. 1981. "The Return of the Sweatshop." New York: Office of State Senator Leichter, Feb. 26.

Leong, Gor Yun. 1936. *Chinatown Inside Out.* New York: Barrons Mussey.

Leong, Russell. 1989. "Asians in the Americas: Interpreting the Diaspora Experience." *Amerasia Journal* 21, 1 & 2: 1–27.

Li, Alexander Kip. 1993. "A History of the Chinese Staff and Workers' Association." Undergraduate thesis in history, Wesleyan University.

Lieberson, Stanley. 1980. *A Piece of the Pie.* Berkeley: University of California Press.

Light, Ivan. 1972. *Ethnic Enterprise in America.* Berkeley: University of California Press.

———. 1974. "From Vice District to Tourist Attraction: The Moral Career of American Chinatowns, 1880–1940." *Pacific Historical Review* 43 (Aug.): 367–94.

———. 1977. "The Ethnic Vice Industry, 1880–1944." *American Sociological Review* 42 (June): 464–79.

Light, Ivan, and Edna Bonacich. 1988. *Immigrant Entrepreneurs: Koreans in Los Angeles, 1965–1982.* Berkeley: University of California Press.

Light, Ivan, and Charles Choy Wong. 1975. "Protest or Work: Dilemmas of the Tourist Industry in American Chinatowns." *American Journal of Sociology* 80, 6 (May): 1342–68.

Lii, Jane H. 1994a. "Parade Underlines Chinatown Split." *New York Times,* Sept. 11, p. CY6.

———. 1994b. "After Tough Start, Bank Seeks New Image." *New York Times,* Oct. 16, p. CY5.

———. 1995a. "Bankruptcy for Silver Palace." *New York Times,* Mar. 5.

———. 1995b. "65 Cents an Hour—A Special Report—Week in Sweatshop Reveals Grim Conspiracy of the Poor." *New York Times,* Mar. 12.

———. 1995c. "Why Is This Bowl of Noodles So Cheap?" *New York Times,* Apr. 23, p. CY4.

Lin, Ching-yuan. 1973. *Industrialization in Taiwan, 1946–1972: Trade and Import-Substitution Policies for Developing Countries.* New York: Praeger Publishers.

Lin, Jan. 1995a. "Polarized Development and Urban Change in New York's Chinatown." *Urban Affairs Review* 30, 3 (Jan.): 332–54.

———. 1995b. "Ethnic Places, Postmodernism, and Urban Change in Houston." *Sociological Quarterly* 36, 4 (fall): 629–47.

Logan, John, and Harvey Molotch. 1987. *Urban Fortunes: The Political Economy of Place.* Berkeley: University of California Press.

Lorch, Donatella. 1990. "Three Are Found Shot in Apparent Gang Execution." *New York Times,* Oct. 16, p. B1.

———. 1991. "Banks Follow Immigrants to Flushing." *New York Times,* Aug. 7, p. A16.

Lovell-Troy, Lawrence A. 1980. "Clan Structure and Economic Activity: The Case of Greeks in Small Business Enterprises." In *Self-Help in Urban America: Patterns of Minority Business Enterprise,* ed. Scott Cummings, 58–85. New York: Kennikat Press.

Lowe, Lisa. 1991. "Heterogeneity, Hybridity, Multiplicity: Marking Asian American Differences." *Diaspora* 1, 1 (spring): 24–44.

Lueck, Thomas J. 1995. "World Trade Center Sale Is Considered." *New York Times,* May 7, p. A48.

Lyman, Stanford M. 1974. *Chinese Americans.* New York: Random House.

———. 1986. *Chinatown and Little Tokyo.* Millwood, N.Y.: Associated Faculty Press.

Lyons, Richard. 1986. "Satellite Chinatowns Burgeon throughout New York." *New York Times,* Sept. 14, section 8, p. 7.

MacFadyen, J. Tevere. 1983. "Exploring a Past Long Locked in Myth and Mystery." *Smithsonian* 13, 10: 70–78.

Maffi, Mario. 1995. *Gateway to the Promised Land: Ethnic Cultures in New York's Lower East Side.* New York: New York University Press.

Maitland, Leslie. 1975. "2,500 Chinese Protest Alleged Police Beating Here." *New York Times.* May 13, p. L.

Man, Glenn. 1994. "Marginality and Centrality: The Myth of Asia in 1970s Hollywood." *East West Film Journal* 8, 1 (Jan.): 52–67.

Marchetti, Gina. 1991. "Ethnicity, the Cinema, and Cultural Studies." In *Unspeakable Images: Ethnicity and the American Cinema,* ed. by Lester D. Friedman. Urbana: University of Illinois Press.

Mark, Diane Mei Lin, and Ginger Chin. 1982. *A Place Called Chinese America.* Dubuque, Iowa: Kendall/Hunt.

Matthews, Fred. 1977. *The Quest for an American Sociology: Robert E. Park and the Chicago School.* Montreal: McGill-Queen's University Press.

Maynes, Charles William. 1996. "The Global Campaign." *New York Times,* Nov. 3, p. E15.

McGee, T. G. 1979. "The Persistence of the Proto-Proletariat: Occupational Structures and Planning of the Future of Third World Cities." in *Third World Urbanization,* ed. Janet Abu-Lughod and Richard Hay Jr., 257–70. New York: Methuen.

———. 1982. "Labor Mobility in Fragmented Labor Markets, the Role of Circulatory Migration in Rural-Urban Relations in Asia." In *Towards a Political Economy of Urbanization in Third World Countries.* Delhi: Oxford University Press.

———. 1985. "Conservation-Persistence in the Two-Circuit System of Hong Kong: A Case Study of Hawkers." In *Theatres of Accumulation,* ed. Warwick Armstrong and T. G. McGee, 168–201. New York: Methuen.

Michael Kwartler and Associates. 1985. "A Re-evaluation of the Special Manhattan Bridge District." Prepared on behalf of the Manhattan Bridge Area Coalition, Aug. New York.

Miller, Stuart C. 1969. *The Unwelcome Immigrant: The American Image of the Chinese, 1785–1882.* Berkeley: University of California Press.

Mollenkopf, John H. 1981. "Community and Accumulation." In *Urbanization and Urban Planning in Capitalist Society,* ed. Michael Dear and Allen J. Scott, 320–37. London: Methuen.

———. 1992. *A Phoenix in the Ashes: The Rise and Fall of the Koch Coalition in New York City Politics.* Princeton, N.J.: Princeton University Press.

Mollenkopf, John H., and Manuel Castells. 1991. *Dual City: Restructuring New York.* New York: Russell Sage Foundation.

Moy, James S. 1993. *Marginal Sights: Staging the Chinese in America.* Iowa City: University of Iowa Press.

Muller, Thomas. 1993. *Immigrants and the American City.* New York: New York University Press.

New York City Department of City Planning. 1976. *Chinatown Street Revitalization.* New York.

———. 1979. *Manhattan Bridge Area Study.* New York.

———. 1992. *The Newest New Yorkers: An Analysis of Immigration to New York City during the 1980s.* New York.

———. 1995. *Annual Report on Social Indicators 1994.* New York.

New York City Voter Assistance Commission. 1994. *Annual Report of the New York City Voter Assistance Commission.* New York.

New York State Banking Department. 1983–88. *Mortgage Activity Reports.* New York: City of New York Commission on Human Rights.

Novak, Michael. 1971. *The Rise of the Unmeltable Ethnics.* New York: Macmillan.

O'Connor, James. 1984. *Accumulation Crisis.* New York: Basil Blackwell.

Oehling, Richard A. 1980. "The Yellow Menace: Asian American Images in American Film." In *The Kaleidoscopic Lens: How Hollywood Views Ethnic Groups,* ed. Randall M. Miller, 182–206. Englewood, N.J.: Jerome S. Ozer.

Okihiro, Gary. 1994. *Margins and Mainstreams: Asians in American History and Culture.* Seattle: University of Washington Press.

Olalquiaga, Celesta. 1992. *Megalopolis: Contemporary Cultural Sensibilities.* Minneapolis: University of Minnesota Press.

Olzak, Susan. 1985. "Ethnicity and Theories of Ethnic Collective Behavior." *Research in Social Movements, Conflicts, and Change* 8: 65–85.

Omatsu, Glenn. 1994. "The 'Four Prisons' and the Movements of Liberation: Asian American Activism from the 1960s to the 1990s." In *The State of Asian America: Activism and Resistance in the 1990s,* ed. Karin Aguilar-San Juan, 19–70. Boston: South End Press.

Omi, Michael, and Howard Winant. 1994. Rev. ed. *Racial Formation in the United States: From the 1960s to the 1990s.* New York: Routledge.

Orleck, Annelise. 1987. "The Soviet Jews: Life in Brighton Beach, Brooklyn." In *New Immigrants in New York,* ed. Nancy Foner, 273–304. New York: Columbia University Press.

Osajima, Keith. 1988. "Asian Americans as the Model Minority: An Analysis of the Popular Press Image in the 1960s and 1980s." In *Reflections on Shattered Windows: Promises and Prospects for Asian American Studies,* ed. Gary Y. Okihiro et al., 165–74. Pullman: Washington State University Press.

Oser, Alan S. 1990. "Growing Asian Presence Inspires a Hotel." *New York Times,* Dec. 23, p. R3.

Palazzo, Anthony. 1994. "Waiting for Justice." *Village Voice,* Mar. 1, p. 9.

Pan, Lynn. 1990. *Sons of the Yellow Emperor: A History of the Chinese Diaspora.* Boston: Little, Brown and Co.

Park, Robert E. 1926. "The Urban Community as a Spatial Pattern and a Moral Order." In *The Urban Community,* ed. Ernest W. Burgess, 3–18. Chicago: University of Chicago Press.

Park, Robert E., and Ernest W. Burgess, eds. 1925. *The City.* Chicago: University of Chicago Press.

Parson, Don. 1993. "The Search for a Centre: The Recomposition of Race, Class, and Space in Los Angeles." *International Journal for Urban and Regional Research* 17, 2: 232–40.

Peattie, Lisa. 1987. "An Idea in Good Currency and How It Grew: The Informal Sector." *World Development* 15, 7: 851–60.

Petras, Elizabeth. 1990. "Third World Workers in the U.S.: Asian Women in the Philadelphia Apparel Industry." Paper presented at the American Sociological Association Annual Meeting, Aug. 1990, Washington, D.C.

Pickvance, Chris G., ed. 1978. *Urban Sociology: Critical Essays.* London: Methuen.

Pomfret, John. 1987. "Letter from Chinatown." *Far Eastern Economic Review* 135, 1: 64.

Port Authority of New York and New Jersey. 1987. *The Regional Economy: Review 1986, Outlook 1987.* New York.

Portes, Alejandro, and Robert L. Bach. 1985. *Latin Journey: Cuban and Mexican Immigrants in the United States.* Berkeley: University of California Press.

Portes, Alejandro, and Leif Jensen. 1987. "What's an Ethnic Enclave? The Case for Conceptual Clarity." *American Sociological Review* 52, 6 (Dec.): 768–71.

Portes, Alejandro, and Robert D. Manning. 1986. "The Immigrant Enclave: Theory and Empirical Examples." In *Competitive Ethnic Relations,* ed. Susan Olzak and Joane Nagel, 47–68. New York: Academic Press.

Portes, Alejandro, and Ruben G. Rumbaut. 1990. *Immigrant America: A Portrait.* Berkeley: University of California Press.

Portes, Alejandro, and Alex Stepick. 1993. *City on the Edge: The Transformation of Miami.* Berkeley: University of California Press.

Portes, Alejandro, et al. 1989. *The Informal Economy.* Baltimore: Johns Hopkins University Press.

Raab, Selwyn. 1975. "New Militancy Emerges in Chinatown." *New York Times,* June 8, p. 1.

Rafferty, Kevin. 1991. *City on the Rocks: Hong Kong's Uncertain Future.* London: Penguin Books.

Reckless, Walter C. 1971. "The Distribution of Commercialized Vice in the City: A Sociological Analysis." In *The Social Fabric of the Metropolis,* ed. James F. Short Jr., 239–51. Chicago: University of Chicago Press.

Republic of China Investment Commission. 1989. *Statistics on Overseas Chinese and Foreign Investment, Technical Cooperation, Outward Investment and Outward Technical Cooperation.* The Republic of China: The Ministry of Economic Affairs, Apr.

Rieder, Jonathan. 1985. *Canarsie: The Jews and Italians of Brooklyn against Liberalism.* Cambridge: Harvard University Press.

Robertson, D., and Dennis Judd. 1989. *The Development of American Public Policy.* Glenview, Ill.: Scott, Foresman.

Robison, Maynard T. 1976. "Rebuilding Lower Manhattan: 1955–1974." Ph.D. diss., City University of New York.

Ross, Robert, and Kent Trachte. 1983. "Global Cities and Global Classes: The Peripheralization of Labor in New York City." *Review* 6, 3 (winter): 393–431.

Safa, Helen I. 1981. "Runaway Shops and Female Employment: The Search for Cheap Labor." *Signs* 7, 2 (winter): 418–33.

———. 1982. *Towards a Political Economy of Urbanization in Third World Countries.* Delhi: Oxford University Press.

Said, Edward W. 1979. *Orientalism.* New York: Vintage Books.

Sakamoto, Janice. 1991. "'Of Life and Perversity': Wayne Wang Speaks." In *Moving the Image: Independent Asian Pacific American Media Arts,* ed. Russell Leong, 71–73. Los Angeles: UCLA Asian American Studies Center.

Sanders, Jimy M., and Victor Nee. 1987. "Limits of Ethnic Solidarity in the Ethnic Enclave." *American Sociological Review* 52, 6 (Dec.): 745–67.

Sanger, David E. 1997. "'Asian Money,' American Fears." *New York Times,* Jan. 5, p. E1.

Sante, Luc. 1991. *Low Life: Lures and Snares of Old New York.* New York: Vintage Books.

Santos, Milton. 1979. *The Shared Space: The Two Circuits of the Urban Economy in Underdeveloped Countries.* London: Methuen.

Sassen, Saskia. 1988. *The Mobility of Labor and Capital.* Cambridge: Cambridge University Press.

———. 1991. *The Global City: New York, London, Tokyo.* Princeton, N.J.: Princeton University Press.

———. 1996a. "Rebuilding the Global City: Economy, Ethnicity, and Space." In *Representing the City: Ethnicity, Capital, and Culture in the Twenty-First-Century Metropolis,* ed. Anthony D. King, 23–42. New York: New York University Press.

———. 1996b. "Analytic Borderlands: Race, Gender, and Representation in the New City." In *Representing the City: Ethnicity, Capital, and Culture in the Twenty-First-Century Metropolis,* ed. Anthony D. King, 183–202. New York: New York University Press.

Sassen-Koob, Saskia. 1979. "Formal and Informal Associations: Dominicans and Colombians in New York." *International Migration Review* 13 (summer): 314–32.

———. 1982. "Recomposition and Reperipheralization at the Core." *Contemporary Marxism* 5 (summer): 88–100.

———. 1987. "Growth and Informalization at the Core: A Preliminary Report on New York City." In *The Capitalist City,* ed. Michael P. Smith and Joe R. Feagin, 138–54. New York: Basil Blackwell.

Scardino, Albert. 1986. "Commercial Rents in Chinatown Soar as Hong Kong Exodus Grows." *New York Times,* Dec. 25, p. A1.

Schaffer, Richard L. 1973. *Income Flows in Urban Poverty Areas: A Comparison of Community Income Accounts of Bedford-Stuyvesant and Borough Park.* Lexington, Mass.: Lexington Books.

Schofield, Ann. 1984. "The Uprising of the 20,000: The Making of a Labor Legend." In *A Needle, A Bobbin, A Strike,* ed. Joan M. Jensen and Sue Davidson, 167–82. Philadelphia: Temple University Press.

Schmalz, Jeffrey. 1986. "Appeals Court Bars Chinatown Building Till Effect Is Studied." *New York Times,* Nov. 19, p. A1.

Schur, Robert. 1980. "Growing Lemons in the Bronx." *Working Papers for a New Society* 7, 4 (July/Aug.): 42–51.

Schwirian, Kent P. 1983. "Models of Neighborhood Change." *Annual Review of Sociology* 9: 83–102.

Seth, Rama, and Robert N. McCauley. 1987. "Financial Consequences of New Asian Surpluses." *Federal Reserve Bank of New York Quarterly Review* 12, 2 (summer): 32–44.

Sheshunoff Information Services. 1990. *The Bank Quarterly: Ratings and Analysis.* Austin, Tex.: Sheshunoff Information Services.

Siu, Paul C. P. 1952. "The Sojourner." *American Journal of Sociology* 58, 1 (July): 34–44.

Smith, Christopher J. 1995. "Asian New York: The Geography and Politics of Diversity." *International Migration Review* 29, 1 (spring): 59–84.

Smith, Michael Peter. 1987. "Global Capital Restructuring and Local Political Crises in U.S. Cities." In *Global Restructuring and Territorial Development*, ed. Jeffrey Henderson and Manuel Castells. London: Sage Publications.

———. 1988. *City, State, and Market: The Political Economy of Urban Society.* New York: Basil Blackwell.

———. 1992. "Postmodernism, Urban Ethnography, and the New Social Space of Ethnic Identity." *Theory and Society* 21, 4: 493–531.

Smith, Michael Peter, and Joe R. Feagin. 1995. "Putting 'Race' in Its Place." In *The Bubbling Cauldron: Race, Ethnicity, and the Urban Crisis,"* ed. Michael Peter Smith and Joe. R. Feagin, 3–27. Minneapolis: University of Minnesota Press.

Soja, Edward. 1990. *Postmodern Geographies: The Reassertion of Space in Critical Social Theories.* London: Verso.

Sontag, Deborah. 1993. "Study Sees Illegal Aliens in New Light." *New York Times,* Sept. 2.

Sorkin, Michael, ed. 1992. *Variations on a Theme Park.* New York: Hill and Wang.

Sterngold, James. 1990. "Hong Kong Empire's 'Junk Tactic.'" *New York Times,* Oct. 8, p. D1.

———. 1996. "For Asian-Americans, Political Power Can Lead to Harsh Scrutiny." *New York Times,* Nov. 3, p. A36.

Strom, Stephanie. 1991. "Thirteen Held in Kidnapping of Illegal Alien." *New York Times,* Jan. 2, p. B3.

Stromgren, Dick. 1990. "The Chinese Syndrome: The Evolving Image of Chinese and Chinese-Americans in Hollywood Films." In *Beyond the Stars,* ed. Paul Loukides and Linda K. Fuller, 61–67. Bowling Green, Ohio: Bowling Green University Popular Press.

Sullivan, Kathleen A. 1986. "The Impact of Real Estate Development on Manhattan-Based Apparel Firms: A Study of Locational Needs, Priorities and Proposed Solutions." Master's thesis, Columbia University.

Sung, Betty Lee. 1967. *Mountain of Gold.* New York: MacMillan Co.

———. 1975. *Chinese American Manpower and Employment.* Washington, D.C.: United States Department of Labor, Manpower Administration, Office of Research and Development.

Suttles, Gerald. 1968. *The Social Order of the Slum: Ethnicity and Territory in the Inner City.* Chicago: University of Chicago Press.

———. 1984. "The Cumulative Texture of Local Urban Culture." *American Journal of Sociology* 90, 2 (Sept.): 283–304.

Takaki, Ronald. 1979. *Iron Cages: Race and Culture in Nineteenth Century America.* New York: Oxford University Press.

————. 1987. *Strangers from a Different Shore.* New York: Penguin Books.

Tanzer, Andrew. 1985. "Little Taipei." *Forbes* 135 (May 6): 68–71.

Tchen, John Kuo Wei. 1984. *Genthe's Photographs of San Francisco's Old Chinatown.* New York: Dover Publications.

————. 1991. "Modernizing White Patriarchy: Re-viewing D. W. Griffith's Broken Blossoms." In *Moving the Image,* ed. Russell Leong, 133–43. Los Angeles: UCLA Asian American Studies Center.

Tefft, Sheila. 1994. "The Perils of Illegal Flight from China." *Christian Science Monitor,* May 18, p. 4.

Thomas, William I., and Florian Znaniecki. 1958. *The Polish Peasant in Europe and America.* New York: Dover.

Thrift, Nigel. 1989. "The Geography of International Economic Disorder." In *A World in Crisis?* 2d ed., ed. R. J. Johnston and Peter J. Taylor, 16–78. Cambridge: Basil Blackwell.

Tilly, Charles. 1990. "Transplanted Networks." In *Immigration Reconsidered: History, Sociology, and Politics,* ed. Virginia Yans-McLaughlin, 79–95. New York: Oxford University Press.

Tobier, Emanuel. 1979. "The New Face of Chinatown." *New York Affairs* 5, 3 (spring): 66–76.

Tolchin, M., and S. Tolchin. 1988. *Buying into America: How Foreign Money Is Changing the Face of Our Nation.* New York: Times Books.

Tsai, Shih-Shan Henry. 1986. *The Chinese Experience in America.* Bloomington: Indiana University Press.

Tyler, Anne. 1985. *The Accidental Tourist.* New York: Knopf.

U.S. Department of Commerce, U.S. Bureau of the Census. 1960–90. *U.S. Census of Population and Housing.* Washington, D.C.

U.S. Department of Commerce. 1974–88. *Foreign Direct Investment in the United States: Transactions.* Washington, D.C.: U.S. Department of Commerce, International Trade Administration, Office of Trade and Investment Analysis.

U.S. Federal Deposit Insurance Corporation (FDIC). 1982–94. *Data Book, Operating Banks and Branches: Summary of Deposits in all FDIC-Insured Commercial and Savings Banks and U.S. Branches of Foreign Banks.* Washington, D.C.

U.S. Office of Management and Budget. 1987. *Standard Industrial Classification Manual.* Washington, D.C.

Van Gelder, Lawrence. 1995. "Merged Bank to Close Seven Offices in Poorer Areas." *New York Times.* Sept. 22, p. B4.

Waldinger, Roger. 1985. "Immigration and Industrial Change in the New York City Apparel Industry." In *Hispanics in the U.S. Economy,* ed. George J. Borjas and Marta Tienda, 323–49. New York: Academic Press.

————. 1986a. "Immigrant Enterprise: A Critique and Reformulation." *Theory and Society* 15: 249–85.

————. 1986b. *Through the Eye of the Needle.* New York: New York University Press.

————. 1986–87. "Changing Ladders and Musical Chairs: Ethnicity and Opportunity in Post-Industrial New York." *Politics and Society* 15, 4: 369–402.

————. 1987. "Beyond Nostalgia: The Old Neighborhood Revisited." *New York Affairs* 10, 1 (winter): 1–12.

————. 1988. "The Ethnic Division of Labor Transformed: Native Minorities and

New Immigrants in Post-Industrial New York." *New Community* 14, 3 (spring): 318–32.

Waldinger, Roger, and Michael Lapp. 1993. "Back to the Sweatshop or Ahead to the Informal Sector?" *International Journal of Urban and Regional Research* 17, 1: 6–29.

Wan, Enoch Yee Nock. 1978. "The Dynamics of Ethnicity: A Case Study on the Immigrant Community of New York Chinatown." Ph.D. diss., State University of New York at Stony Brook.

Wang, John. 1979. "Behind the Boom: Power and Economics in Chinatown." *New York Affairs* 5, 3 (spring): 77–81.

———. 1981a. "Periling Chinatown." *New York Times,* May 15, p. A31.

———. 1981b. "Developers Readying Three Towers in Chinatown." *New York Times,* Sept. 20.

———. 1982. "Chinatown's Changing Fortunes." *Village Voice* 27 (June 8): 28.

Warner, Sam Bass, Jr. 1972. *The Urban Wilderness: A History of the American City.* New York: Harper and Row.

Weberman, Ben. 1985. "The Best of Two Worlds." *Forbes* 136 (July 29): 98.

Weinstein, Jay. 1984. "Fu Manchu and the Third World." *Society* 21, 2, 148 (Jan.–Feb.): 77–82.

Whyte, William Foote. 1943. *Street Corner Society.* Chicago: University of Chicago Press.

Williams, Monte. 1995. "Labor Dept. Hears Tales of Sweatshops, Restaurants, and Fear." *New York Times,* Aug. 6.

Wilson, Kenneth L., and W. Allen Martin. 1982. "Ethnic Enclaves: A Comparison of the Cuban and Black Economies in Miami." *American Journal of Sociology* 88, 1: 135–60.

Wilson, Kenneth L., and Alejandro Portes. 1980. "Immigrant Enclaves: An Analysis of the Labor Market Experiences of Cubans in Miami." *American Journal of Sociology* 86, 2 (Sept.): 295–319.

Winnick, Louis. 1990. *New People in Old Neighborhoods.* New York: Russell Sage Foundation.

Wirth, Louis. 1927. *The Ghetto.* Chicago: University of Chicago Press.

———. 1938. "Urbanism as a Way of Life." *American Journal of Sociology* 4: 1–24.

Wohl, R. Richard, and Anselm L. Strauss. 1958. "Symbolic Representation and the Urban Milieu." *American Journal of Sociology* 63: 523–32.

Wolfe, Gerald R. 1988. *New York: A Guide to the Metropolis.* New York: McGraw-Hill Book Co.

Wong, Bernard. 1982. *Chinatown: Economic Adaptation and Ethnic Identity of the Chinese.* New York: Holt, Rinehart and Winston.

———. 1987a. "The Chinese: New Immigrants in New York City's Chinatown." In *New Immigrants in New York,* ed. Nancy Foner, 243–71. New York: Columbia University Press.

———. 1987b. "The Role of Ethnicity in Enclave Enterprises: A Study of the Chinese Garment Factories in New York City." *Human Organization* 46, 2: 120–29.

———. 1988. *Patronage, Brokerage, and the Chinese Community of New York City.* New York: AMS Press.

Wong, Sau-Ling Cynthia. 1994. "Ethnic Subject, Ethnic Sign, and the Difficulty of

Rehabilitative Representation: Chinatown in Some Works of Chinese American Fiction." *Yearbook of English Studies* 24: 251–62.

———. 1995. "Denationalization Reconsidered: Asian American Cultural Criticism at a Theoretical Crossroads." *Amerasia Journal* 21: 1 & 2: 1–27.

Wong, Scott. 1995. "Chinatown: Conflicting Images, Contested Terrains." *MELUS* 20, 1 (spring): 3–16.

Wu, Yuan-Li, and Chun-hsi Wu. 1980. *Economic Development in Southeast Asia: The Chinese Dimension.* Stanford: Hoover Institution Press.

Yancey, William L., Eugene P. Ericksen, and Richard N. Juliani. 1976. "Emergent Ethnicity: A Review and Reformulation." *American Sociological Review* 41, 3 (June): 391–402.

Yoshihara, Kunio. 1988. *The Rise of Ersatz Capitalism in Southeast Asia.* Singapore: Oxford University Press.

Yu, Renqui. 1992. *To Save China, To Save Ourselves: The Chinese Hand Laundry Alliance of New York.* Philadelphia: Temple University Press.

Zhou, Min. 1992. *Chinatown: The Socioeconomic Potential of an Urban Enclave.* Philadelphia: Temple University Press.

Zhou, Min, and John R. Logan. 1989. "Returns on Human Capital in Ethnic Enclaves: New York City's Chinatown." *American Sociological Review* 54 (Oct.): 809–20.

Zorbaugh, Harvey W. 1926. "The Natural Areas of the City." In *The Urban Community,* ed. Ernest W. Burgess, 219–29. Chicago: University of Chicago Press.

Zukin, Sharon. 1980. "A Decade of the New Urban Sociology." *Theory and Society* 9: 539–74.

———. 1989. Paperback ed. *Loft Living: Culture and Capital in Urban Change.* New Brunswick, N.J.: Rutgers University Press.

———. 1995. *The Cultures of Cities.* Cambridge, Mass.: Blackwell Publishers.

Index

Abeles, Schwartz, Haeckel, and Silverblatt, Inc., 40, 43, 63, 64, 114, 115, 156
Abramson, Jill, 199
Abu-Lughod, Janet, 9–10, 14, 189
African American enclaves, 43
Aiming, Zhou, 54
Allen, Irving L., 174, 175
Amalgamated Clothing and Textile Workers Union (ACTWU), 63, 67–68
Anchor Savings Bank, 104
Anderson, Kay J., 20, 21
anti-Asian violence, 135–37
anti-urbanism, 8
Apana, Chang, 179
Appo, Quimbo (Lee Ah Bow), 30
Ardener, Shirley, 46
Armstrong, Warwick, 13, 14
Asia Bank, 116
Asiagate scandal, 200
Asian American International Film-Festival, 187
Asian American Legal Defense and Education Fund (AALDEF), 131, 144
Asian American movement, 127–32
Asian Americans for Equal Employment (AAFEE), 134–35, 136
Asian Americans for Equality (AAFE), 129, 130, 135, 141–43, 162, 163

Asian Americans for Equality v. *Koch*, 154
Asian American studies, 21, 128
Asian Cine-Vision, 187
Asian Immigrant Women Advocates (AIWA), 193
assimilation, human ecology theory on, 8

bachelor sojourners, 23, 24–27, 46–47, 48
backward linkages, 42
Bagli, Charles V., 100
Bahr, Howard M., xii
banking industry: in Chinatown, globalization of, 88–92; deregulation of, 88, 89; overseas Chinese investment in, 86–87, 88; restructuring of, 104–5
Bank of China, 69, 95, 99
Bank of East Asia, 5, 99, 100, 102
Bank of the United States, 213n.8
banks: barriers to use of American, 48; deposits in Chinatown, 4–5, 89–92, 103; fraudulence and instability in history of immigrant, 212n.8; Golden Pacific Bank, 95–97; International Banking Facilities (IBFs), 88; local Chinese American, 89–98; mortgage activity reports, 92–94, 212n.6; overseas Chinese, 5, 89–94, 98–100, 116;

Jan Lin is an associate professor of sociology at Occidental College.